M000119606

THE NEW GROVE®

VIOLIN FAMILY

THE NEW GROVE®

DICTIONARY OF MUSICAL INSTRUMENTS

Editor: Stanley Sadie

The Grove Musical Instruments Series

EARLY KEYBOARD INSTRUMENTS

ORGAN

PIANO

VIOLIN FAMILY

in preparation

BRASS

WOODWIND

THE NEW GROVE®

VIOLIN FAMILY

David D. Boyden   Sonya Monosoff
Boris Schwarz   Klaus Marx
Rodney Slatford   Carleen M. Hutchins
and others

M
MACMILLAN

Copyright © 1980, 1984 and 1989 Macmillan Press Ltd, London

Copyright © 1980, 1984 and 1989 David D. Boyden, Boris Schwarz,
Klaus Marx, Rodney Slatford, Sonya Monosoff, Carleen M. Hutchins,
J. C. Schelleng, Ann Woodward, Werner Bachmann, Malcolm Boyd,
Peter Cooke, Alastair Dick

All rights reserved. No part of this publication
may be reproduced or transmitted, in any form or by any means,
without permission.

Parts of this material first published in
The New Grove® Dictionary of Musical Instruments,
edited by Stanley Sadie, 1984

and

The New Grove Dictionary of Music and Musicians®,
edited by Stanley Sadie, 1980

The New Grove and The New Grove Dictionary of Music and Musicians
are registered trademarks of Macmillan Publishers Limited, London

First published in UK in paperback with additions 1989 by
PAPERMAC
a division of Macmillan Publishers Limited
London and Basingstoke

First published in UK in hardback with additions 1989 by
MACMILLAN LONDON LIMITED
4 Little Essex Street London WC2R 3LF
and Basingstoke

A CIP catalogue record for this book is available from the British Library

ISBN 0-333-44451-5 (hardback)
ISBN 0-333-44452-3 (paperback)

First American edition in book form with additions 1989 by
W. W. NORTON & COMPANY
500 Fifth Avenue New York NY 10110

ISBN 0-393-02556-X

ISBN 0-393-30517-1   {PBK.}

Printed in Hong Kong
1 2 3 4 5 6 7 8 9 0

Contents

List of illustrations

Cover: detail from 'A Musical Party at Melton Constable': painting
(first half of the 18th century) by D. Heins (private collection)

Illustration acknowledgments

We are grateful to those listed below for permission to reproduce illustrative material. The drawings were prepared by Brian and Constance Dear and Alan Forster.

W. E. Hill & Sons, Great Missenden (figs.1, 6, 13; figs.1, 13 photo Desmond Hill); Hermann, Paris, and University of Toronto Press (fig.4: after E. Leipp, *Le violon, historique, esthétique, facture et acoustique*, Eng. trans., 1969); British Piano Museum Charitable Trust, Brentford/photo Times Newspapers Ltd (fig.7); photo Bildarchiv Foto Marburg (fig.8c); The Photo Source, London (fig.8d); Civico Gabinetto Fotografico, Ferrara (fig.9a); Mansell Collection, London, and Alinari, Florence (figs.9b, 10, 48); Musée des Beaux-Arts, Strasbourg (fig.11); David D. Boyden (figs.12a, 49, 54); photo Michael Baines, London (fig.12b); Ashmolean Museum, Oxford (figs.15, 28a, 29, 52); RCA Ltd, London (fig.25); photo Bálint Sárosi (fig.26); photo Jitendra Arya, Bombay (fig.27a); Music Division, Library of Congress, Washington DC (fig.27b); Mrs Lionel Tertis, London/photo Sotheby's, London (fig.28b); HM the Queen (fig.31); National Gallery of Victoria (Everard Studley Miller Bequest, 1961), Melbourne/photo Schweizerisches Institut für Kunstwissenschaft, Zurich (fig.32); British Library, London (figs.33, 50); Musikwissenschaftliches Institut, University of Cologne, and Gustav Bosse Verlag, Regensburg (fig.35: from J. Eckhardt, *Die Violoncellschulen von J. J. F. Dotzauer, F. A. Kummer und B. Romberg*, Kölner Beiträge zur Musikforschung, li, 1968); Vivien John, London / photo Tate Gallery, London (fig.36); Novosti Press Agency, London (fig.37); Tiroler Landesmuseum Ferdinandeum, Innsbruck (fig.38); Germanisches Nationalmuseum, Nuremberg (fig.39); Horniman Museum (Dolmetsch Instrumental Collection), London (fig.40a); Kunsthistorisches Museum, Vienna (fig.40b); Raymond Elgar, St Leonards on Sea (fig.41: from R. Elgar, *Looking at the Double Bass*, St Leonards on Sea, 1967); Biblioteca Nacional, Madrid (fig.44); Soprintendenza alle Gallerie, Florence (fig.45); Real Academia de la Historia, Madrid (fig.46); Glasgow University Library (Hunterian Collection) (fig.47); C. M. Hutchins (figs.55, 60); W. H. Freeman & Co., San Francisco (figs.56–9; 56, 57, 59 after J. C. Schelleng, 'The Physics of the Bowed String', *Scientific American*, ccxxx (Jan 1974); fig.58 from J. C. Schelleng, 'The Physics of the Bowed String', © 1974 by Scientific American, Inc.); Kenneth Marshall and the American Institute of Physics (fig.61: from K. Marshall, 'Modal Analysis of a Violin', *Journal of the Acoustical Society of America*, lxxvii/2, Feb 1985); William Y. Strong (fig.62); Karl A. Stetson (fig.63)

General abbreviations

b	born		n.	note
BWV	Bach-Werke-Verzeichnis [Schmieder, catalogue of J. S. Bach's works]		n.d.	no date of publication
			orig.	original(ly)
c	circa [about]		*R*	photographic reprint
			r	recto
D	Deutsch catalogue [Schubert]		repr.	reprinted
d	died		rev.	revision, revised (by/for)
diss.	dissertation		RV	Ryom catalogue [Vivaldi]
facs.	facsimile		suppl.	supplement, supplementary
fl	floruit [he/she flourished]			
			trans.	translation, translated by
H	Hoboken catalogue [Haydn]			
Hz	Hertz [cycles per second]		U.	University
incl.	includes, including		*v*	verso
Jg.	Jahrgang [year of publication/ volume]		WOO	Werke ohne Opuszahl [works without opus number]
			WQ	Wotquenne catalogue [C. P. E. Bach]
K	Köchel catalogue [Mozart]			

Bibliographical abbreviations

Preface

This volume is one of a series of short studies derived from *The New Grove Dictionary of Musical Instruments* (London, 1984). Some of the texts were originally written for *The New Grove Dictionary of Music and Musicians* (London, 1980), in the mid-1970s. For the present volume, all the material has been critically re-read and much of it has been substantially modified, with corrections and changes in the light of recent work.

Sadly, two of the principal authors of this volume – David Boyden, who contributed the first two chapters, the original version of Chapter 5 and the latter half of Chapter 8, and Boris Schwarz, author of Chapter 3 – have now died. We are specially grateful to Sonya Monosoff for her work in reconciling parts of Professor Boyden's essays with the findings of more recent research; her own material on fingering technique has been incorporated into Chapters 2 and 6.

The material in the appendices is based on articles published in *The New Grove Dictionary of Musical Instruments*.

S. S.

CHAPTER ONE

The Violin

The violin is the soprano member of the family of string
instruments that includes the viola, cello and double bass. It
is one of the most perfect instruments acoustically and has
extraordinary musical versatility. In beauty and emotional
appeal its tone rivals that of its model, the human voice, but at
the same time the violin is capable of particular agility and
brilliant figuration, making possible in one instrument the
expression of moods and effects that may range, depending on
the will and skill of the player, from the lyric and tender to the
brilliant and dramatic. Its capacity for sustained tone is remarkable, and scarcely another instrument can produce so many
nuances of expression and intensity. The violin can play all the
chromatic semitones or even microtones over a four-octave
range, and, to a limited extent, the playing of chords is within
its powers. In short, the violin represents one of the greatest
triumphs of instrument making. Composers, inspired by its
potential, have written extensively for it as a solo instrument,
accompanied and unaccompanied, and also in connection with
the genres of orchestral and chamber music. Possibly no other
instrument can boast a larger and musically more distinguished
repertory, if one takes into account all forms of solo and
ensemble music in which the violin has been assigned a part.

Historically the 'strings' have constituted the backbone of the
Western orchestra for more than three centuries, ever since the
rise of an orchestra (of sorts) in the 17th century (the 'strings'
comprised the violin family – strictly speaking, violin, viola and
cello – plus the double bass, which was sometimes constructed
like a viol and sometimes like a violin). The violin (and violin
family), however, had originated well before the 17th century
– the three-string violin was certainly in existence in the 1520s
and perhaps even earlier – and by the early 17th century the
reputation and universal use of the violins were such that

1. *Instruments of the violin family by Antonio Stradivari, Cremona: (right to left) violins (1708, 1670), viola (1696) and cello (1725)*

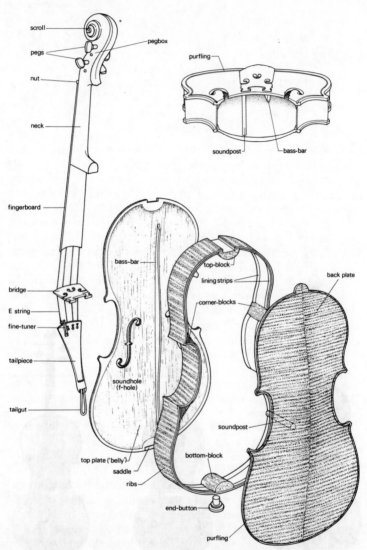

2. *Diagram of the component parts of the modern violin*

STRUCTURE

Praetorius declared (2/1619): 'And since everyone knows about the violin family, it is unnecessary to indicate or write anything further about it'.

1. STRUCTURE

(i) Components

The violin gives an appearance of deceptive simplicity to the eye, but is in fact constructed of some 70 parts, which require the skill of a master craftsman to cut and assemble. Acoustically it is one of the most complex of instruments (see Chapter Nine, §1). The body is a hollow box (see fig.2) about 35.5 cm long, consisting of an arched top plate ('belly') and arched back plate, joined by sides ('ribs') of slightly varying heights (a typical Stradivari measurement is 2.8 cm at the top end of the instrument and 3.2 cm at the bottom). The edges of the belly and back are not flush with the ribs (as is usual in a viol of authentic design), but project beyond, overhanging the ribs slightly. The belly is made of softwood, generally European spruce, and the back and sides are fashioned of hardwood, usually maple. The neck, pegbox and scroll are also customarily of maple. The fingerboard runs along the neck and extends over the belly towards the bridge; modern ones are normally made of ebony. The fingerboard is unfretted, a feature that distinguishes the violins from the viols.

Both top and back may be made of one piece of wood, or (much more usually) of two pieces joined. The wood may be cut either in layers ('on the slab') or radially 'on the quarter'. A one-piece back (either quarter- or slab-cut) is not uncommon, but a one-piece slab-cut top is rare because for technical acoustical reasons it seldom gives satisfactory results. The appearance of the wood surface depends on which of the two methods of cutting is used; fig.3 (p.6) shows both methods, and the resulting appearance of two violin backs made by each. The 'waves' in the veined wood are generally called 'curls', and in fig.3c these are seen to run continuously upwards from left to right; in the example in fig.15 (p.30) they run downwards from left to right. In two-piece backs, of course, the curls (if there are any) would not be continuous because they would be interrupted by the join

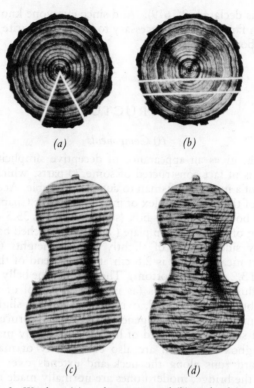

(a)   *(b)*

*3. Wood cut (a) on the quarter, and (b) on the slab,
with the resulting appearance of violin backs (c, d)
made from each*

(c)   *(d)*

in the middle (as in the 'Messiah' Stradivari violin). Radial
cutting is generally favoured, especially for tops, because the
properties of the various radial sections are about the same from
one piece to another. Fig.4 shows how a radial section is split
from the top and the resulting two sections then glued base to
base. In this way the resulting piece of wood will have the same
properties relative to the join in the middle.

'Grain' in wood is distinct from 'figure', the latter being
figured patterns such as the curls mentioned above, while 'grain'
refers to the arrangement or direction of the fibres of the wood.
In a violin body the grain runs longitudinally from top to

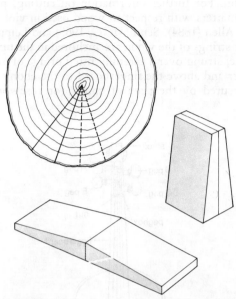

4. Radial section split (cut on the quarter) and glued base to base

bottom and is generally more prominent in the top plate (i.e. belly) than in the back. This is so because the top, typically of spruce, seldom has 'figures' to distract the eye from the parallel lines of the grain, which, under a fine varnish, constitute an important element of the visual beauty and appeal of a superior violin. The distance between the parallel grain lines varies, sometimes being narrow ('close' grain), sometimes wider ('open' grain). In a typical two-piece top the spacing of the grain tends to be symmetrical outwards from the centre join, the distance between the grain lines being 'closer' (narrower) at the centre.

The grain also runs longitudinally in the back, but it is far less obvious to the eye, partly because of the less prominent character of the grain itself and partly because in a typical maple back there are figures in the wood, often strikingly handsome, which catch the attention. These figures generally run at right angles, more or less, to the longitudinal grain – that is, across the back of the violin. For further information on cutting, preparation and other matters with respect to wood used in violin making, see Heron–Allen (1884), Senn (*MGG*, 1965) and Leipp (1965).

The four strings of the violin are anchored in the upper end of the tailpiece, strung over a carefully fitted bridge of maple, then carried over and above the fingerboard to the ebony (or ivory) nut and secured by the pegs of ebony (or rosewood) in the

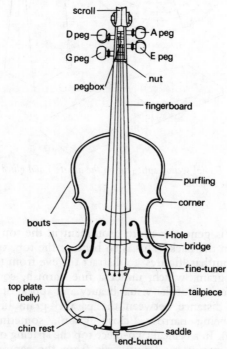

5. Features of the modern violin

pegbox (see figs.2 and 5). The latter is crowned by an ornamental scroll. At the lower end of the violin, the tailpiece is secured by the tailgut (traditionally a heavy piece of gut, but now sometimes wire or nylon) that runs over the ebony saddle (see figs.2 and 5) and is looped over, and secured by, the end-button ('endpin'). The tension of the strings is regulated by turning the pegs to bring the four strings to their proper pitches: g, d', a' and e''. In modern violins the steel E string is generally 'fine-tuned' by means of an E-string tuner, located where the E string is secured by the tailpiece (see figs.2 and 5). The chin rest is made of wood (usually ebony or rosewood) or vulcanite.

The strings of the violin were originally all gut, and remained so for some time. However, from the 1660s the lowest (G) string was commonly wound with silver wire to give a better response. Today violinists generally use wound strings for the D and A strings as well and also use a steel E string, the latter being generally more durable and quicker to respond in the higher registers.

Inside the violin, the top-, bottom- and corner-blocks and the side-linings (see fig.2) strengthen and stabilize the structure. The soundpost and bass-bar give additional support from the interior of the instrument. The soundpost, ordinarily of spruce, stands vertically between back and top and is located under the right foot of the bridge – not directly under the bridge's foot but on a line with it, slightly towards the tailpiece. The position of the soundpost is a critical factor in producing the best sound from the instrument. The bridge too must be fitted exactly to the contours of the belly, between the f-holes. The bass-bar, also normally of spruce, is glued to the undersurface of the top, running under the left foot of the bridge. Like the soundpost, the bass-bar helps support the top and also serves an acoustical purpose (see Chapter Nine, §1).

The beautiful design and shape of the violin are not merely ornamental but are functional to a considerable degree. The vaulting of the back and belly is essential for strength and for acoustical reasons, the whole body being designed to furnish the best amplification of sound. The narrow waist – that is, the 'middle bouts' – permits ease of playing on the highest and lowest strings. The scroll is decorative, although in earlier times the instrument was often hung up by it. The line of purfling which runs just inside the outer edge of back and belly not only emphasizes the beauty of the outline but also minimizes cracks and prevents any damage to the over-hanging edges from going further into the body. Some modern acoustical experts (see Backus, 1969, p.178) think that purfling may be a factor in the fine tone of a violin. The soundholes (f-holes) and the bridge are basically acoustical in function (see Chapter Nine, §1), but their actual forms are probably determined by partly decorative

considerations. In any case, early bridges vary in design somewhat from modern bridges (see fig.6).

Finally, the varnish, so beautiful in the finest violins, is
functional as well as decorative, being indispensable as a preservative. Varnish cannot improve the tone, although it may affect
it adversely since a varnish that is too hard, too soft or badly
applied may prevent the best tone qualities inherent in the
instrument from being realized. (See also Chapter Nine, §4.)

6. Back (left) and front views of the bridge of Stradivari's 'Tuscan' viola
compared with a modern viola bridge (right)

The composition of the Cremona varnish, which contributes
so much to the visual beauty of a Stradivari and other Cremonese violins, remains something of a mystery, although there
could not have been anything very mysterious about it in its
time. Jacob Stainer (c1617–83) in the Austrian Tyrol, for
instance, knew all about it, and the Venetian makers used an
equally fine varnish. However, easier and quicker methods of
varnishing were later applied, and by 1750 or 1760 the old
process had nearly disappeared, G. B. Guadagnini being one of
the last (c1780) to use Cremona varnish. Nevertheless, excellent
varnishes are once again being used today.

Distinctive structural characteristics of the violin from c1600
to c1785 ('Baroque violin') are described below (see §3).

(ii) Sound production

Any violin has a certain potential of volume, whose realization
depends on the type of strings and their tension, the type of
bridge, the degree of pressure the player exerts on the bow, the
relative speed with which he bows and the location of the bow
relative to the bridge or fingerboard. The full realization of the
tone and other qualities inherent in the instrument itself depends

on the player's skill in bowing and fingering and on the expressiveness of his vibrato.

When the bow sets the string or strings in motion, the vibrations are transmitted to the belly and the back via the bridge and the soundpost. The total area of the soundbox then further transmits the amplified vibrations eventually to the ear of the listener. The soundholes operate as a secondary and complementary acoustical system, adding considerably to the resonance.

The quality and character of tone depend on the vibrating string and how well its fundamental pitch frequency and upper partials are received and transmitted by the wood of the violin's body. The string vibrates not only as a whole – that is, as stopped between nut and bridge or by the player's finger – but also in various parts of its length so as to produce the other harmonics of the fundamental, thus giving richness and complexity to the timbre. Some individual tones are the result of the complex interaction of as many as 20 upper partials in addition to the fundamental.

The role of the violin body is to transmit the string vibrations to the outer air; and a violin is good in the degree that it transmits the string vibrations of the fundamental and its harmonics with equal response over the whole register of the instrument. The tone of a violin, then, depends initially on the wood of which it is constructed, on the many resonance frequencies of the wood and on their capacity to respond to the string vibrations.

Many experiments have been made to determine which factors affect the timbre of a single note or of all the notes of a particular violin, thus distinguishing one violin from another. There are still major questions regarding the acoustics of the violin that are not yet completely or satisfactorily answered – for example, what makes a violin a 'good' one, and whether old violins are better than modern ones (at present, the best available answer to the second question is 'Not necessarily'). (See also Chapter Nine.)

Since its origins, the violin has undergone a considerable evolution of detail to meet the changing requirements of successive generations of performers and composers. The first century and a half of the 'true' violin culminated in the magnificent 'classical' model of Antoni Stradivari shortly after 1700. But this was not the end of the instrument's evolution; by the early 19th

7. *Mechanical violin: Hupfeld's 'Phonoliszt-Violina', Leipzig, c1912*

century it had been altered in a number of respects to attain greater power and brilliance (see §4 below and Chapter Nine); in the early 20th century attempts to reproduce the sound of the violin by mechanical means resulted in inventions such as the violina (see fig.7), the violinista and the virtuosa. Today the violin is a more powerful instrument, supporting greater tensions and pressures; the strings are generally steel or wire-wound; and the instrument is played with a different type of bow and a different technique. These changes in the violin (and bow) were occasioned by new styles of music and new techniques of playing. Fig.8 (pp.14–15) shows how different violinists from the 17th century onwards held their violins and bows, and it is obvious from the pictures of Geminiani and Isaac Stern that the 16th and 20th centuries are worlds apart in this as in many other matters. Not all the changes, however, were necessarily improvements. At best the instrument, bow and technique of each age have been those that players and makers have believed to be best suited to the music of their own time.

2. THE 1520s TO *c*1600

By about 1550 the four-string ('true') violin must have been a familiar part of the musical scene; the instrument and its tuning were described explicitly by Jambe de Fer in his *Epitome musical* (Lyons, 1556). A three-string violin, whose strings were tuned to the pitches of the lower three strings of the true violin, had preceded the four-string instrument by about a generation and appeared in paintings of Garofalo's school at Ferrara around 1508 and others by Gaudenzio Ferrari in the Milan area around 1529–30 (see fig.9, p.16). Almost as early as this, there are references to the violin in France and in Poland, but the preponderance of evidence points to northern Italy as the cradle of the violin, especially the general area of Milan (including Brescia and Cremona) and Venice. The viola and cello appeared by about 1535, as is proved by the fresco of Gaudenzio Ferrari in the cupola of Saronno Cathedral (fig.10, p.18). Just as Jambe de Fer in his treatise of 1556 described the four-string violin, viola and cello as a family, similarly Gaudenzio depicted in the Saronno fresco the three-string violin and viola (and a cello in which the number of strings cannot be distinguished) as a

(d)

(c)

8. *Violinists from the 17th century to the 20th: (a) French violinist using the typical 17th-century breast position and thumb-under-hair grip: lithograph after a painting (1665) by Gérard Dou; (b) Francesco Geminiani: frontispiece from the French translation (1752) of his treatise 'The Art of Playing on the Violin' (1751); (c) Joseph Joachim accompanied by Clara Schumann: detail of a chalk drawing by Adolf Menzel (1815–1905); (d) Isaac Stern*

15

(a)

(b)

9. (a) Violin depicted in a wall painting (1505–8) by Garofalo, or his school (Sala del Tesoro, Palazzo di Ludovico il Moro, Ferrara); (b) three-string violin: detail from 'The Madonna of the Orange Trees' (1529) by Gaudenzio Ferrari (S Cristoforo, Vercelli)

family. This and other evidence suggests strongly that the violin, viola and cello emerged at about the same time. There is no convincing evidence that the viola (alto violin) appeared before the violin proper, as is often claimed.

The earliest violins were an amalgam of the features of certain well-known instruments in vogue about 1500: the rebec, the Renaissance fiddle and the *lira da braccio* (a developed form of the fiddle). (See fig.46, p.202, and fig.47, p.203.) The violin combined the sonority and efficient playing potential of the *lira da braccio* (whose middle bouts made the instrument easier to bow than the rebec) with the musical advantage and simplicity of the rebec's three strings and uniform tuning in 5ths. The viols, on the other hand, were not ancestors of the violins in any decisive aspect of construction, tuning or playing technique. While the violin gradually made its ancestor forms of rebec and *lira da braccio* obsolete, the viols persisted for a century and a half after the origin of the violin – that is, to the end of the 17th century, when the polyphonic forms, for which the viols were most suited, themselves fell into neglect. The bass viol in its role as a continuo instrument and, to some extent, as a soloist continued to flourish until the mid-18th century or a bit later.

No-one knows who invented the violin, and it is most unlikely that a single person did so. Possibly certain Brescian makers like Giovan Giacobo dalla Corna and Zanetto Montichiaro had a hand in the first violins, since both were mentioned by Giovanni Lanfranco (*Scintille di musica*, Brescia, 1533) as makers of 'lutes, lyras and the like'. The first famous maker was probably Andrea Amati (born before 1511 and possibly as early as 1500–05), the founder of the Cremonese school of violin making.

Nearly as baffling as the origins of the violin is its 16th-century terminology. About 1500, for instance, 'viola' did not mean 'alto violin' as it does today, but rather a string instrument in general or, more specifically at times, a Renaissance 'fiddle'. When the Italians (e.g. Ganassi, 1542–3) sought to distinguish the instruments of the viol family from those of the violin family, they used 'viola' with different qualifiers. 'Viola da gamba' ('leg viola') referred to the viol family, and 'viola da braccio' ('arm viola') to the violin family, the particular members of each family being designated by such terms as 'soprano', 'alto' and so on. 'Soprano di viola da braccio' then meant the 'soprano arm viola' or 'violin'. The specific Italian

10. *Possibly the earliest depiction of the violin (left), viola (right) and cello (centre) as members of the same family: detail of a fresco (1534–c1537) by Gaudenzio Ferrari in the cupola of Saronno Cathedral*

diminutive form 'violino' had appeared by 1538; the equivalent form in French ('violon') is found in documents at least 15 years earlier. The Italian word 'violone' referred in the 16th century to viols as a class. Jambe de Fer (1556) said that the Italians first called the violin 'violon da braccia' (*violone da braccio*) or 'violone'. 'Violone da braccio' ('arm viol') seems a reasonable term for 16th-century Italians to have used to distinguish the violin from the plain violone, the 'ordinary viol' played at the leg. The French at that time were the political masters of northern Italy, however, and consequently French was the language of officialdom; therefore when French chroniclers of Savoy or Piedmont, where the first violins evidently originated, tried to describe the new 'violins', they simply adopted the Italian 'violone da braccio'. But since the French already had a term in common usage for viol ('viole'), they simply dropped the 'da braccio' as redundant, leaving 'violon(e)' to mean 'violin'. This French usage became the source of extraordinary confusion because the French term was so easily confused with 'violone' – often shortened in Italian to 'violon' – the Italian term for viols as a class.

In any case 'violino' rarely, if ever, meant anything but violin proper. The one clear exception occurs in Venetian usage (see Zacconi, 1592, and G. Gabrieli, *Sonata pian e forte*, 1597), where 'violino' may mean either the violin proper or the alto violin (the modern viola). 'Violino' does not mean 'viol'. In modern German the term for alto violin (viola) is 'Bratsche', a derivative of 'braccio'.

In Italian, diminutive and augmentative endings might be used to designate either particular instruments or families as a whole. Thus 'violone', used to refer to violas as a class, was later, in the 17th century, used to mean the double bass in particular; and 'violetta', which was used for violins as a class, came to mean 'alto violin' (the modern viola) in particular.

In German there was a close parallel to the Italian use of 'violone' for viols as a class and 'violetta' for violins as a class, in that 'grosse Geigen' meant viols, while 'kleine Geigen' meant violins. Occasionally other qualifiers were used, such as 'Polish Geigen' (fiddles) for violins (the probable meaning in Agricola, *Musica instrumentalis deudsch*, 5/1545, and the certain meaning in Praetorius, 2/1619). 'Violino piccolo' meant what the name implies: a small violin. It also implied a higher tuning than the violin: that is, in 5ths upwards from $b\flat$ or c', a 3rd or 4th above the ordinary violin. (On the other hand, a 'three-quarter' violin is smaller than a regular one but is tuned to the same pitch.) The two *violini piccoli alla francese* specified by Monteverdi in his opera *Orfeo* (1607) may have been boat-like pochettes (kits), tuned an octave above the violin (and treated as transposing instruments, their music being notated an octave below the actual sound), while his specification *violino ordinario* meant the violin (not the viola, as some scholars have inferred).

Just as the violin proper was the most standardized of the string instruments with respect to its size and construction, so after 1550 it was the most stable in terminology. 'Violino' was the constant in Italy, although such terms as 'lira', 'violetta' or 'rebecchino' might mean the violin proper in certain contexts. In England 'viol' was clearly distinguished from 'violin', although both have a number of variant spellings; individual members were described by such expressions as 'bass viol', 'tenor violin' and so on.

In the first century of its existence the violin served two principal functions: doubling vocal music (an occasional off-shoot of this practice was 'doubling' without the voices) and playing for dancing. 16th-century printed music for either type of violin music is practically non-existent. In vocal music the violinist doubtless played directly from the vocal part, and hence no separate instrumental parts were needed or made. Dance musicians played largely from memory and many violinists could not read music. It was only the great occasion of a royal marriage at the French court in 1581 (the entertainment for which was called the *Balet comique de la Royne*) that caused a description of the whole affair, which included two dances explicitly set for ten 'violins' in five parts, to be published in 1582. 16th-century documents mention numerous other occasions graced by music – although almost none of the music described has survived – theatrical entertainments (such as masques, *ballets de cour*, Italian *intermedi*), weddings, private house music, and occasions or festivities connected with a town, church or court. In all this, violinists functioned primarily as professionals, engaged by the court, the authorities of a town or church or by a prosperous individual for his household. By contrast, viol players were partly professional, partly amateur. The latter, often of aristocratic rank, played the viols as a worthy avocation, hence the difference in the social status of viols and violins before 1600. Jambe de Fer wrote: 'We call viols those [instruments] with which gentlemen, merchants, and other virtuous people pass their time . . . The other type [of instrument] is called violin; it is commonly used for dancing.'

From its origin to about 1550 information about the violin is somewhat sketchy, being derived mainly from iconography, the theorists and stray references. After 1550 the evidence becomes more telling. A certain number of violins survive from the late 16th century, as well as a fair number of documents and paintings. With the establishment of the standard four-string violin, progress was relatively rapid after 1550. The first of the great makers appeared, among them Andrea Amati and Gasparo da Salò (see fig.28*a*, p.138 and fig.29, p.142), the respective founders of the Cremonese and the Brescian schools of violin making. Other famous makers were V. Linarol in Venice, the sons of Andrea Amati in Cremona and G. P. Maggini, the pupil of Gasparo da Salò, in Brescia.

At the same time the violin was more in evidence throughout the European countries, and was quite probably made increasingly by local makers in those countries that used the instrument. In France for instance there was almost certainly a 'school' in Paris and Lyons. References to violins before 1550 in countries other than Italy do not always make clear whether the instrument in question was of local manufacture or imported from Italy. However, it is evident that shortly after 1550 Italian violin makers enjoyed a lucrative export business to England, France, the Low Countries, Germany and elsewhere. Andrea Amati of Cremona, for instance, reputedly made a set of 38 instruments (12 'small' violins, 12 'large', 6 violas and 8 cellos) for the French court of Charles IX in the 1560s and 1570s. (In its early days there were two models of the violin, one slightly shorter and one slightly longer than the average (35.5 cm) violin body now.) A large viola from this set and one of the small violins are in the Ashmolean Museum, Oxford. Gasparo da Salò of Brescia reported in his tax returns of 1588 that his export business to France was falling off; figures given in these returns reveal that he received high prices for his best instruments – in one instance four times the sum he paid for a housemaid's annual wage.

By 1600 the violin had come a long way from the three-string violins depicted about 1530 by Gaudenzio Ferrari. It was being made by craftsmen of the first rank in Italy, and exported (and probably made) throughout Europe. The best specimens were highly prized by the knowing and the wealthy. As a dance instrument the violin was much sought after, whether played in the meanest tavern or in the palace of a king.

FROM c1600 TO c1785

In the 17th century and most of the 18th, the tradition of violin making did not change radically from the norms already established by 1600. In fact the 17th-century violin had a playing potential beyond the technical demands then made on it, although 17th-century composers and violinists began to develop modes of musical expression more idiomatic to the violin and more demanding of it than previously. The birth of opera, and especially the violin sonata and concerto, brought new technical demands which were, however, still within the capabilities of the violin as inherited from the 16th century. Two prominent composers were Monteverdi (in the opera) and Biagio Marini (in the sonata). As an expansion in the violin's range was called for by composers, some adjustments had to be made – for example, the fingerboard had to be lengthened somewhat. In essence, however the old schools of violin making continued with few changes.

The popularity of the violin is attested by its appearance in a large number of paintings, especially in Italy and the Low Countries, and by the accounts of such theorists as Praetorius (2/1619) and Mersenne (1636–7) – who was moved to designate the violin 'the King of Instruments'.

(i) Characteristics and use

To judge by extant instruments and paintings of the 17th century, the body length of the violin was abut 35.5 cm, as it is today. It was less standardized with respect to arching and other details. The old-style neck, slightly shorter and somewhat thicker than the modern neck, projecting straight from the body, persisted until the late 17th century, when makers experimenting with increased string tension as a means of achieving greater volume of tone began tilting the neck back at a slight angle and increased its length. Pegboxes sometimes ended in carved heads instead of scrolls. The fingerboard was shorter than it was to become in the 18th century, when composers

11. *Violin (with bridge placed closer to the tailpiece than on the modern instrument), recorder and tambourine: detail from the painting 'Musicians and Soldiers' by Valentin de Boullongne (1591–1634)*

increasingly called for the 7th and higher positions. Because tensions on the bridge were relatively low, the violin used a shorter and thinner bass-bar and a thinner soundpost than those required under the much heavier tensions from the strings on a modern violin.

The old bridges also differed from the modern one. Indeed, before 1800 they varied so much that it is very difficult to make definite statements about them. Height, thickness and curvature varied, as they still do, but in general bridges were probably a bit lower, somewhat flatter and slightly narrower. The 'eyes' were placed higher, the central opening was larger and lower, and the entire effect was more open (see fig.6). In paintings (see fig.11) the bridge is often shown placed not in line with the notches in the middle of the f-holes, as the modern bridge is, but further down towards the tailpiece. There are too many instances of this bridge placement for it to have been accidental or casual. Possibly a longer string length was being sought; possibly a certain tone quality. It was 17th-century violinists who discovered that tone could be muted by a device affixed to the bridge. The existence and use of the violin mute were first mentioned by Mersenne (1636–7). A typical mute is a metal or wooden three-pronged clamp that is placed on the bridge when required (some modern mutes are attached to the strings between the tailpiece and the bridge and are pushed onto the bridge as needed; see fig.12). Mutes are specified in all five string parts in several passages in Act 2 (scenes iii and iv) of Lully's *Armide* (1686), among them the famous air 'Plus j'observe' (scene iii). Similarly Purcell specified mutes for the violins in the air 'See, even night herself is here' from *The Fairy Queen* (1692).

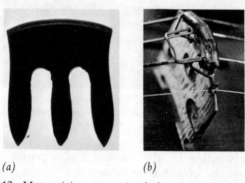

(a)   (b)

12. Mutes: (a) a conventional three-pronged mute;
(b) a Roth (or Roth-Sihon) mute

The strings were all gut until towards the end of the 17th-century, when the G string was wound with silver or copper wire, vastly improving its response by increasing the string's rigidity while allowing for a decrease in thickness. Presumably the gut strings were thinner than today's strings, but the variations from one country to another were in some cases considerable; violin strings in Italy, where the ideal was a full, powerful tone, were regular ropes compared to those used in France. (For further details on construction as, for instance, in the contemporary manuscript by James Talbot, see Boyden, 1965; see also Chapter Eight, §1.)

The appreciation of the violin grew constantly during the 17th and 18th centuries because of the instrument's inherent tonal beauty and aptness for dramatic figuration and because of its versatile application to a variety of musical uses. It was especially suited to the new forms of opera, the instrumental sonata and the concerto; and it began its life as an instrument suited to dance music. It was also useful in doubling voice parts and in playing a kind of neutral music 'apt for viol or violin'. The violin gradually made certain instruments (like the rebec and *lira da braccio*) obsolete, and it diminished the popularity of the viol except in such genres as the contrapuntal 'fancy' for which viols were so well suited. Thomas Mace (*Musick's Monument*, 1676) complained of the 'scolding Violins' and their 'High-Priz'd Noise fit to make a man's Ear Glow, and fill his brains full of frisks'; but he could not turn back the tide of the times. The violin was the mainstay of the opera orchestra, and the purely instrumental forms of sonatas and concertos encouraged the development of an idiomatic form of expression. The formation of the 24 Violons du Roi (1626) in France and a similar group in England helped to raise the social status of the violin and violinists.

The bow used for Italian sonatas was relatively long compared to the short French dance bow and the much greater volume of sound favoured by the Italians as opposed to the French required Italian violins to be much more strongly strung.

(ii) Leading makers

In Brescia G. P. Maggini (*c*1581–*c*1632) followed the example set by his master, Gasparo da Salò, including the use of double purfling (and other decorative touches), and attained a comparable degree of resonance. Maggini was the last of the great Brescian makers; by the end of the 1630s Cremona's reputation had far outdistanced that of Brescia. The Amati dynasty continued to flourish in Cremona with the two sons (and pupils) of Andrea Amati, Antonio and Girolamo, and Girolamo's son Nicolo (1596–1684).

No great violin maker appeared outside Italy until Jacob Stainer (*b c*1617) began making violins in the Austrian Tyrol. For German-speaking lands Stainer represents a peak of violin making which parallels the distinguished achievement and tech-

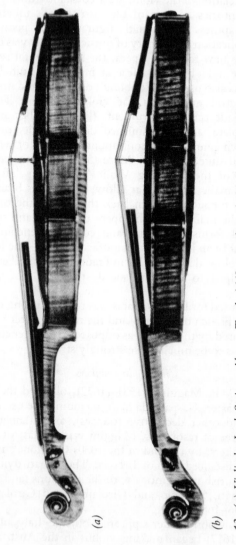

13. (a) Violin by Jacob Stainer, Absam, Tyrol, 1668; note the arched belly and back, short fingerboard with wedge, and short, straight neck; (b) violin (Stradivari model) by Jean-Baptiste Vuillaume, Paris, 1867; note the comparatively flat belly and back, the more elongated fingerboard with no wedge, and the somewhat longer, tilted neck

(a)

(b)

nical demands of such late 17th-century German-Austrian composers as Biber and Walther. There was no comparable French, Dutch or English maker in the 17th century.

Between 1650 and 1750 violin making enjoyed its most illustrious century. This period embraced the heyday of the most celebrated makers: Nicolo Amati (the last and greatest of the Amati family of Cremona), Jacob Stainer, Antonio Stradivari (generally conceded to be the greatest of all violin makers), and the five members of the Guarneri family, the most famous being the fifth and last, Giuseppe Guarneri 'del Gesù' (1698–1744). There was also, of course, a host of lesser-known masters. Amati and Stainer favoured a more highly arched back and (especially) top than did Stradivari and Guarneri (see fig.13). For the modest-scale performances for which the instruments of the time of Amati and Stainer were designed, their tone quality can hardly be surpassed; both achieved a bright and woody soprano. To the eye as well their violins presented a flawless beauty of finish.

Nicolo Amati was the teacher of almost every important master of violin making in the late 17th-century, including Andrea Guarneri (*c*1626–1698) and presumably Stradivari. In view of the present-day exaltation of Stradivari and Guarneri violins, it seems remarkable that both Stainer and Nicolo Amati violins fetched far higher prices in London auction rooms of the early 18th century than those of either Stradivari or Guarneri, and continued to do so through most of the 18th century. It was not until Viotti championed the Stradivari violins late in the 18th century (and until his teacher Pugnani, and later Paganini, favoured the Guarneri 'del Gesù' violins) that the violins of these two makers began to achieve the fantastic admiration and reputation which they enjoy today. The relatively flat-modelled bodies of the Stradivari and Guarneri instruments withstood the higher tensions of modernization better than the highly arched Stainers and Amatis, and met more fully the demand for greater carrying power which became essential, particularly in large halls and for concertos, after about 1800. Ironically Nicolo Amati was ahead of his time when he experimented (from about 1640) with the notion of increased volume in his so-called 'grand' model (see fig.14*a*, p.29), widening the upper and lower bouts rather than lengthening the body appreciably (later he preferred a small model). Amati was closely rivalled in favour by Stainer: An extraordinary number of players and musicians owned Stainer violins, including Biber, F. M. Veracini, Locatelli, Leopold Mozart and J. S. Bach.

Stradivari's early violins show the influence of his presumed teacher, Nicolo Amati (some were fashioned in the Amati 'grand' pattern), hence those made before about 1690 are generally called 'Amatisé'. About 1690 Stradivari, evidently seeking to supply violins of greater power for the new breed of concerto players (for example, Corelli, Torelli and Albinoni), produced his so-called 'long-model' violin, increasing the normal body length from 35.5 cm to a typical 36.4 cm, but keeping the upper and lower bouts somewhat narrower in proportion, thus giving the impression of an elongated instrument. This long model did not produce the desired results, however, and Stradivari returned to a 35.5 cm model of classic proportions, first embodied in the 'Betts' violin of 1704 (fig.14b). This instrument marks the beginning of Stradivari's 'golden' period, and served as a prototype for his later violins.

Stradivari invariably made instruments of the finest materials and to the highest standards of craftsmanship. Sometimes he increased the brilliant appearance of an instrument with such additional decoration as inlays of mother-of-pearl or ivory (see fig.15, p.30).

Although it is impractical to describe here the merits and characteristics of more than a handful of the distinguished makers from the period 1650–1750, some of the best known should be enumerated. In Milan were members of the Grancino and Testore families and in Mantua, Camillus Camilli and Tomaso Balestrieri. In Bologna the best-known maker at this time was Giovanni [Joannes] Tononi; in Venice, Sanctus Seraphin, Matteo Goffriller and Domenico Montagnana were the most celebrated; in Rome, David Tecchler and Michael Platner; in Naples, the Gagliano family, of whom the best was probably Gennaro; in Florence, Lorenzo and Tomaso Carcassi; in Treviso, Pietro Antonio dalla Costa; and in Piacenza, Lorenzo Guadagnini and his son Giovanni Battista [J. B.] (who signed himself 'the pupil of Antonio Stradivari' and also worked in Milan, Parma and Turin).

With the successive deaths of Stradivari in 1737, Guarneri 'del Gesù' in 1744, and Carlo Bergonzi in 1747, the greatest glory of Cremona was over. The death of Pietro Guarneri 'of Venice' in 1762 marked the end of the great Venetian makers and a general

(a)   (b)

14. (a) Nicolo Amati's 'grand' model violin, made from about 1640; (b) Antonio Stradivari's 'Betts' violin, 1704

15. *Three views of an inlaid violin by Antonio Stradivari, Cremona, 1683*

decline of violin making in Italy. For while the 19th century still produced a certain number of distinguished Italian makers, commissions were no longer as rich, cheaper violins were being made more commonly in Italy, and violin makers in other countries showed more talent, activity and proficiency.

4. SINCE *c*1785

At the end of the 18th century the leadership in violin making passed gradually from the Italians to the French. Aided particularly by the English, the French also led the way to a new level of perfection of the bow. During this period the violin was remodelled in certain respects to achieve greater power and brilliance. These changes were occasioned by the musical needs of the time and by the great social changes accompanying the French Revolution and related events.

For the first time in France a great violin maker appeared, Nicolas Lupot (1758–1824); he took Stradivari as his model, thus linking French and Italian craftsmanship. Similarly Viotti was to fuse the Italian style of violin playing with that of his French colleagues and pupils such as Baillot, Rode and Kreutzer in Paris. Meanwhile François Tourte (1747–1835) succeeded, about 1786 in Paris, in perfecting and standardizing the bow with respect to length, weight, shape and action. In this triumph Tourte was aided greatly by the advice and example of many others, including his father (Tourte *père*), Tartini, Wilhelm Cramer (a virtuoso violinist who was born in Mannheim and lived in London from 1772 to 1799), John Dodd (also in London) and, according to Fétis (*Biographie universelle*, 2/1860–65), Viotti, the most celebrated violinist of his time; it should however be noted that a drawing in the British Museum, London, representing Viotti late in his career, shows him holding a Baroque-type bow. The process of change leading to the 'modern' bow of Tourte's had required nearly half a century. The development of the modern violin and bow reflected certain musical developments, during the lifetime of Haydn, Mozart and Beethoven, that favoured both a more sustained cantabile and a greater variety of bowstrokes, including the *martelé* (bowed *sforzando*) effect.

During the 18th century, and perhaps the early 19th, the

process of angling, thinning and lengthening the neck was continued (see fig.13); the fingerboard was lengthened and its shape ·somewhat altered; the bridge was made slightly higher and with a more pronounced arch; and stronger strings were favoured in order to bear higher tensions (the wound G string had long been in use; the E string was normally gut until around 1920, when it was replaced by steel). These changes were made because of a need for greater power (and possibly to accommodate a higher concert pitch). The longer and heavier strings increased the pressure exerted downwards on the belly as well as the longitudinal string tension from nut to bridge. Consequently, the bass-bar had to be lengthened and made thicker and stronger, and the diameter of the soundpost was increased for added strength. Because the longitudinal tension was now greater, the neck had to be thrown back and mortised into the top block for greater strength. Throwing back the neck entailed dispensing with the old wedge inserted between neck and fingerboard (see fig.13). Various clues indicate that the modern violin as just described had come into being by the beginning of the 19th century, yet it is very difficult to document exactly when and by whom the changes were accomplished. The new-model violin was complemented by the new and more powerful Tourte bow.

After the old system of royal and aristocratic patronage collapsed in the wake of the French Revolution (1789–99), it was replaced gradually by middle-class (sometimes city or state) support of musical life, including the commercial concert with its almost inevitable appendage of the travelling virtuoso like Liszt or Paganini – 'stars' who dazzled and attracted the public and charged fees of corresponding magnitude. These concerts and their soloists had to be supported by an audience large enough to pay the bills. The natural result was the advent of larger halls and correspondingly larger orchestras and more powerful solo instruments. It should however be noted that Paganini, in a lithograph by Begas, is depicted using a transitional-style bow and in a painting of 1830 by Friedrich Kersting he plays a Baroque violin; his Guarneri instrument is preserved as he last played it, with its original short neck and fingerboard.

The old bows were gradually discarded since they could not be remodelled; hence comparatively few genuine old bows remain. Those that were saved were, as a rule, of intrinsic worth apart from their musical value – those, for instance, with ivory, gold or special fittings.

Old violins, on the other hand, could be strengthened and refitted without too much difficulty by an expert craftsman. Consequently, most of the better instruments were modernized and preserved. The more valuable the violin, the more likely it was to be refitted and modernized. As far as is known, not a single Stradivari violin has come down to us in completely original condition – an ironic endorsement of excellence. (As noted above, the flat-modelled violins like the Stradivaris and Guarneris survived their modern transformation with better results as to carrying power than the more highly arched violins like the Amatis and Stainers.) As a result, it is a rare concert virtuoso today who does not play an old (but modernized) Italian violin with a Tourte (French) bow. (And to play what music? Probably a violin concerto by one of the great German composers who was not primarily a violinist at all: Bach, Mozart, Beethoven, Mendelssohn or Brahms!)

Although major changes were complete by about 1800, the violin has subsequently undergone some minor changes in detail. The chin rest, which Spohr claimed to have invented about 1820, has become a standard addition. By making the grip on the violin more secure through chin pressure, thus somewhat freeing the left hand from its previous role in supporting the instrument, the chin rest allows the left hand greater freedom in fingering, shifting and vibrato. Spohr's illustration of the chin rest (in his *Violin-Schule*, 1832; see fig.16, p.34) shows it coming directly over the tailpiece, not to the left side of it as one might expect. Mutes of various types (but all applied to the bridge) have been used successfully – most recently one attached to the violin, for easy access when not in use (see fig.12*b*). Steel strings and strings wound over various types of cores have become commonplace; the 20th-century steel E string is generally less subject to the hazards of breakage than the old gut E, and responds better in the highest registers.

Attempts to improve or alter the body or the acoustics of the violin in one way or another have not yet proved markedly successful. François Chanot patented (1817) a violin of guitar-shaped body and small crescent soundholes. This met with no more success than the experimental instrument (also of 1817) by Félix Savart, a well-known physicist who made a trapezoidal violin with straight sides and straight slits for soundholes. A

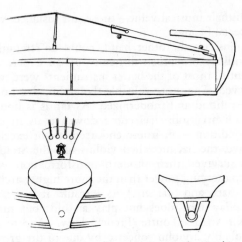

16. *Chin rest as illustrated by Spohr in his 'Violin-Schule' (1832)*

serious attempt at improving the acoustics of the viola was Hermann Ritter's *viola alta*, an exact enlargement of the violin, introduced in 1876 (see also Chapter Five, §1(iv)). During the 1960s and 1970s Carleen Hutchins and associates made a serious effort to re-form, improve and even revolutionize the entire violin family; Hutchins has built a new-style family of eight basic members (differing in size). As promising as some of the acoustical results have been and as admirable as the intent, the practical hurdles to instituting so formidable and sweeping a change, at least relative to existing repertory, stagger the imagination. It would perhaps be as foolish to say, however, that the violin (and violin family) cannot be improved as to predict that it will be (for a description of these instruments see Woollen, 1974, and Taylor, 1978; see also Hutchins, 1962 and 1967, and Hutchins and Bram).

Finally, violins have been made of a wide variety of materials including metals, plastics and ceramics. None has seriously challenged wood as the basic material of construction.

The founding of conservatories after 1795 and the growing need for cheaper and more plentiful instruments encouraged the increased output of 'factory fiddles', mass-produced in France at Mirecourt and in Germany at Mittenwald and Markneukirchen.

There also remained many fine individual violin makers in the 19th century, including G. F. Pressenda of Turin (?1777–1854), but none equalled an Amati or a Stradivari, although Nicolas Lupot continued to make fine violins in Paris in the early years of the century.

More conspicuous, however, was Jean-Baptiste Vuillaume (1798–1875), famous as a maker of violins, often copying existing instruments (by Nicolo Amati, Guarneri 'del Gesù', Maggini and Stradivari), and one of the most influential figures in violin and bow making in the 19th century. He also employed others to make instruments, and especially bows, under his name and direction (and even label); among them were bow makers as famous as Dominique Peccatte and F. N. Voirin. Ironically, it is not positively known that Vuillaume made a bow himself. Vuillaume was a supremely astute businessman, one of those international dealers who served an important role in the process of finding and extracting many beautiful violins (some unused) from their resting or hiding places in homes, churches or collections, and putting them, for an appropriate consideration, into the hands of players, museums or collectors. Another celebrated dealer who scoured Italy for valuable old violins was Luigi Tarisio (*c*1790–1854).

In recent years this recurrent cycle of violin hunting, dealing and collecting has led to a scarcity of valuable old instruments and to a manipulative commercial psychology like that cultivated in the diamond market. Prices have been inflated to such fantastic levels that the 'Lady Blount' Stradivari violin of 1721 fetched £84,000 at auction in 1971 at Sotheby's in London, at the time nearly four times the previous auction record; in the 1980s some violins have been sold for half a million pounds. Only wealthy collectors, heavily endowed institutions, or rich musicians can afford to participate in this game, which is now preventing many young and gifted violinists (who are mostly impecunious) from acquiring the first-class instrument and bow essential to play to the highest potential of their ability. There are, however, many excellent contemporary makers to whose instruments and bows many young players are turning.

CHAPTER TWO

Violin Technique

1. ORIGINS TO THE LATE 18TH CENTURY

(i) Historical outline

Jambe de Fer, the earliest theorist (1556) to describe the four-string violin, implied that the violin was used primarily in the performance of dance music, that it was played mainly by professionals and that it enjoyed a low social esteem. In addition, it was used to double the parts of vocal music or to play vocal pieces alone, and certain instrumental forms of the time exhibit traces of their vocal origin. There is no written or printed violin music known before 1582. One reason is that dance music was generally played from memory, and doubling vocal music required no separate violin part. Extant treatises from before about 1590 discuss playing the viol, not the violin; and even after that date the information regarding the violin is fragmentary. In the professional tradition of the violin, instruction was given orally from master to pupil, and when violin methods first appeared in the 17th century they were aimed primarily at the amateur, not the professional violinist. Methods for advanced players hardly appeared before 1750.

But from the viol treatises (notably Ganassi's *Regola rubertina*, 1542–3) one can deduce certain general principles of string playing that were doubtless applied to violin playing from earliest times. Moreover, iconography furnishes important clues to the playing habits of the 16th century. From these various sources one can be relatively certain that a basic though elementary discipline of violin playing had developed by 1600, especially as it applied to dance music.

As yet there were no pronounced national differences in technique, the basically Italian technique for dance music having been copied by other nations. Catherine de' Medici imported

(1554–5) to the French court at Paris Italian violinists as well as dancers, and later the Italian leader of the violins, Balthasar de Beaujoyeux, was put in general charge of the famous *Balet comique de la Royne* (1581) for a royal wedding. This ballet, printed in 1582, included violin music (two dances).

Shortly after 1600 the violin began to develop its idiomatic potential in connection with the instrumental sonata and related forms (e.g. Marini) as well as opera (Monteverdi) and other concerted vocal genres. An extension of range and a development of figuration characterized Italian violin music of the early 17th century. The technique of playing the instrument became the subject of considerable attention and experimentation, entailing a rational discipline of bowing, different types of bowstrokes (among them legato slurs), scale passages, and a much greater use of rapid figurations and positions above the 1st. For the most part the lowest string was little used, probably because the gut G string was relatively unresponsive. Such special effects as pizzicato, tremolo, *col legno*, *sul ponticello* and *sul tasto* were sometimes called for in the music although not always by these names (see §§(iv)*j* and (v) below); and on occasion, vibrato and dynamic nuance were not only used but marked in the interests of expression. The voice was regarded as the model of tone.

As the violin developed in the 17th century, violin technique tended to polarize around two ways of playing: a mannered, rhythmic and relatively simple style used for dance music, and a more technically advanced but rhythmically freer style of sonata playing, which in slow movements required a cantabile line modelled on the voice (e.g. G. B. Vitali, Corelli). These two styles became closely associated with the French and the Italians respectively and other nations tended to follow their lead. More exactly, composers of all nations, including the Italians, used the first style for dance music until the 18th century; but with few exceptions the French did not compose or play in the style of the Italian sonata until about 1720 (Leclair).

Before 1650 the Germans copied the Italians, but by 1700 some German violin music (e.g. Biber and Walther) required a more advanced technique than that of the Italians. Special features of the German development were chord playing, scordatura tuning (in which the tuning of one or more strings is different from the established tuning; see §(vii) below), the variation as a favourite form, and the use of descriptive titles and

VIOLIN TECHNIQUE

effects. The progress of the violin (Nicolo Amati, Stainer and, later, Stradivari) and the bow kept pace with these musical developments, and during the 17th century the violin permeated all ranks of society to a much greater degree than in the 16th century, as paintings and documents show. Moreover, the social position of the violin and violinists was improved by the establishment of such groups as the 24 Violons du Roi (1626) in Louis XIII's court.

By 1700, the violin had already enjoyed a virtuoso technical development, at least among the Germans and Italians. Begun in the sonata and the variation in the 17th century, virtuosity was encouraged after 1700 by the newly invented instrumental concerto, especially the concertos of Vivaldi and Locatelli. The advent of the virtuoso soloist in opposition to the 'orchestra' (no matter how small) demanded greater power and technique. Virtuoso technique took the form of more elaborate figurations and bowstrokes, playing in the highest positions (7th position was generally regarded as the highest normally used in the early 18th century, but Locatelli required the 14th position in his Caprice no.22), the use of multiple stops of all kinds, and a more expressive kind of playing in melodies, particularly in slow movements, where the employment of vibrato was developed (see §2(vii) below). The ad libitum use of unwritten improvisation (as in cadenzas) doubtless implies still higher levels of virtuosity. Some cadenzas were written out, but the majority were left to the fancy of the performer (the place for one normally being indicated by a fermata).

In the technical development after 1700 the Italians were again pioneers, but the contributions of the Germans and the French were also significant. Bach's sonatas for unaccompanied violin, for example, make the greatest musical and technical demands on the player. After 1720 the French began to compose and play in the style of the Italian sonata and concerto, and they experimented with such special effects as natural and artificial harmonics. In the mid-18th century, the traditions of violin playing were summarized in three treatises: Geminiani's (1751) represents the Italian tradition; Leopold Mozart's (1756), the German; and that of L'abbé le fils (1761) points to the gradual ascendancy of the French, who were to take the lead in violin playing in the 19th century. The modern bow was perfected about 1786 by the Frenchman François Tourte, around the same time that Viotti (who is rightly called 'the father of modern violin playing') went to Paris, nurturing the French school of Baillot, Rode and Kreutzer.

(ii) Holding the violin and bow

Before 1750 there were several ways to hold the violin: at the breast (see fig.8*a*; a grip used for many years in dance music and generally limited to 1st position), at the shoulder and at the neck. In the neck position the player commonly placed his chin at the right of the tailpiece, the chin steadying the violin, especially in downward shifts of position. It is possible to shift downwards without chin pressure by using a special method of crawling downwards with the left hand, but this method was not entirely satisfactory and gradually became obsolete. According to the treatises of Corrette (1738) and Leopold Mozart, gripping the instrument with the chin would give greater security in shifts, though this was not essential; and L'abbé *le fils* recommended holding the violin at the left side of the tailpiece in a way approaching the modern method, albeit with no chin rest. In such technical matters there was as little standardization as in the violin itself, its fittings, or the bow.

In general, the scroll of the violin was held somewhat below the level of the tailpiece, and the right (E-string) side of the violin was tipped a bit lower than the G-string side to make it easier for the player to bow on the G string. The left hand grasped the neck of the violin between the thumb and the first finger without letting the instrument fall into the hollow between them. The actual position of the left hand was adjusted to suit the individual player by means of the so-called 'Gemini-ani' grip, which automatically determined the hand position from the position of the fingers indicated (ex.1).

Ex.1

Before the universal adoption of the modern bow there were many types and models. Similarly, there were different ways of holding the bow, depending on the physical characteristics of the bow itself and the function for which it was being used. Bows varied in length from very short to longer than the modern variety. Most early ones had a marked outward curvature, but by 1700 many were practically straight and by 1750 some exhibited an inward curve as in the modern bow.

The thumb-under-hair or so-called 'French' grip used in all countries for dance music during the 16th century and to at least the mid-17th century – even later in France – was associated with the short bow. The hand grasps the bow at the frog, with three fingers on the top of the stick and the thumb under the hair (see fig.8a); the little finger may be braced in the back of the stick. This grip gives a vigorous, precisely articulated individual stroke, particularly applied to the 'rule of down-bow' (see below) and to emphasize the strong beats in dances. Longer bows, normally used for playing sonatas, were usually held by the 'Italian' grip, which was adopted by sonata players in Italy soon after 1600 and came into increasing vogue after 1650 (though players in France used the French grip until well into the 18th century). In the Italian grip all four fingers are on top of the bowstick and the thumb presses against the stick below – in principle, the modern grip. In this grip, and especially with long bows, the bow was often held 2 or 3 cm or more above the frog.

(iii) Aspects of bowing before Tourte

Generally, the unstandardized 'old' bow had a straight or convex bowstick. The latter was usually lighter than in the modern (standardized) bow, whose stick is concave and stronger. The yielding property of the hair on the string meant that every tone could have 'a small softness' at the beginning of a stroke, as Leopold Mozart recommended; in his view, 'this same softness must also be heard at the end of the stroke'. The modern-bow hair may be tightened to a markedly greater tension; this is made possible by the concave bowstick and the screw mechanism of the modern frog which make the bow stronger at the tip and the frog. At this greater tension the hair 'yields' very little when pressed on the string by the player; consequently the modern bow can produce more strongly accented strokes, for example the true *martelé* (a bowed *sforzando* effect), which is therefore a modern stroke. The characteristics of the early bow favour a non-legato stroke. Modern taste and technique characteristically join one note to the next in a seamless continuum of individual strokes; this was not impossible with the early bow, which did however lend itself more readily to the clean, natural separation of a series of fast notes and light, rapid execution of arpeggiated chords. The musical effect of a series of individual strokes with an early bow is analogous to a string of pearls, each of which appears to be separated from, while actually just touching, its neighbours – Leopold Mozart's 'small although scarcely noticeable softness' at the beginning and end of each stroke.

The natural non-legato of the early bow results in a brilliant and effortless articulation of rapid notes, especially when short strokes are applied in the middle of the bow. This is so because the balance point of the early bow, compared with that of the modern bow, is closer to the player's hand, and because the head of the early bow is lighter. The resulting articulation and natural clarity of individual notes, though produced by an 'on-string' stroke, resembles the sound of a modern *sautillé*, which is an 'off-string' stroke. The early bow is, however, capable of bounding strokes, but they were apparently used less before 1750 than afterwards. Being lighter and shorter than the modern bow and having a narrower hair-ribbon under less tension, the early bow can produce a *pianissimo* tone more easily; and because of its lightness and shape, chords can be more rapidly spread and double and triple stops can be more easily managed without scratching.

Before about 1750 the elbow of the bowing arm was held quite freely – not as close to the body as in the 19th century nor as high as today. The bow was drawn at right angles to the string, the stick sloping somewhat away from the player. The bow motion proceeded 'from the joints of the wrist and elbow in playing quick notes' (Geminiani). In long notes, the joint of the shoulder was also a little employed. The bow was not held as firmly as is customary now, nor was the pressure as heavy on the string. Nevertheless, the best violinists advocated a virile tone – something modern Baroque 'bowers' would do well to remember. Leopold Mozart, for instance, urged a 'manly' tone. The power came from the pressure of the index finger; the speed of the bow's movement as a factor in the volume of tone was not mentioned before Leopold Mozart's *Violinschule* (1756). For *forte* the player bowed near the bridge; for *piano*, nearer the end of the fingerboard.

On instruments of the violin family, 'down-bow' means that the player pulls the bow so that its point of contact with the string moves from the frog end towards the tip, whereas in 'up-bow' the player pushes the bow so that the point of contact moves from the tip towards the frog. Down-bow is more heavily weighted than up-bow, partly because of the downward force of gravity and partly because of the weight exerted on the bowstick by holding it from above by the hand in a palm–down position; the natural weight of the arm is also a factor. Down-bow for stressed notes must have been used from the earliest times by violinists, especially to make the strong accent needed by dancers on the first beat. In general the down-bow, because it is naturally a weightier stroke than the up-bow, has been found appropriate for the stressed note (or even stressed part of one). Hence, unless a bar begins with a rest, a down-bow is normally used for the first (stressed) note; this is the basic tenet of the so-called 'rule of down-bow'. Leopold Mozart said that it should be followed 'even if [by so doing] two down-bows come together' (see ex.3). Similarly, an up-beat implies an up-bow.

Over the centuries, violinists have toiled to equate the aural effect of down-bow and up-bow when it is musically desirable to do so. But the natural difference in emphasis was embodied in the fundamental rule of down-bow formulated by the Italians early in the 17th century (or perhaps even before) – the rule was implicit in treatises for the viol in the early 16th century (e.g. Ganassi) and was mentioned briefly by Riccardo Rognoni (1592) as applied specifically by violinists. With the rapid development of the violin in the 17th century, the rule and its applications were amplified. Instances may be found in various treatises, among them those of Francesco Rognoni (1620), Mersenne (1636–7), Bartolomeo Bismantova (1677) and Georg Muffat (1698) – the last a compendium of the practices of the French violinists under Lully. Sometimes important clues are given by markings in music, as in Zanetti's *Il scolaro* (1645), where specific marks for down-bow (T) and up-bow (P) were printed. (The modern signs for down-bow and up-bow, used here in ex.3, did not appear before the 19th century.) The same principles contin-ued in the 18th century although partly repudiated by some writers. Geminiani, for instance, spoke of 'that wretched Rule' of down-bow. Of course, the vestiges of the rule may be seen today.

Beginning the bar with a down-bow works well if there is an even number of notes in the bar, because by playing each note alternately with down-bow and up-bow a down-bow will naturally occur on the first note of the following bar. But if there is an odd number of notes in the bar, as happens most often in triple time, some adjustment has to be made to conform to the rule: notes can be slurred together or played portato (ex.2); or

Ex.2

two down-bows or two up-bows can follow each other, either by using different regions of the bow or by taking the bow off the string and replacing it ('replaced bow'). These adjustments were related to tempo, it being easier to slur the notes together in fast time and to replace the bow in slow time. Sometimes the bowing was adjusted so that the down-bow occurred on the first beat of every second bar; in 3/4, however, with continuous triplets, this would happen naturally.

A specific application of the rule of down-bow is shown in ex.3, given by Georg Muffat as an example of how Lully bowed a minuet. According to the rule, a down-bow is used at the beginning of each bar. After a preliminary first bar, the remaining six bars in ex.3 are organized into three similar bowing patterns of six beats each (i.e. two bars of music), so as to conform to the six-beat pattern required in dancing the minuet.

Ex.3 G. Muffat (1698)

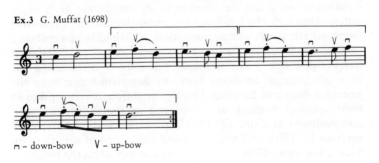

⊓ – down-bow   V – up-bow

In the second bar, second and third beats, the two notes under dots and a slur are played in one up-bow stroke, distinctly articulated in successive regions of the bow – an effect called *craquer* in French (similar to portato; see §(iv)*d* below). In the fourth and sixth bars the beginning of the new pattern is emphasized by a 'replaced' down-bow, the replacing being essential because the last bowstroke of the old pattern is also down-bow. Since a replaced bow requires a lifting and replacing of the bow, the articulation between patterns includes a heavy stress which signals to the dancers the beginning of the next six-beat pattern. The bowing indicated in ex.3 would have been understood by any French violinist of the day without bow markings, even though a modern violinist would never think of such a bowing without specific instructions – hence the value of knowing how written music of earlier times was played according to unwritten convention. While the complications of applying the rule of down-bow were considerable and often differed from modern practice – especially when a dance pattern or an uneven number of notes in a bar was involved – the rule also resulted in instances of bowing that have become more usual, such as the consecutive replaced up-bows of ex.4.

Ex.4 L. Mozart: *Violinschule*, chap.4, §5

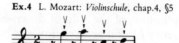

(iv) Bowing techniques

Bowing determines the length of a note, its basic character, its dynamic nuance and the manner of its connection with other notes. Although the left hand is responsible for the expressive device of vibrato as well as intonation, it should be remembered that vibrato was less of a factor in expression before 1750 than it has become since. The manifold possibilities of handling the bow give rise to so many types of bowstroke that only the principal ones can be given here. (The different bowstrokes in their musical context are displayed systematically in such compositions as Corelli's 'Folia', a 'theme' and 24 variations, op.5 no.12, 1700, or Tartini's *L'arte del arco*, a set of variations on a Corelli theme, 1758.) There is no generally accepted terminology or notation for every bowstroke and type of bowing described below. Probably for this reason, only the most common of these terms are used by players, and when the notation is ambiguous the player uses the bowing suggested to him by the musical context.

(a) The basic stroke. The effect of using one bowstroke per note was essentially non-legato, though it was not impossible to change the bow smoothly (depending on the speed and length of the stroke). In the tradition of the time, a certain amount of dynamic nuance was applied (see Geminiani, 1751, ex.XX).

Long notes were often played with a crescendo–diminuendo effect (*messa di voce*) sometimes combined with vibrato. Leopold Mozart described four dynamic 'divisions of the bow' with the purpose of producing the sounds so that 'they are beautiful and moving' – evidently using the whole length of the bow, to judge by his illustrations. The general purpose of these 'divisions' was to cultivate purity of tone, variety of expression and mastery of the bow in all its parts. The first of the four, the crescendo–diminuendo, was used to sustain a long note in *adagio* purely and delicately. The second, a bowstroke starting loudly and then decreasing through the whole bow-length, was more for 'shortly sustained notes in quick tempo' than for *adagio*. The third started softly and made a crescendo throughout to the end of the bowstroke. The fourth alternated crescendo and diminuendo. Besides these four divisions, Mozart admitted, as 'a very useful experiment', the technique of sustaining a perfectly even tone 'with a slow stroke'. (For a later meaning of 'division of the bow', see §2 (iii) below.)

(b) True legato. Before 1750 (as after), this could be achieved by connecting two or more notes with a slur, playing the notes concerned smoothly with one bowstroke.

(c) Staccato. When a composer wished a greater degree of detachment than the normal non-legato bowstroke he placed a dot or little vertical stroke over or under the notes concerned (see ex.5*a* and *b*, p.46), or used such terms as staccato (from *staccare*, to detach), stoccato, spiccato, or *détaché* (the last literally meaning 'separated'). Such terms were probably synonymous; spiccato did not imply the much harder, bouncing stroke for which the term is used today. (For the meaning of 'staccato' from the late 18th century onwards see §2(iii) below.)

Leopold Mozart (1756) said that staccato notes were to be played 'well separated from each other, with short strokes, and without dragging the bow' and Tartini (*Lettera*, 1760) indicated that the written notes were to be played half as sound and half as rest (see ex.5*c*.). A dot generally meant a lesser degree of separation than a stroke, but they were often used interchangeably. Quantz (1752) states that 'the notes with strokes must be played with completely detached strokes, and those with dots simply with short strokes and in a sustained manner'. The technique used for playing staccato was dependent on the speed of the notes. For a series of staccato quavers (or faster notes) in *allegro*, and for semiquavers in *allegretto*, Quantz said that quite a short bowstroke was used, but the bow was 'never lifted or separated from the string'. For a slower tempo he recommended a lifted 'off-string' bowing (*Absetzen*) 'as time permits'. He also adds that in the bass line of an Adagio 'the notes that provide motion beneath the concertante part may be considered as half-staccato, even if no little strokes stand above them, and hence a little pause may be observed after each note'. Geminiani (1751) devotes the whole of his Exercise XX to showing the different styles of bowing appropriate to different tempos; he recommends off-string strokes for crotchets in an Adagio or Andante, and for quavers in an Allegro.

Ex.5

(a) Handel: *Concerto grosso* op.6 no.7, Allegro

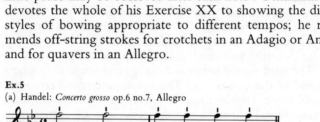

(b) L. Mozart: *Violinschule*, chap.1/iii, §20

(c) Tartini: *Lettera . . . alla Signora Maddalena Lombardini*

written   played

(d) L. Mozart: *Violinschule*, chap.1/iii, §10

The above may seem to imply the absence of a *sautillé* bowing before 1750 – a *sautillé* being a rapid, off-string stroke in which the bow bounces slightly off the string of its own accord. The fact is that the old bow is perfectly capable of this bouncing stroke, but the documentary evidence is ambiguous as to its use and extent. In any case, the *sautillé* was evidently not included in the meaning of staccato before 1750. To be sure, *sautillé* may have been used without a name; and the basic 'plain', non-legato stroke, when played rapidly, gives an articulated stroke whose musical effect is similar to that of the *sautillé* stroke.

Sometimes the conventions of the time dictated 'lifted' bow without any staccato indication. Leopold Mozart (1756, chap.1/iii) said in reference to the passage shown in ex.5*d*: 'In rapid pieces the violin bow is lifted [*aufgeheben*] at each dot; therefore each note is separated from the other and performed in springing style'.

(d) Slurred staccato. A distinct separation between two or more notes within the same bowstroke was indicated by dots or strokes over or under individual notes, all within a slur. Again, the degree of separation and the technique used to achieve it were dependent on the tempo and character of the music. Quantz says that the notes under a slur 'must be taken in one bowstroke and stressed with a pressure of the bow'. In an Andante or Adagio, the notes were usually played on the string with a portato stroke (see ex.2), later called the *louré*; the French *craquer* was similar, but generally used in faster tempos. Leopold Mozart gives many examples of these slurred staccato bowings, including the lifted bowstroke in down-bow as well as in up-bow, a stroke rarely used today (ex.6*a*). He also gives a virtuoso elaboration in which 12 notes are played in an up-bow, separated 'by a quick lift of the bow' (ex.6*b*). Similar examples involving as many as 24 notes under one slur may be found before 1700 in the music of Biber and Walther.

Ex.6
(a) L. Mozart: *Violinschule*, chap.7/i, §14

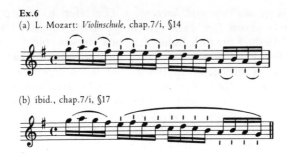

(b) ibid., chap.7/i, §17

(e) Tremolo. This term can have several meanings, but here refers merely to repeated notes, slurred or unslurred. The unslurred variety is played with individual strokes in the rhythm indicated by the notation. The slurred tremolo, more problema-

tical in notation and in manner of performance, is often indicated by a wavy line as in ex.7*a*, a passage performed by taking the four notes in one bowstroke, barely stopping the bow between each note. In ex.7*b*, a 'legato' slurred tremolo without dots or strokes, the separation is even less distinct (for modern tremolo, see §2(iii) below).

(f) Ondulé (ondeggiando). *Ondulé* refers to a 'wavy' motion of the bow back and forth between two strings. Ex.8*a* shows a slurred *ondulé*, but the stroke may also be unslurred. Bariolage is a special type of *ondulé* bowing in which a tone of the same pitch is played alternately on two strings, one being stopped, the other open; it may be performed either slurred or unslurred (ex.8*b*).

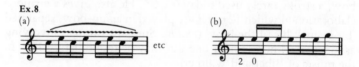

(g) Arpeggiando (arpeggio, harpeggio). This refers to the arpeggiation of a chord (see ex.9). Such a passage might be played slurred (*legato*) or with light, detached strokes, but Geminiani (1751) lists 18 ways in which to arpeggiate. Sometimes a passage of chord progressions implies a continuous arpeggiation (see Geminiani, ex.XXI); sometimes the word 'arpeggio' indicates that a chord passage is to be played as continuous arpeggios; and sometimes the manner of arpeggiation is made explicit, as in the Chaconne from Bach's Partita in D minor, where a few bars are written out as a model for the rest.

(h) Mixed bowings. Several types of bowstroke might be combined in the execution of a particular passage. Ex.10, for instance, contains slurred staccatos, slurs within slurs, and the same pattern played both down-bow and up-bow. In addition, the bowing pattern is syncopated, being produced 'off the beat' and consisting of four quavers in 3/4.

Ex.10

etc

(i) Bowing of triple and quadruple stops. The collective term for all chords played on the violin is 'multiple stops', the specific terms being double stops (using two strings), triple stops and quadruple stops. Few of the triple stops and none of the quadruple stops were ever meant to be played in fully sustained style, even when they were so notated. Rather, three-part and four-part chords were written in sustained note values largely to show the violinist the chord progression and the part-writing of the music. These multiple stops are generally performed by 'breaking the chord as shown in ex.11*a* (with the lower two notes coming just before the beat), but before about 1750 they were conventionally arpeggiated swiftly by playing as shown in ex.11*b*, emphasizing the lowest note (presumably on the beat) and dwelling on the top note only. If one of the middle notes was a continuing melody note, the top note obviously could not be held, and some adjustment had to be made so that the melody note sounded at the end of the chord. (In some instances, players

Ex.11

(a)   (b)

today break chords downwards when the melody note continues in the lowest voice, but there is no solid evidence for the authenticity of the practice.) The yielding qualities and greater manoeuvrability of the early bow (as compared with the quick attack of the modern bow) made multiple stops distinctly easier to play without scratching.

In the 20th century a so-called 'Bach' bow (see fig.17) was created to play the Bach solo violin sonatas and partitas 'precisely as written'. This goal was based on the misconception that the chords in these works were intended to be sustained precisely as written. The bow is of very high arch and has a mechanical lever, worked by the thumb; the lever enables the player to adjust the hair to play on individual strings, or on all the strings at once and thus sustain multiple stops continuously.

Apart from the problems of rendering triple and quadruple stops authentically, there are other questions that affect all multiple stops, the two most perplexing being whether to insert slurs in order to hold out notes to their full written values (ex.12), and whether to break ties, especially those in chains of suspensions (ex.13). There is no general answer to these questions. The treatises say nothing about such matters, and each perplexing case must be resolved on its own merits.

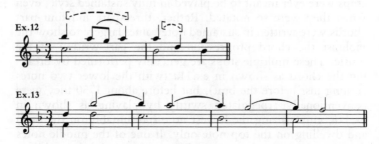

(j) Special effects. Certain methods of bow manipulation in tone production were used occasionally, and are still used, for special effects. The instruction to play *col legno* (It.: 'with the wood') means that the strings are to be set in motion with the wood of the bow, rather than the hair, by tapping the stick on the string (*col legno battuto*) or drawing it across the string (*col legno tratto*), producing a dry, staccato effect with a relatively small sound. It was known early in the 17th century (it occurs in compositions by Tobias Hume, 1605, and Carlo Farina, 1627) but was not much used until the late 19th century. *Sul ponticello* (It.: 'on the bridge') is an instruction to bow close to the bridge (or, as defined by Schoenberg, to play so that the wood of the bow actually touches the bridge); it produces a thin, nasal, glassy sound. *Sul tasto* (It.: 'on the fingerboard'), or *flautando*, means that the player is to bow (or occasionally pluck) near or over the

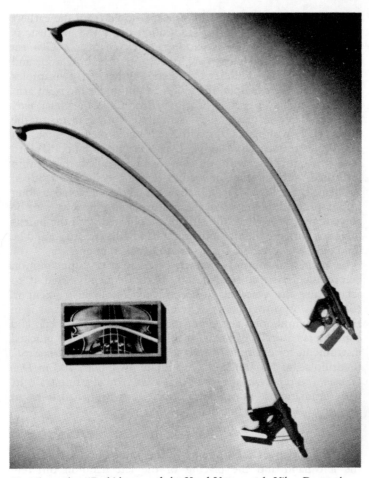

17. *The modern 'Bach' bow, made by Knud Vestergaard, Viby, Denmark*

fingerboard to obtain an ethereal tone. (See also Chapter Nine, §2.)

(v) Pizzicato

Pizzicato (normally abbreviated to 'pizz.') is a direction to pluck the string (or strings) with the fingers, usually of the right hand. It is mentioned in treatises for the viol in the 16th century

VIOLIN TECHNIQUE

(Ganassi, 1542–3) and must have been known from the earliest times of the violin. The first indication of its use in music is found in Monteverdi's *Combattimento di Tancredi e Clorinda* (1624), in which the players are asked to put the bow aside and 'pluck the strings with two fingers'. Other early examples require that, for example, the violin be put under the right arm and plucked like a guitar (Carlo Farina: *Capriccio stravagante*, 1627) or that the player play 'senz'arco' with 'the tip of the finger' (J. J. Walther: 'Capriccio X', *Hortulus chelicus*, 1688). In *Musick's Recreation on the Viol, Lyra-way* (1669) John Playford said that plucking with the left hand is called the thump (executed with the first or second finger and limited to open strings). Leopold Mozart (*Violinschule*, 1756) devoted a long paragraph to defining pizzicato and explaining how it is to be played, and wrote that 'the strings are plucked with the index-finger or with the thumb of the right hand'; the thumb should be used only when 'whole chords are to be taken in one'.

In orchestral music, pizzicato was relatively uncommon before the Classical era, though Bach frequently used it to accompany the voice or to accompany a solo instrument in concerto slow movements. There are many examples of it in Haydn's symphonies and other music of the Classical era, and composers naturally came to use it in operas to imitate a plucked instrument, for example Mozart in *Die Entführung aus dem Serail* (Pedrillo's 'Im Mohrenland', to imitate his guitar) and in *Don Giovanni* to represent the serenade ('Deh vieni alla finestra'). Its truly dramatic use in orchestral music, however, had to await the age of Beethoven (see §2(iv) below).

(vi) Fingering

Fingering involves the stopping of the strings by the fingers of the left hand and the placing of the left hand in different 'positions' on the fingerboard. It is closely allied to intonation, tone-colour and expression.

In any one position the fingers can play from 1 on the lowest string to 4 on the highest without a shift (i.e. without moving the hand to another position) or an extension. On the violin the 1st position covers *a* to *d'* on the G (*g*) string, *e'* to *a'* on the D (*d'*) string, and so on. Thus the violin can be played in a range from (open) *g* to *b''* (on the E (*e''*) string) without leaving 1st position. The 2nd position is achieved by moving a semitone or tone up, so that the first finger on the G string plays *b♭* or *b* and the fourth finger on the E string plays *c'''* or *c♯'''* and so on. 'Half' position lies between the nut and first position. Leopold Mozart called the 2nd, 4th and 6th positions collectively 'halb Applicatur', the 3rd, 5th and 7th 'ganz Applicatur'; the French 18th-century word was 'ordre'; the English called 2nd position the 'half' shift, 3rd position the 'whole' or 'full' shift, 6th position the 'double' shift and 7th position the 'last' shift.

Position changes are usually indicated by composers and theorists by fingerings, with the roman numerals I, II, III, IV designating the four strings (from highest to lowest). Unless some special effect is desired, however, composers usually leave the choice of positions to players.

A method of changing from one position to another is the slide, which is effected by moving the finger already on the string (usually the first or second finger if the direction is upwards and the third or fourth if downwards) to within a short distance of the new note to be taken by another finger. The audible result of the slide depends on the speed at which it is executed and the way it is bowed. (A smooth and rapid, but audible, slide is known as portamento, or glissando; see §2(vi) below.)

The idea of extensions and contractions of the hand in fingering was implicit in certain of the fingerings found in the treatises for the viol in the 16th century. These notions were greatly expanded by violinists, and reached a very sophisticated level by 1750. Extensions and contractions were used with the notion of gliding from one position to another without formal shift, a point made explicitly by L'abbé *le fils* (see below and fig.20*a*, p.58). Leopold Mozart and others recommended that in shifting one should take advantage of open strings, repeated notes and dotted notes as places to shift to advantage. To compensate for the relative insecurity of the violin grips, a special technique of crawling downwards by an adroit manipulation of the thumb, first finger and wrist was cultivated for large shifts downwards. Geminiani (1751) was one of the few to furnish a special shifting exercise training the violinist in going back and forth from one position to another (ex.14).

Ex.14

53

VIOLIN TECHNIQUE

Fingering systems and conventions have changed from one period to another in response to other changes: in the instruments themselves, in the material out of which strings are made, in the manner in which instruments were held and in musical taste. Musicians began to explore the technical possibilities of the violin at the beginning of the 17th century, and to deal with it in treatises. In his *Harmonie universelle* (1636–7), Mersenne gave his opinion that the violin was 'more perfect than the fretted instruments, in which one is forced to use some temperament and to decrease and increase the greatest part of the consonances'. His fingering examples are elementary. The one for a chromatic scale, 0112233, was used intermittently until the beginning of the 20th century; an astonishing slide is the E-string extension, 4444. One of the most interesting French innovations was the use of the thumb for certain chords; the earliest example (1715) appeared in the *Premier livre de sonates* of Louis Francoeur (ex.15).

Ex.15 L. Francoeur: Sonata VIII, 2nd movt (*Premier livre de sonates*, 1715)

Numerous fingerings are given in Michel Corrette's *L'école d'Orphée* (1738). Like Mersenne he recommended a sliding fingering for chromatic-scale passages. He was the first to establish the division of the fingerboard into seven positions, a practice adopted by the French school (see fig.18).

Several practice pieces are with 'cordes ravallées' or scordatura, a favourite device of certain 17th- and 18th-century composers, notably Biber (see §(vii) below). Corrette's *L'art de se perfectionner dans le violon* (1782) includes instructions for a more advanced technique, including precise fingerings for passages in higher positions and for double stops. Corrette indicates a shift of position by the letter D (*démancher*) and the string to be used by dots (two dots for the A string, three for D, four for G). Many examples give alternative fingerings which we could consider quite modern (fig.19, p.56). In the preface to *L'art de se perfectionner* Corrette says that his lessons 'can serve as

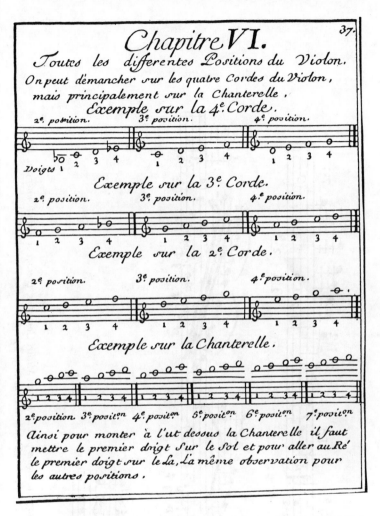

Chapitre VI.

Toutes les differentes Positions du Violon.

On peut démancher sur les quatre Cordes du Violon, mais principalement sur la Chanterelle.

Exemple sur la 4ᵉ Corde.

2ᵉ. position.   3ᵉ. position.   4ᵉ. position.

Doigts

Exemple sur la 3ᵉ Corde.

2ᵉ. position.   3ᵉ. position.   4ᵉ. position.

Exemple sur la 2ᵉ Corde.

2ᵉ. position.   3ᵉ. position.   4ᵉ. position.

Exemple sur la Chanterelle.

2ᵉ. position 3ᵉ. positⁿ 4ᵉ. positⁿ 5ᵉ. positⁿ 6ᵉ. positⁿ 7ᵉ. positⁿ

Ainsi pour monter à l'ut dessous la Chanterelle il faut mettre le premier drigt sur le Sol et pour aller au Ré le premier doigt sur le La, La même observation pour les autres positions.

18. Fingerings for positions above 1st position, from the violin method 'L'école d'Orphée' (1738; Chapter VI, p.37) by Michel Corrette, who was the first to establish the division of the fingerboard into seven positions: 'L'Exemple sur la Chanterelle' shows the fingerings for the 2nd to 7th positions on the E string

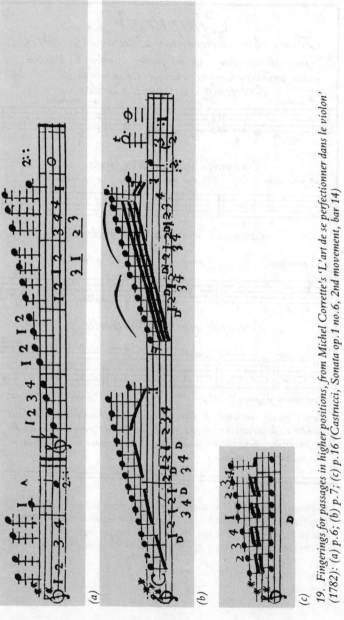

19. Fingerings for passages in higher positions, from Michel Corrette's 'L'art de se perfectionner dans le violon' (1782): (a) p.6; (b) p.7; (c) p.16 (Castrucci, Sonata op.1 no.6, 2nd movement, bar 14)

general rules for executing all present and future [violin] music'.

The French virtuoso Jean–Marie Leclair *l'aîné* marked only a few fingerings in his sonatas, but large leaps, complicated double stops, chords, arpeggios and double trills, which are abundant in his works, speak for a left-hand technique previously unsurpassed in virtuosity. In his *Premier livre* (1723) he indicates the use of the thumb in an arpeggio passage. The fingerings in Jean–Marie Leclair *le cadet*'s only book of sonatas (1739) are numerous and consistent with those given by Leopold Mozart in his *Violinschule* (1756). They are particularly instructive for extension fingerings (ex.16*a*), shifting between articulations (ex.16*b*), finger patterns in sequences (ex.16*c*), avoidance

Ex.16 J.-M. Leclair *le cadet: Premier Livre de Sonates* (1739)

(a) Sonata III, 5th movt, Menueto, bar 17

(b) Sonata XII, 2nd movt, Corrente, bars 73–5

(c) Sonata VIII, 3rd movt, Aria, bars 30–1

(d) Sonata I, 4th movt, bar 22

(e) Sonata VIII, 4th movt, bars 92–3

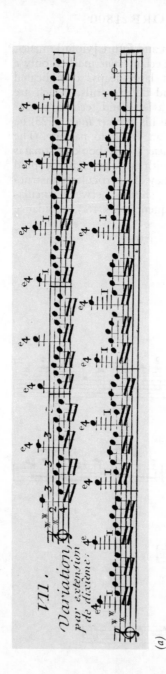

20. Fingerings from 'Principes du violon' (1761) by L'abbé 'le fils': (a) extensions, indicated by the letter 'e' (VII. 'Variation, par extension de dixième', p.55); (b) half position (p.5): 'R' probably stands for 'reculer', to draw back (this instruction is missing from the second edition, 1772); the dot (•) before figure 3 occurs throughout 'Principes' and appears to be an indication that the third finger is to be used (presumably for a note that would not normally be played by the third finger)

58

of open strings (a common 18th-century requirement; ex.16*d*), and shifting by means of an open string (ex.16*e*). An unusually difficult, and carefully fingered, passage occurs in *le cadet*'s Sonata no.12 (ex.17). Other French violinists, such as J.-B. Cupis and L. Aubert, also indicated fingerings in their sonatas. Peter Walls (1984) has listed many 18th-century violin sonatas with fingerings marked by the composer.

Ex.17 J.-M. Leclair *le cadet*: Sonata XII, 2nd movt, Corrente, bars 79–87

L'abbé *le fils* (Joseph-Barnabé Saint-Sévin), in his treatise *Principes du violon* (1761), was the first to state that the chin should be placed next to the G string: 'Le violon doit être posé sur la Clavicule, de façon que le Menton se trouve du côté de la quatrième corde'. Previously, the chin was usually located on the E-string side and sometimes over the tailpiece. The manner of holding the violin in the 18th century varied considerably, as evidenced in contemporary treatises and in paintings, prints and drawings. L'abbé quotes examples which include high positions, extension fingerings identified by the letter e (fig.20*a*), double stops and double trills. He was also the first to illustrate fully the use of half-position as we know it (see fig.20*b*; 'R' above the stave presumably means 'reculer', since L'abbé's instruction for this position is that 'il faut observer de Reculer [draw back] la main contre le Sillet [nut]') and to explore the use of natural and false harmonics. By mixing natural and artificial harmonics, L'abbé produced chromatic as well as diatonic scales in harmonics. Trills, double stops and whole pieces in harmonics were not beyond him; and he gave a minuet composed entirely in harmonics of both kinds.

A. B. Bruni, although Italian-born, lived most of his professional life in France. His *Caprices et airs variés en forme d'étude*

(1787) and his *Cinquante études* (*c*1790) were the first publications for the violin to use the word 'étude' in their titles. Fingerings are plentiful, and both works require an advanced left-hand technique. Some of the fingerings seem modern in conception, using fewer, large leaps of the hand rather than numerous small shifts and utilizing high position notes on lower strings (ex.18).

Ex.18   A. B. Bruni: Caprice no.3, bars 22–5

Fewer violin treatises and methods were written in Italy than in France, despite the existence there of numerous composer–performers. Among the most important works by Italians are those of Tartini, Geminiani, Galeazzi and Campagnoli. Tartini's contributions apply chiefly to bowing and ornamentation, but his letter to his pupil Maddalena Lombardini (1760) recommends that she practise 'upon the half-shift [second position]' and then in 3rd, 4th and 5th positions. Geminiani's *The Art of Playing on the Violin* – published in 1751 in London, where the composer lived for most of the time from 1714 until his death in 1762 – is one of the most frequently cited sources for 18th-century performing practice. The various fingerings for scales and for shifting through the now standard seven positions are inventive and thorough, giving (to quote David D. Boyden's introduction to his facsimile edition) 'a bewildering confusion of choice'. While the text does not always perfectly clarify the examples, there is much information on contractions, extensions, finger-changes on the same note, and half-position. Geminiani insisted, as did the great viol players, that fingers should not be raised 'till there is a Necessity of doing it, to place them somewhere else'. Among the left-hand possibilities discussed are alternative fingerings for the same note or groups of notes, unusual (and sometimes impractical) fingerings for shifting, the use of open strings for shifting, and the playing of chromatic scales with a new finger to each note rather than by sliding from note to note with the same finger. He also gave some unusual alternative fingerings for what he called 'Scales . . . of the *Diatonick* and *Cromatic Genera*' (ex.19). In Geminiani's revisions (1739) to his op.1 sonatas (1716), fingerings are added. They are also included in his sonatas op.4, published in 1739.

Ex.19 F. Geminiani: *The Art of Playing on the Violin* (1751)

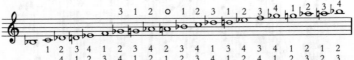

Campagnoli's *Nouvelle méthode* (op.21, begun in the 1790s but not published until 1824) is an important source of information. Extension fingerings on double stops (ex.20*a*) as well as on single notes, half-position (ex.20*b*), and exercises in shifting into high positions on one string (see fig.21, p.62) are all discussed and provided with extensive examples.

Ex.20 B. Campagnoli: op.21
(a) Study no.188, bar 6

(b) Study no.140, Fantasia, bars 64–5

The second volume of Galeazzi's *Elementi teorico-pratici di musica* (1796) is notable for its advocacy of high positions, including G–string fingerings up to the 8th position. One may conjecture that the G was a wound string of good quality. It is interesting to compare the advice of Galeazzi with that of Leopold Mozart, whose *Versuch einer gründlichen Violinschule* (1756) is perhaps the most authoritative violin treatise of the 18th

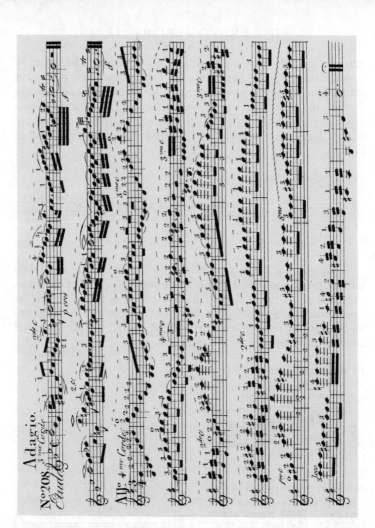

21. An exercise for shifting into high positions on one string: from Campagnoli's 'Nouvelle méthode de la mécanique progressive du jeu de violon, op.21 (1824; Etude no.208)

62

century. Galeazzi dealt more thoroughly with the 2nd, 4th, 6th
and 8th positions, whereas Mozart, more conventionally, was
concerned primarily with the 1st and 3rd but gave fingerings up
to the 7th and included a few paragraphs on the 'half-position'
(modern 2nd). In semiquaver passages Mozart's shifts were
usually made on the beat or between phrases or bowing articulations (see ex.23, p.64). The result is more musical than with
Galeazzi, who was less careful in such matters (ex.21). Galeazzi
gave extension fingerings, fingerings for large leaps, examples
of bad fingerings, and a table of all positions on each string,
beginning with the 2nd and ending with the 11th.

Ex.21 F. Galeazzi: *Elementi teorico-pratici di musica*, vol. ii, table V, ex.10

18th-century German treatises, despite the new advice they
contain on holding the violin, described a technique far more
conservative than existed in practice. Leopold Mozart's advice
about fingerings was always practical and musical. He cited the
important principle that 'one must remain in the position as long
as it is at all necessary . . . [and] await a good and easy
opportunity to descend in such fashion that the listener does not
perceive this change. This can be most conveniently achieved if
you wait for a note which can be taken on the open string'. This
principle has been important in both viol and violin playing
since Ganassi (1542–3). In addition, Mozart gave the advice that
'it is . . . easy to descend [and ascend] if similar passages be
played with similar fingerings' (ex.22*a*) and 'when two similar

Ex.22 L. Mozart: *Violinschule*
(a) chap.8/i, §9

(b) chap.8/i, §18

notes occur consecutively, they afford very good opportunity for descending' (ex.24b). As an example of the connection between fingering, bowing and articulation, Mozart showed seven different ways of treating the same short phrase (ex.23). There are also examples of upwards and downwards extensions, contractions, 9ths and 10ths, awkward chords and arpeggios, and exercises beginning in various positions.

Ex.23 ibid., chap.8/ii, §14

A hitherto neglected source of information about string fingering is found among the string quartets of Haydn. His wit and his feeling for sonority and articulation are well illustrated in ex.24. The first two passages (*a* and *b*) are from Pleyel's edition of the *Collection complette des quatuors* (1804); the third (*c*) occurs in an autograph manuscript in the National Széchényi Library, Budapest.

An unusual fingering, to modern violinists, is given in Beethoven's Sonata for violin and piano, op.96 (ex.25). This uncommon use of the 4th finger is a clue to performance: the fingered violin notes cannot be played as fast as they usually are nowadays. The gut E string (which would have been used at that time) takes longer to speak clearly and the 4th finger must have time to shift.

SCORDATURA

The Russian violinist Ivan Khandoshkin (1744–1804), in his *Russian Songs with Variations*, showed the first use, according to Yampol'sky (1933), of the 'virtuoso technique of playing on one string only (the G string)'. This extended use of the G string in all registers was based on the 'dynamic mobility of the hand' over the fingerboard, rather than the exhaustion of 'all possible finger movements within any one given fixed hand position'.

Ex.24 Haydn String Quartets

(a) H III: 49 (op.50 no.6), finale, from Pleyel: *Collection complete de quatuors d'Haydn, nouvelle édition* (Paris, 1804)

(b) H III: 76 (op.76 no.2), finale, ibid.

(c) H III: 81 (op.77 no.1), 2nd movt, from MS in National Széchényi Library, Budapest

Ex.25 Beethoven: Sonata op.96, 4th movt, bars 270–1

(vii) Scordatura

Scordatura (from Italian: *scordare*, 'to mistune') is any tuning of string instruments other than the established tuning. (The established tuning of the violin is *g-d'-a'-e''*.) It was first used early in the 16th century and enjoyed a vogue between 1600 and 1750. Thereafter it was used less and less, and it is now rare. It is generally applied to single instruments, but occasionally several instruments of the same ensemble are in scordatura. The French

VIOLIN TECHNIQUE

term *avallé* or *ravallé* (or *avalé*, *ravalé*) was used from the 16th century by French lutenists to refer to a 'lowered' string but was later used by French violinists to mean any scordatura. The first use in violin music occurs in Biagio Marini's Sonata op.8 no.2 (1626). An established tuning that has been mistuned by being transposed literally up or down may be called a 'transposition scordatura': a striking instance is in Mozart's Sinfonia concert-ante for violin and viola (κ364/320*d*), in which all the strings of the viola are tuned a semitone higher than usual (see Chapter Five, p.147). In Carl Stamitz's Sinfonia concertante for violin and viola both solo instruments are tuned up a semitone. The cello tuning *B♭'-F-c-g*, common in the 16th and 17th centuries, cannot be regarded as a scordatura because it was an established tuning together with the *C* tuning, which finally prevailed. The Hardanger fiddle (see p.129) has several recognized tunings, which may themselves be transposed.

Scordatura has certain advantages which prompted its use:

(1) To extend the range downwards by tuning the lowest string a tone lower. This type of scordatura, the original, occurred first among Italian lutenists in the 16th century. In the 18th century Antonio Lolli lowered the G string of the violin to *d* (ex.26), thus allowing the violin to accompany itself; pieces in this particular scordatura were called 'in the style of Lolli'. Carl' Ambrogio Lonati was another Italian violinist who used scorda-tura extensively.

Ex.26

(2) To make certain passages easier or possible. With the astonishing violin scordatura shown in ex.27 (from Biber's 'Mystery' Sonata no.11, *c*1674) the violinist can play difficult 10ths (and octaves) with relative ease; with this tuning and with Lolli's (ex.26) one can achieve sounds impossible with the normal tuning.

(3) To produce special effects. By tuning to the key of a piece, tonic chords and others are reinforced by the resonance of open strings. A violin piece in C major played with a C major scordatura (ex.28) sounds quite different from the same piece played in the normal tuning. The tuning of ex.29*a* is often used

by Scottish reel players (among others), and it is good in the key of A. Tunings of this kind are also advantageous for chord-playing and arpeggio.

Certain scordaturas are designed to aid the production of effects characteristic of other instruments, such as the trumpet (ex.28, from Biber's 'Mystery' Sonata no.12) or the viola d'amore (ex.30, from E. Barbella; later used by B. Campagnoli).

(4) To increase brilliance. If the strings of an instrument are all tuned higher than normal, the tension is greater, the volume of sound is increased, and that sound is more brilliant (e.g. the

viola in Mozart's Sinfonia concertante; the violin in Paganini's Violin Concerto no.1). The advantages of such tunings in helping the soloist compete with the orchestra are obvious.

(5) To produce mixed sonorities. In certain scordaturas (e.g. those shown in exx.28, 29c and 29d) some strings are tuned higher and others lower than in normal tuning; this results in a new sonority. In general, the more a scordatura differs from the normal tuning, the less the instrument sounds like itself. This is especially true of the violin.

The advantages of scordatura are offset by pronounced dis-advantages, and these gradually led to its abandonment. By 1752 Quantz (*Versuch*) considered scordatura obsolete. The principal limitations of scordatura are as follows: a given scordatura may lessen the range (ex.28); a special notation and playing rules have to be observed (see below), lacking which the player has to learn a new fingering for each scordatura; the lack of a set tuning means that the instrument is hard to keep and to play in tune: if several pieces with different scordaturas are used in the course of a concert, the player must use different instruments or retune at the beginning of each piece; *outré* scordaturas may require a restringing of the instrument (ex.27); higher tensions than normal are hard on the strings and, if continued, hard on the instrument; and finally, in scordatura the instrument loses its characteristic sound.

Those scordaturas which are used most frequently show a balanced consideration of the advantages and disadvantages explained above. Of the more than 30 known violin scordaturas, the four shown in ex.29 are the most used (in descending order of popularity). They reflect an interest in attaining sonorous and special effects without resorting to extremes of alteration, the A string not being altered at all. It is also remarkable that in three of these tunings the lower three strings are tuned to a-e'-a', presumably favouring the sonority of A major/minor. The vogue of the tunings in ex.29 shows that extreme scordaturas (as in ex.27) were used only by a few specialists like Biber, whose imagination far transcended the simple purposes of the original scordaturas. In any case, at least from Biber's time onwards, the scordatura was aimed primarily at tonal effects and secondarily at ease of fingering. Indeed, scordatura was never intended to simplify the technical problems of amateurs. It was a device for the 'masters', as Georg Falck explicitly wrote in his *Idea boni cantoris* (1688).

SCORDATURA

In scordatura pieces the appropriate 'mistuning' is invariably indicated at the beginning of the piece and the music is generally written so that the player reads it as he would if playing in the normal tuning – in effect, a species of tablature for a kind of transposing instrument. This method of notation presupposes that the player will use 1st-position fingering and the open strings unless the contrary is indicated, a point illustrated by ex.31 (from Ariosti's Third Lesson for viola d'amore, whose 'scordatura' notation is tied to violin fingering). Ex.31 makes clear, especially at the asterisk, that the appearance of the score of a scordatura piece may have little relation to its actual sound.

Furthermore, the accidentals in key signatures of scordatura pieces apply only to the specific note, not to its octave above or below. Some strange signatures result (as in ex.27).

Ex.32 shows the scordatura and curious notation of a piece for solo violin entitled *Sonate énigmatique* attributed to Pietro Nardini. A note on the score says: 'By means of this tuning one can play his own bass'. The upper two strings, normally tuned, are played with the normal fingering from the G clef, on the upper stave, but the lower two strings, raised to the pitches shown, are notated in the bass clef on the second stave, an octave below normal. Thus the first note (*d*) in the lower staff is played

on the open '*d''* string (sounding *f'* in this scordatura), and similarly *G* in the second bar is played on the '*g*' string (here sounding *c'*).

In a few cases the actual sounding notes in a scordatura piece are given by the composer, and the player must work out his own fingering (e.g. B. Marini, op.8 no.2 and Szigeti's transcription for violin and piano of M. Gnesin's *Spielmannslied*), but 'sounding-notation' is impractical for the player, and consequently it has seldom been used. For similar reasons few composers require a string to be retuned in the course of a piece, although there are a few such instances (Marini; P. M. Baillot; Biber, no.6 of *Sonatae violino solo*, 1681; Schumann, on the cello in his Piano Quartet op.47; and Stravinsky, in the *Firebird Suite*).

Early in the 17th century, a period of intense experimentation for instruments, scordatura is found in lute collections. Violinists, doubtless inspired by the lutenists, also introduced scordatura early in the century (in Marini, the *e''* string is tuned down to *c''*). Many others followed suit in Italy (M. Uccellini, Bononcini, C. A. Lonati), in Germany (C. H. Abel, G. Arnold, Johann Fischer, J. E. Kindermann, Pachelbel, J. H. Schmelzer, N. A. Strungk, J. P. von Westhoff), and in England (Playford's *The Division Violin*, 1685, no.1: tuning as in ex.29*c*). Viols and violins were sometimes played in scordatura in the same piece (J. Theile, 1667). Biber, however, made the most extensive and imaginative use of scordatura in the history of music. Of the 15 'Mystery' Sonatas (DTÖ, xxv, Jg.xii/2, 1905), 14 use scordatura; of his *Acht Violinsonaten* (DTÖ, xi, Jg.v/2, 1898), two employ scordatura; and six of the seven suites of his *Harmonia artificiosa-ariosa* (DTÖ, xcii, 1956) use scordatura in various combinations (two violins, violin and viola, two violas d'amore). Biber's scordaturas are related to the key of his pieces, and they use practically all the devices and possibilities of scordatura playing mentioned above.

From the 18th century there are relatively few German uses of the scordatura (e.g. Bach's Cello Suite no.5). On the other hand the French and Italians exploited it. Corrette was the first to use it in French violin music ('Pièces à cordes ravallées' in *L'école d'Orphée*, 1738). Others were J. Lemaire (1739), Tremais (op.4, *c*1740), and I. Bertheaume ('Sonate pour le violon dans le stile de Lolli', after 1769 and before 1786). Among the Italians who demanded scordatura are: P. Castrucci, E. Barbella, Lolli, Lonati, Vivaldi, Tartini, Nardini and B. Campagnoli – Vivaldi used scordatura, including that of ex.29*a*, in a few of his violin concertos.

In the 19th century scordatura was used infrequently, and was limited mainly to transposition scordaturas or a downward extension of the lowest string. One of the most remarkable of all scordatura effects was used by Baillot in *L'art du violon* (1834) where, at the end of a violin study, he introduced a cadenza-like passage by tuning the G string downwards through semitones to *d* (while playing), then continued with this tuning to the end (ex.33).

Ex.33

en tournant la cheville ritardando e diminuendo

Scordatura is rarely used in 20th-century art music. However, examples may be found in the works of Mahler (scherzo, Fourth Symphony), Kodály (Sonata for unaccompanied cello), Stravinsky (*Firebird Suite*), and Bartók (Contrasts for violin, clarinet and piano, last movement).

(viii) Tone qualities

How the violin sounded before the middle of the 18th century is a matter of informed conjecture. Obviously, the sound of the old violin differed from that of the modern violin because the tension was less, the strings were mainly of gut, and the technique and ideas of expression were different. In addition, there were pronounced differences relating to the structure of the instruments, with their lighter bass-bars and other distinctive features. As a rule, the Italian and German violins were probably tuned higher than the French, and this is one of several reasons why violins playing in the sonata style sounded different from those playing in dance style. Also, the sound made by a village fiddler playing a nondescript box of a violin must have differed considerably from a Corelli, Biber or Vivaldi playing an instrument made by an Amati, Stainer or Stradivari. The old sound was also sometimes modified by the use of a mute, first described by Mersenne in 1636.

The sound of the violin was first mentioned in early sources in connection with the viol, compared with whose tone that of the violin was considered powerful, penetrating and assertive. Although the violin's sprightly tone and its power of rhythmic articulation made it a natural vehicle for the performance of dance music, the old violin must have sounded less intense in tone, purer, mellower and smaller in volume than a modern violin. Because of this and the sparse use of the vibrato, the tone must also have been more transparent. At first the range of violin music was comparatively limited, and the instrument was heard less in the higher registers of the E string and much less on the G string, especially in the upper register, than it is today. The G string was unresponsive when made of gut and hence was relatively little used before the advent of the silver-wound G string in the 1660s. The differing pitches used in early times also made a difference in the sound, but the standards of pitch were so variable that this matter cannot be discussed in any specific detail.

The old technique of playing was a primary factor in the sound of the violin. The ornamental vibrato of the left hand was more sparing and less continuous. The right hand was considered 'the soul of the violin' (Bismantova). The nuanced bowstrokes of the right hand were more expressive than the typical evenly-sustained modern strokes, and the articulated non-legato bowstroke was rather more varied than the 'seamless' legato used now. Other contributing factors to the sound of the violin before 1750 were the occasional use of scordatura, the greater stress on the accented notes of the bar, the use of *notes inégales* in French music and double-dotted notes in certain situations, and the conventional use of the *messa di voce* (and vibrato) on long notes.

The modern violin has gained in power and, in certain respects, in range and expression compared with the old violin. The modern violin has also lost something in sweetness, nuance and natural articulation, and if its varieties are different they are perhaps no greater.

2. SINCE THE LATE 18TH CENTURY

(i) Historical outline

It is interesting to observe, at various points in the history of music, the changing relationship of the composer to the performer. The virtuoso sometimes pushes ahead of the composer technically, as in the case of Paganini; and sometimes composers advance beyond the accepted technical horizon of performers, as in the case of the 'impossible' concertos of Brahms, Tchaikovsky and Schoenberg.

Mid-18th-century violin technique was sufficiently developed to satisfy the needs of the Rococo period and the ornamental style of such composers as Tartini, Nardini and Stamitz. But the broader cantabile of the developed Classical style (Haydn, Mozart), and such features as the long crescendo and the *sforzando* required a technical change. The establishment of the modern bow by François Tourte about 1786 was a result of new musical conditions; and Woldemar (2/*c*1800) implied that the bow (and bowing) of Tartini, Leopold Mozart and Geminiani were inadequate for 'modern' music. Tourte standardized the modern concave bow, capable of a more powerful bowstroke and more suited to that *martelé* which the bowed *sforzando* and an amplified technique of the right and left hand demanded. Similarly, after 1800 the violin was adjusted to produce a more powerful tone in order to match the larger orchestra and to fill the larger concert halls characteristic of the increasingly commercial concerts of the 19th century.

The future development of violin playing was focussed in the person of G. B. Viotti, the 'father of modern violin playing'. Trained in the classical Italian tradition by Pugnani, Viotti first went to Paris in 1782, and there taught or influenced the founders of the French violin school (Baillot, Rode and Kreutzer), who exerted an immense influence on violin playing in the 19th century. Viotti's cantabile was based on Tartini's maxim 'per ben suonare, bisogna ben cantare'. Viotti was also one of the first to appreciate the specific beauties of the lowest (G) string, including its high positions; and his concertos unite the singing style, the brilliance of passage-work, and such specialized bowings as the 'Viotti' stroke (see §(iii)*l* below). In addition, Viotti persuaded the Parisians of the beauty of the Stradivari violins; and he may have assisted Tourte in creating the modern bow.

A benign feature of the French Revolution was its concern with public instruction, an example of which was the founding of the Paris Conservatoire in 1795. This in turn inspired or forecast the founding of similar institutions in other cities, encouraging and standardizing technical and musical training:

for example, in Prague (1811), Brussels (1813), Vienna (1817), London (1822, the Royal Academy of Music), St Petersburg (1862), Moscow (1866) and Berlin (1869, the Hochschule für Musik).

Under the French Revolutionary government, the Paris Conservatoire commissioned books of instruction for violinists, the first two being J. B. Cartier's *L'art du violon* (1798) and the *Méthode de violon* by Baillot, Rode and Kreutzer (1803). Cartier's text is a compilation of the principal earlier violin treatises, but the bulk of the work is a larger and valuable anthology of some 154 pieces of Italian, French and German violin music of earlier masters, including the Bach C major (unaccompanied) fugue and Tartini's 'Devil's Trill' sonata. The *Méthode* of Baillot, Rode and Kreutzer was the approved violin text for some years, but it was completely superseded 30 years later by a greatly amplified *L'art du violon* (1834), written by Baillot alone. This work epitomizes the Paris school of the time and is perhaps the most influential violin treatise of the 19th century. Baillot's teachings were carried on by his successor, Delphin Alard, also the author of a violin treatise and the teacher of Sarasate. The celebrated études of Rode and Gaviniès (and those of Kreutzer also) represent the teachings of the Paris violin school.

In the meantime, the Italian school was drawing to a close in the virtuoso displays of Antonio Lolli and his pupil G. M. Giornovichi. Bartolomeo Campagnoli, a pupil of Nardini, summarized the teachings of the Italian school in his études and in his important *Nouvelle méthode*, op.21, which he worked on from the 1790s (it was published in Leipzig in 1824 and there were later editions and translations). The real end of the Italian school, however, was Nicolò Paganini (1782–1840), who aroused audiences to hysterical enthusiasm by the technical perfection and verve of his playing and by the intense projection of his hypnotic personality. His music, including the 24 caprices and the concertos, uses practically all known technical devices in a grand, virtuoso and frequently novel manner, including fingered octaves, glissandos, harmonics of all types, pizzicatos of both right and left hand, octave trills, the solo on the G string alone (a speciality of his), multiple stops, extensions and contractions of the hand, and the scordatura. Staccato, ricochet and mixed bowings of all sorts were also among the stock in trade of his amazing technique.

Paganini and Baillot (through his 1834 treatise) set the techni-

cal standard of the early 19th century. Moreover, in spite of a
penchant for technical bravura (typical of the *air varié*, étude and
caprice), the Classical tradition was not neglected by the French,
and Baillot's treatise is filled with selections (bowed and fingered) from the Haydn quartets and Viotti concertos, among
others. Baillot's treatise is also a monument to Gallic sentiment:
according to him, a true performer prefers to be understood
rather than praised – 'un sourire, une larme, lui en disent assez'.

A school of violin playing similar to the Paris school was
founded in Brussels in 1843 by Charles-Auguste de Bériot, who
like the Parisians was heavily indebted to Viotti. Among
Bériot's illustrious successors were Léonard, the pupil of
Habeneck at Paris, himself the pupil of Baillot; Vieuxtemps, the
pupil of Bériot; Wieniawski, the celebrated Polish violinist, who
had trained in Paris under Massart; and Ysaÿe, the pupil of both
Vieuxtemps and Wieniawski and one of the most famous of all
violinists, whose bowing facility, energetic personality and
golden tone became legendary.

The adverse side of the technical virtuosity in the early 19th
century did not go unnoticed. Bériot wrote in the preface of his
Méthode (1858):

> The fever of technique which, in the last years, has seized the violin, has
> often diverted it from its true mission, that of imitating the accents of the
> human voice, a noble mission which has earned for the violin the glory of
> being called the King of instruments.

These sentiments, doubtless a reaction to the more technical
'fevers' of Paganini, were shared by others, particularly in
Germany – for example, by Spohr, David and Joachim.

The Germans were generally more conservative in technique
and more serious in musical attitude than the French, whose
virtues included great technical facility, elegance and imagination. Spohr was astonished by the accuracy of intonation of
Paganini and Ole Bull but was unimpressed with such 'tricks' as
their elaborate harmonics, intense vibrato, bounding bow, and
the air played solely on the G string. Spohr himself wrote a
violin method, and at least one of his concertos (no.8, the
'Gesangsszene') is still played today. Ferdinand David, his pupil,
was the central figure in the Leipzig Conservatory; and Mendelssohn in writing his Violin Concerto (1844) assiduously
sought the advice of David, who played the solo part in the first
performance. In his *Hohe Schule des Violinspiels* (1867–72), an
edited (and indeed sometimes rewritten) anthology of 17th- and

18th-century masterworks, David made an important contribution to the violin repertory. Joseph Joachim (1831–1907), a giant among violinists, was first a pupil of Joseph Böhm in Vienna and afterwards of David at Leipzig. Superbly gifted and splendidly trained, Joachim was as great a musician as a violinist – a sad but necessary distinction. He revived the Bach unaccompanied sonatas and the Beethoven concerto, and at Leipzig he studied the Mendelssohn concerto under its composer. The close adviser to Brahms in the composition of the latter's violin concerto, Joachim also founded the famous string quartet bearing his name; and on the opening of the Hochschule für Musik in Berlin (1869) he became its director. In his cadenzas and his editions of such works as the Mendelssohn and Beethoven violin concertos there is much to be learnt about the technique of the 19th century and the implied ideas of expression (including the deliberate portamento slide in shifting). In short, about the middle of the 19th century, as Leopold Auer wrote, 'a nobler, more artistic trend made itself evident'; and of this trend David and Joachim, among others, were prominent examples.

Although one may sometimes speak quite properly of 'schools' and their characteristics, and although great violinists like Joachim and Ysaÿe played in markedly different styles, sharp distinctions in schools of instruction became less clear in the course of the 19th century. There was a strong tendency to mix the teachings of various schools, to amalgamate their styles and, under outstanding teachers, to select the best from all methods – a process that had been going on for some time. The old Italian training was grafted on to the newer precepts in France and Belgium, and the results, in turn, to various teachings in Vienna, Prague, Leipzig and Budapest.

This trend is illustrated by the background and training of Leopold Auer (1845–1930), who became in turn the most successful teacher in the early 20th century, to judge by the attainments of his pupils (Heifetz, Elman, Milstein, Zimbalist and others). Auer was born in Hungary and studied with Ridley Kohne at the Budapest Conservatory, using Alard's *Ecole de violon* – an indication of the fact that the goal of every violinist was (as Auer said) the Paris Conservatoire. Then Auer studied in Vienna with Jacob Dont (who had studied in Vienna with Joseph Böhm, a Hungarian). His formal training was completed with Joachim at Hanover (1863–5), and in 1868 he succeeded Wieniawski at the St Petersburg Conservatory. Auer's fundamental training was French in origin, and by inviting him to Russia St Petersburg was continuing a French tradition. Rode had taught there, as had Vieuxtemps (1846–51). Böhm too had studied under Rode at St Petersburg, going later to Vienna (and, as noted above, Böhm taught Dont, a teacher of Auer's). Thus the central tradition was Franco-Belgian, but there were many other influences at work. This central tradition defined clearly the technique of the time, including its limitations; and this may explain why Auer considered unplayable the novel difficulties in the violin concerto that Tchaikovsky dedicated to him (the concerto was first played by Adolf Brodsky, to whom Tchaikovsky re-dedicated it).

While Auer was undoubtedly a great teacher, he did not really found a school; and, as he and his pupils have said, he had no particular 'method'. Part of his greatness as a teacher was his ability to bring out the best in each pupil treated as an individual. Hence the 'Russian' school of Auer comprised essentially a great teacher and a group of pupils some of whom were endowed with natural gifts of the highest order.

On the other hand Otakar Ševčík (1852–1934), who was chiefly associated with Prague, though also with Kiev and Vienna, brought something new to violin instruction. He revolutionized and systematized basic technique, especially of the left hand, by a system of numberless exercises based on the semitone system (rather than the diatonic system, as previously); and all possible permutations and combinations of this system were applied to fingering, bowing and technique in general. The introduction and gradual acceptance of Ševčík's exercises led to a great increase in the efficiency of basic technique, and as a result the technical proficiency of the average violinist rose considerably. It is a moot point whether Ševčík was as interested in musical as in technical questions; and although he trained many virtuosos, including Jan Kubelík, none of them made the lasting impression of an artist such as Heifetz. Nevertheless, from a technical point of view at least, Ševčík's achievements were of the highest order, and every violinist is in his debt.

No matter how great, the teacher is but a means to the end of training the violinist. Given the technical tradition obtaining in the early 20th century, the ultimate models for young violinists were the great players of the time, especially Ysaÿe and Kreisler. Kreisler (1875–1962), trained in Vienna by Auer and Hellmesberger and in Paris by Massart (a pupil of Kreutzer), was also

VIOLIN TECHNIQUE

greatly influenced by Joachim in his musical ideals in spite of their vast difference in playing styles. But his real idol was Ysaÿe (1858–1931). Kreisler's playing was unique and his tone was perhaps the most favoured of modern times. He introduced the vibrato on fast notes as well as in cantabile passages – a practice of continuous vibrato generally followed since. He endeared himself to violinists and audiences alike by his contributions to the repertory: attractive, eminently violinistic short pieces or arrangements which he sometimes promoted under the names of Classical composers – a practice that was discovered and viewed with moral indignation by some, while Kreisler himself maintained an air of innocent bewilderment over the whole thing. In any case his playing of the great concertos, especially those of Beethoven and Brahms (for which he wrote cadenzas), was an unforgettable experience.

Kreisler, whose fundamental interests were musical rather than technical, markedly influenced the repertory, but he had little taste for 'modern' music. On the other hand, Joseph Szigeti (1892–1973), a pupil of Hubay in Budapest, while also interested in the Classics, supported modern composers by playing their music and, in some cases, commissioning new music (e.g. from Bartók, his friend and compatriot).

In the course of the 20th century a number of distinguished teachers appeared, among them Carl Flesch (1873–1944). Trained in Vienna and Paris, Flesch exhibited his gifts as a pedagogue early in his career, his *Urstudien* (1911) being revolutionary in their rational approach to basic left-hand finger motions. His most influential work was *Die Kunst des Violin-Spiels*, which embodies a systematic approach to instruction and many thoughtful solutions to technical problems, combined with the highest musical ideals. His pupil Max Rostal continued the Flesch tradition in London and on the Continent. In France, Lucien Capet wrote a noteworthy contribution to the art of bowing (*La technique supérieure de l'archet*, 1916). In the USSR the successes of Auer were continued by P. Stolyarsky (1871–1944) and later by such celebrated virtuosos as David Oistrakh (1908–75) in Moscow. In the USA, violin instruction is an amalgam of European systems. Among the most successful teachers one may mention Louis Persinger, who taught Menuhin and Stern (the latter was also the pupil of Naoum Blinder in San Francisco), and Ivan Galamian, possibly the most influential teacher in the USA during the third quarter of the 20th century, and the author of an important work on violin playing (*Principles of Violin Playing and Teaching*, 1962). Born in Iran, Galamian was trained in Moscow and Paris.

Since 1945 the emphasis in the recital repertory has shifted somewhat from 'small pieces' to a greater interest in sonatas, both classic and modern; and the most conspicuous changes in the sound of the violin have been brought about mainly by the demands of composers. Even among the works of Debussy and Ravel there are many interesting uses of mutes, tremolos and harmonics to produce impressionistic sound among the strings, but after 1918 the exploitation of many special effects by composers such as Stravinsky, Bartók, Hindemith, Schoenberg, Berg and Webern was more striking. Stravinsky often treated the violin percussively, and Bartók was especially ingenious in suggesting new sounds (e.g. the pizzicato rebounding from the fingerboard; see §(iv) below) or old sounds used in new ways – among them the glissando employed with structural significance (as a device of imitation in the Fourth Quartet). Bartók also contrasted vibrato and non-vibrato to juxtapose a vibrant and a 'white' tone.

Music of the 12-note composers confronts the violinist with difficult problems of intonation, often insoluble by a traditional 'position' technique geared to the chord progressions of tonal music. In atonal music, the old signposts have been removed, and control of intonation must be achieved partly by intense concentration on hearing and partly by a greater reliance on extensions and contractions to solve such difficulties as those posed by the multiple stops in the Schoenberg Violin Concerto.

Serial composers have also been intensely interested in expanding the range of possible sound-effects on the violin. One of the most interesting features of Schoenberg's String Trio is the fascinating use of rather *outré* effects for tone-colour: for instance, *col legno, sul ponticello* and numerous harmonics. The rapid alternation of these and similar effects is often a severe test of the mental and technical agility of the player. Difficulties of this sort invite specialization and certain violinists (e.g. Louis Krasner, Robert Gross and Paul Zukofsky) have accordingly specialized in contemporary music.

Modern violin playing is also remarkable for its use of the very high registers on all strings. Violinists today (particularly the younger players) generally oppose the sliding shift and seek to eliminate unwanted slides by a 'creeping fingering' (see §(v) below) involving extensions and contractions. But the expressive portamento, especially upwards, is still used as a special effect. Fingering and sometimes shifting is determined more often by a desire to emphasize phrasing than by the technical convenience of many older fingerings. In seeking a bigger and more sonorous ('Russian') tone, characteristic of Auer's pupils, violinists today have resorted to higher tensions on the instrument and bow, firmer bow grips, higher positions on the strings (especially the G string), and a broader and more intense vibrato.

(ii) Holding the violin and bow

By the later 18th century most violinists held the violin under the chin, which more or less secured the instrument. There was no clear preference as to placing the chin to the right of the tailpiece (Tartini) or to the left (Viotti). Spohr (*Violin-Schule*, 1832) claimed that he invented the chin rest in about 1820 to increase security. However, the illustrations in his method show the chin rest directly over the tailpiece, and Spohr said that this middle position allows greater freedom and regularity in bowing. But Baillot (1834) recommended that the chin be on the left side, 'not over the tailpiece', and thereafter holding at the left side became the normal method. Baillot also mentioned the use of some sort of shoulder pad for people of small stature (particularly women and children), for the sake of greater security and convenience. Later, the use of shoulder pads and other supports between the shoulder and the violin became general. Among players today there has been some reaction to such rigid security in gripping the violin, which, although it has the advantage of complete freedom of the left hand, has the disadvantage of tension and sometimes of causing sores on the neck. Thus a number of the best players today grip strongly with the chin only when necessary, as in downward shifts, and still others avoid a shoulder pad on the grounds that it dampens the tone.

The scroll of the violin is held horizontal to the floor, rather higher than formerly, and the E-string side is tilted somewhat downwards, although this matter is dependent on the position of the bow arm. When the latter is close to the player's side (as in the 19th century), a steeper downward tilt of the E-string side is needed for ease of playing on the G string, and vice versa when the right arm is held away from the side as is more usual today. The position of the left hand as it grips the violin neck is shown

22. *The old German grip, in which the bow was held relatively lightly:*
lithograph from Ferdinand David's 'Violinschule' (1864)

in fig.22. The hand position changes, of course, in the higher
positions, and the thumb tends to disappear under the neck
(fig.25, p.84). The Geminiani grip (fig.8*b* and ex.1 above) was
used for a long time to give the proper hand position for 1st
position.

By 1800 the old 'French' bow grip was completely obsolete,

and the old 'Italian' grip with thumb and fingers gripping the bowstick became the basis for future development. Although there are some vestiges of a grip with the thumb several centimetres above the frog (sometimes used by Paganini), the normal method is one in which the thumb is held at the frog. The firmness and power of the bow grip depend on the position of the thumb relative to the fingers and the 'pressure point' of the index finger on the stick. In the old German grip (see fig.22) the bow was held relatively lightly. In the grip favoured by the French and Belgians, the thumb is about opposite the second (i.e. 'middle') finger or between the second and third fingers, and the middle of the second joint of the index finger presses against the bowstick (see fig.23); the fingers are fairly close together. In the 20th century, still stronger grips have sometimes been used with the thumb under the third (or even fourth) finger and with a corresponding adjustment in the index finger (as by Spivakovsky, for instance), but these grips are not regarded as advantageous for the anatomy of most players. The little finger is used as a balancing device when playing in the lower part of the bow (see figs.23 and 25).

In the 18th century the right arm was held loosely at the side, in the 19th century closer to the side (compare Geminiani with Joachim in fig.8 above). As Spohr said, when bowing at the frog, the wrist is high, the elbow is low and as near the body as possible. The illustration in fig.8c of the young Joachim shows this position very clearly. In the 20th century the elbow is held more loosely away from the body (as by Heifetz in fig.25) and the high wrist at the frog is flattened out. The modern position of the right arm also implies a greater degree of turning inwards (pronation) of the hand (see fig.24). The position of the arm and the bow grip also depend on such factors as whether one is playing *forte* or *piano*, *détaché* or legato.

(iii) Bowing techniques

The bow is held at a right angle to the strings, near the bridge for loud tones and away from it for soft ones. With the modern bow the 'small softness', characteristic of the old bow attack, has disappeared and the tone may start more abruptly – a kind of sharp attack first used by Viotti. The non-legato bowstroke characteristic of the old bow has been replaced by a 'seamless' legato, an ideal made possible by a super-legato bow change. This style entails a greater use of the fingers (especially at the frog), as cultivated by the Franco-Belgian school (see also the special finger exercises in Flesch's *Urstudien*). The fingers are also used more than previously in bowstrokes like the *martelé* required for *sforzando* effects. In the long bowstroke the fingers, wrist and upper arm all come into play. The long bowstroke is also useful to equalize up-bow and down-bow and for practising bow-strokes nuanced or evenly sustained. In the 19th century the upper arm was used less than it is in modern times, when the shoulder has been used by 20th-century players to equalize tone (Kreisler, Heifetz, Szigeti).

Before 1750 the usual method of increasing the volume of tone consisted in pressing the index finger harder on the bowstick. This method is still common, but some violinists also use the middle finger, which, when opposite the thumb, creates what Isaac Stern described as a 'circle of pressure'. Increased bow speed, mentioned for the first time by Leopold Mozart, is another way to increase volume. A slight spread to the fingers promotes added pressure on the bow, as does the pronation of

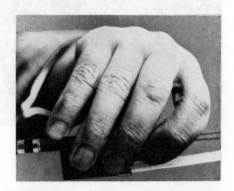

23. The Franco-Belgian grip

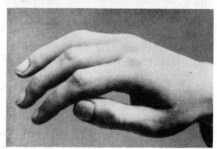

24. Pronation of the right hand in the Franco-Belgian grip

25. Jascha Heifetz playing in a high position

the hand, the application of the bow hair more flatly on the string, and the use of a high-tension adjustment of the bow hair (practised by Kreisler).

The old 'rule of down-bow' is still valid in that down-bow is equated with the accented (especially, first) beat of the bar. But the rule is not as rigidly applied as in earlier times and sometimes special bowings are introduced which violate it altogether. Ex.34, for instance, reverses the normal usage of down-bow and up-bow to bring out the short notes clearly. One may also use a series of successive up-bows or down-bows for special reasons. Two cardinal developments have been, first, the concept of 'divisions of the bow', a phrase used in the 19th century to refer

Ex.34

to the use of particular segments of the bow under various conditions of tempo (whole bow, half-bow, upper half-bow, upper third, etc, in *adagio, moderato, allegro*, etc); and, second, the standardization of bowing, one of the great accomplishments of the French school, as important to the orchestra as to the soloist.

In the 17th century the bow was proclaimed the soul of the violin, and this affirmation of faith was reiterated with monotonous regularity through the 19th century. The bowstrokes of the modern bow differ from those before 1750, partly because the action of the modern bow is different and partly because since about 1800 dynamic nuance has been considered a separate aspect of bowing technique rather than an inherent aspect of it, as earlier. The immense variety of modern bowstrokes arises from a number of basic factors which may be used in combination. Apart from the length or part of the bow used or the dynamic nuance sought, these basic factors are: whether one bowstroke plays one note; whether two or more notes played in a single stroke are legato or detached; whether the bow plays on or off the string and, if off the string, whether the bow is controlled or uncontrolled.

The bowstrokes listed below assumed prominence after 1750 while several already established bowstrokes continued basically unchanged (these are not described again here; see §1(iv) above). The term 'coup d'archet', used in French 18th- and 19th-century treatises for a bowstroke in general, is occasionally found in such qualified forms as *coup d'archet articulé* (e.g. in L'abbé *le fils*, 1761). Castile-Blaze (*Dictionnaire de musique moderne*, 3/1828) defined the *coup d'archet* as the manner of producing (*lancer*) the sound by means of the bow; he said the bowstroke ought to be distinct, firm and full-bodied (*moelleux*). The special term *le premier coup d'archet* (late 18th century) usually refers to the bowstroke used at the opening of a symphony beginning with a loud tutti passage, often in unison (Mozart made fun of this device in a letter to his father from Paris, 12 June 1778: 'what a fuss the oxen here make of this trick! The devil take me if I can see any difference! They all begin together, just as they do in other places').

VIOLIN TECHNIQUE

(a) The legato slur. The playing of several notes with a smooth continuity in one bowstroke gained in prominence after 1750.

(b) Détaché. This term signifies the basic stroke in which one note is bowed by one bowstroke. Because of the quick response of the modern bow and the almost imperceptible change from one bowstroke to another that is taught in modern technique, these strokes may not be 'detached' at all in the old sense of 'separated'. Instead, in the 'simple *détaché*' the notes may be imperceptibly joined to sound legato even though the bow changes direction. For this stroke there is no special marking. *Détaché* may refer to a bowstroke of any length; sometimes a long *détaché* is called *le grand détaché*. Sometimes the individual notes are marked by a line over or under the note (ex.35), which generally denotes a broad, vigorous stroke. In other types of

Ex.35

détaché (for which there are no generally recognized signs), the notes are really 'detached' (i.e. separated) by means of accents of various types or by lifting the bow off the string as in *fouetté* ('whipped'), where, after being lifted, the bow is struck down again vigorously ('whipped') on to the string.

(c) Martelé. The literal meaning of this term is 'hammered', referring to a percussive on-string stroke produced by an explosive release following heavy initial pressure ('pinching') on the string, and a subsequent stop of the arm (and tone) before the next 'pinching'. The result is a sharp, biting, *sforzando*-like attack and a rest between strokes. The early bow, with its comparatively gentle attack, cannot produce this stroke effectively. *Martelé* can be played in any region of the bow (but is best between middle and point). However, it cannot be executed in excess of a certain speed because of the preparation required for each stroke. *Martelé* may be indicated by dots or by arrow-head strokes as in ex.36.

Ex.36

(d) Sautillé. This is a rapid detached stroke played in the middle of the bow so that the bow bounces of its own volition. *Sautillé* is usually indicated by dots, sometimes by arrow-head strokes.

(e) Spiccato. The term is used either as a synonym for *sautillé* or to mean a controlled thrown-and-lifted stroke as in staccato before 1750 (see §2(iv)*c* above).

(f) Staccato. The modern staccato can be separate strokes, or a series of *martelé* strokes taken in one bowstroke, as in ex.37. This gives a brilliant effect, more easily executed up-bow than down-bow. It is usually notated with dots under a slur.

Ex.37

(g) Flying staccato (staccato volante). In this stroke the bow is allowed to spring slightly off the string. As in staccato taken in one bowstroke, up-bow is more usual and easier than down-bow. The notation is the same.

(h) Flying spiccato. This stroke consists of a number of spiccato notes (i.e. thrown strokes). Consequently, it is more limited in speed than the flying staccato. Flying spiccato is usually performed up-bow, and can be executed in one place on the bow by a 'recovered' stroke.

(i) Ricochet (jeté). In this bowstroke the bow is thrown on the string, making contact in its upper third, so that it will bounce or 'ricochet' off the string two to six times, or even more, as indicated in Paganini's Ninth Caprice (ex.38).

Ex.38 Paganini: Caprice no.9

(j) Tremolo. The modern, unmeasured, tremolo bowstroke is generally used in the orchestra but also (after the mid-19th century) in some chamber music and solo playing: the same note

VIOLIN TECHNIQUE

is reiterated very rapidly with very little bow, at the point. The notation is as in ex.39.

Ex.39

(k) Bowing of multiple stops. There is considerable variety in performing triple and quadruple stops. Some players break the chord (as in ex.11*a*, p.49), the lower notes being played before the beat like a grace note. Others try to perform all the notes together (especially triple stops) or in such a manner that the lower note or notes come on the beat, the rest following very quickly after. A few players have returned essentially to the earlier method of arpeggiation and holding the top note, as in ex.11*b*. In polyphonic playing the chord may have to be played so that a note other than the top note emerges to continue the polyphony.

(l) Special effects. There are many other types of specialized bowing, including the *bariolage, col legno, sul ponticello* and *sul tasto* (see §1(iv)*j* above, p.50) – all of these are often used as special effects in contemporary music. *Col legno* was little exploited before the late 19th century, although a notable example occurred as early as 1830 in the finale of Berlioz's *Symphonie fantastique*; among the many 20th-century compositions that require its use is Schoenberg's String Trio (op.45, 1946), which calls for *col legno battuto* in double stops in violin and cello, *col legno tratto* in double stops in the violin, *col legno tratto ponticello* in double stops in all parts (to be played so that the wood of the bow actually touches the bridge), and *col legno tratto ponticello* in double stops in the violin and viola, also played tremolo. Notable examples of the use of *sul ponticello* include bars 470–86 of the Presto in Beethoven's String Quartet op.131, the opening scene of Wagner's *Tristan und Isolde*, the 'Marche au supplice' in Berlioz's *Symphonie fantastique* and 'Marche des pèlerins' in his *Harold en Italie*, and several passages in Schoenberg's *Pierrot lunaire* and the string quartets of Bartók. Other types of bowing include using an extra short length of bow at frog or tip for an additional stroke in the same direction to play such rhythmic figures as are shown in ex.40. Certain

special bowings have taken the name of their author, a famous instance being the 'Viotti' stroke, a syncopated bowing combined with dynamic accent, as indicated in ex.41.

Ex.40

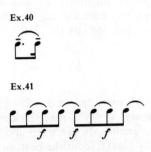

Ex.41

(iv) Pizzicato

In the late 18th century the usual pizzicato was that of the right hand (see §1(v) above). More rare are the left-hand pizzicato and special effects like pizzicato with the violin muted (described by Löhlein, 1774). Paganini (1782–1840) was the first composer to make extensive use of left-hand pizzicato (usually indicated by a +); he asked for it either simultaneously or in alternation with bowed notes (e.g. in the 24th Caprice). Duport (in his cello method, c1813) and Baillot (1834) wrote of left- and right-hand pizzicato. There is a short paragraph dealing with left-hand pizzicato in Galamian's *Principles* (1962, 2/1985; p.30). To execute the usual right-hand pizzicato, players preferred the first finger (the thumb being braced under the fingerboard); but sometimes – as in whole sections played entirely in pizzicato – the violin was held like a guitar and the fleshy part of the thumb was used (Baillot). Berlioz suggested plucking with the middle (second) finger, and the first and second fingers were sometimes used alternately to simplify fast passages in pizzicato. Sometimes cantabile passages were accompanied by left-hand pizzicato; sometimes right-hand and left-hand pizzicato were used in alternation.

Notable examples of the dramatic use of pizzicato in orchestral music are the passage linking the third and fourth movements of Beethoven's Symphony no.5 and the concluding pages of the Allegretto of his Symphony no.7. Particularly striking later uses include the Scherzo of Tchaikovsky's Fourth Symphony, where the strings are exclusively pizzicato, and the thrummed pizzicato accompaniment to the cadenza in Elgar's Violin Concerto.

In the 20th century, new types of pizzicato have appeared. Bartók showed special ingenuity in this respect. He used rebounding pizzicato, in which a string is snapped back onto the fingerboard, a device indicated by the sign:

♂

His music also calls for pizzicato *sul ponticello* (plucking close to the bridge, producing a dry sound lacking in resonance), pizzicato glissando, harmonics pizzicato and pizzicato chords. The last are normally played from the bottom string to the top, though in some cases, for example where there are repeated chords (e.g. in works of Glazunov, Prokofiev and Ravel and in Bartók's *Music for Strings, Percussion and Celesta*), alternate bottom-to-top and top-to-bottom may be indicated, usually by upward and downward arrows (though the signs for up- and down-bow have occasionally been used for this). In jazz and dance-band music of the 20th century, the double bass part is often pizzicato throughout, sometimes requiring such techniques as 'slapping' the string. Another special pizzicato effect used in 20th-century music is plucking with the fingernail, to produce a rather sharp sound. (See also Chapter Nine, §5.)

(v) Fingering

The 19th century brought a demand for bigger sounds and greater virtuosity. Bass-bars and soundposts were altered; necks were set at steeper angles to produce greater string tension; instruments were held in a manner to ensure perfect freedom of the left hand. Quick passages and high positions on the lower strings became common. Tourte bows drew more brilliant sounds from refurbished instruments.

The Italian violinist G. B. Viotti, who went to Paris towards the end of the 18th century, had a great impact on what was to become the French school of violin playing. The Paris Conservatoire was founded in 1795, and in 1803 the official *Méthode de violon*, by Pierre Baillot, Pierre Rode and Rodolphe Kreutzer, was published. Together with Baillot's *L'art du violon: nouvelle méthode* (1834) it became the model for all future methods. The manner of holding the violin, with the chin left of the tailpiece and the instrument rather horizontal, is modern, as is the idea that the left hand should be held away from the neck so that left-hand freedom is guaranteed. Scale and arpeggio exercises are given in each of seven positions. There are three-octave chromatic scales with the sliding fingers first advocated by Mersenne (the third octave is fingered 1212121223344), scales in 3rds, double trills in 3rds, and 6ths with alternative fingerings. Not all the fingerings would be acceptable to violinists today (ex.42). In Baillot's method there are studies in octaves

Ex.42 P. Baillot: *L'art du violon*, p.35

and 10ths, broken 10ths and fingered octaves (which, according to Flesch, were invented by Wilhelmj). The many examples from the violin literature of the period include fingerings that show a 19th-century liking for warm, rich sounds produced by lower strings in high positions, and for sliding in both directions (ex.43). Baillot gave the register of the G string as a whole two

Ex.43 P. Baillot: *L'art du violon*
(a) Haydn: String Quartet op.74 no.2, H III: 73, 1st movt, from Pleyel: *Collection complete de quatuors d'Haydn, nouvelle édition* (Paris, 1804)

(b) J. S. Bach: Sonata no.4 in C minor BWV 1017, 3rd movt

octaves above the open string. He also fingered the Adagio from Bach's C minor Sonata for violin and harpsichord entirely on the G string (ex.43*b*). Baillot distinguishes among fingering choices of contemporary violinists, maintaining that Viotti remained almost always in the same position whereas Kreutzer changed positions frequently. Fingering choices were made according to personal taste, technical· necessity and expressive inclinations. His method also includes much of the information on harmonies in Guhr's book on Paganini (see below).

Les vingt-quatres matinées (*c*1800) of Pierre Gaviniès, a teacher at the French Conservatory, show a remarkable penchant for high-position playing on all strings, finger pattern repetitions in sequences (ex.44*a*), extension fingerings and the replacement of one finger for another on the same note (ex.44*b*). Remarkable examples of finger replacement occur in the third movement of Beethoven's String Quartet op.95 (ex.45). Although Beethoven did not mark fingerings, it is clear what he intended. The finger replacements involve string changes that colour the tone for a special effect.

Ex.44 P. Gavinis: *Les vingt-quatre matinées*
(a) no.2, bars 13–16

(b) no.12, bars 1–2

Ex.45 Beethoven: String Quartet op.95, 3rd movt, bars 49–52

The *Méthode de violon* (1858) by Charles-Auguste de Bériot formed the basis of the Franco-Belgian School. He emphasized fingering as 'an individual means of artistic expression' (Yampol'sky, 1933). He suggested that teaching should begin with the G major scale instead of the more usual C major, because the disposition of the fingers is more natural in the former. His fingerings for chromatic scales were based on the use of each finger in succession, an important step towards present-day technique.

The innovations of Paganini had tremendous influence on all aspects of violin playing. He rejected the classic concept of positions, thus opening up unlimited possibilities for the left hand. Guhr (1829) gave many astonishing fingerings used by Paganini to play passages on one string (ex.46), double stops and chords. Paganini also gave a new impetus to the use of

Ex.46 K. Guhr: *Über Paganinis Kunst*, p.45

(a)

1 2 1 2 1 2 1 2 1 2 1 2 3 3 3

(G string)

(b)

0 1 2 3 4 3 2 1   1 2 3 4 3 2

harmonics, though Spohr rejected artificial harmonics (harmonics of a stopped string) as 'useless' because they differed so much from other tones. Guhr set forth the most advanced use of harmonics in his book, which actually proceeds beyond the usage in Paganini's printed music. Guhr, who said he was dealing only with what was unique to Paganini, gave not only the artificial harmonic of the 5th but also that of the octave, as well as double harmonics (sometimes double artificial harmonics, which require all four fingers to execute) and trills in harmonics. With the resources of both natural and artificial harmonics he devised fingerings of diatonic and chromatic scales entirely in harmonics. Guhr wanted the harmonics written as they sound, but this impractical advice was followed by few. While recent composers have used them extensively, it is scarcely possible to add to the arsenal exhibited by Guhr

VIOLIN TECHNIQUE

(Stravinsky's glissando using natural harmonics in *The Firebird* is a remarkable exception).

One of the most important 19th-century methods is Spohr's *Violin-Schule* (1832), which carried into central Europe the French conservatory standards. Spohr seems to approach open strings with the same caution as his 18th-century counterparts, saying that the open strings, especially the E and A, give a sharper sound than stopped notes and should therefore often be avoided. However, using open strings as means of getting from one position to another and in scale and arpeggio passages is commonplace. Despite words of caution to avoid sounding the slides in position shifts – except when portamento is used for expressive purposes – the fingering in ex. 47 seems to go out of its way to create a slide. Spohr also favours repeating finger patterns in sequences (ex. 48).

Ex. 47 L. Spohr: *Violin-Schule*, no.45 (6th position), bar 58

Ex. 48 ibid., no.47, bars 27–8

In the 19th century methods were not the only, or necessarily the most interesting, means of communicating fingering technique and musical style; there were also the many editions by violinists such as H. W. Ernst, Joseph Joachim, Ferdinand David, Hubert Léonard and August Wilhelmj). David's *Die hohe Schule des Violinspiels* (1867–72) is a remarkable collection of Baroque and Classical works fingered in 19th-century style, with expressive slides, high-position playing on all strings and additions to the original texts of double stops and chords. By the second half of the 19th century, extensions and contractions were well established as means of avoiding unwanted slides and

of moving smoothly over the fingerboard. Alternative fingerings were given for scales and arpeggios in many methods.
Joachim, for example, suggested that each three-octave diatonic
scale, except for those of G and A, should begin with the second
finger, but he also advised the student to learn each scale
beginning in the 1st position.

At the beginning of the 20th century Otakar Ševčík's publications dealing with aspects of standard violin technique were very
influential and they are still used today, despite the fact that his
conception of set positions is somewhat outmoded. Perhaps the
most important modern book dealing specifically with violin
fingering is Carl Flesch's *Alta scuola di diteggiatura violinistica*
(1960), which incorporates many ideas from his *Die Kunst des
Violin-Spiels* (i, 1923; ii, 1928). He rejected the traditional concept
of hand positions indicated by numbers and encouraged the
player to adapt standard fingerings to his own style and technique. He admitted to a prejudice against stretching (extension),
but indicated extension fingerings when they are necessary to
avoid slides. He discussed the merits of open strings and fourth
fingers in runs, fearing that the new steel E string might cause
'whistling'. (Gut D, A, and E strings were commonly used until
around 1920.) He preferred to play chromatic scales with conti-
guous fingers and used half-position to mitigate slides. The type
of fingered chromatics shown in ex.49 were recommended by
Flesch in 1923 and have since been generally adopted. But

Ex.49

similar fingerings were advocated earlier by Achron, occasionally by Bériot and Spohr, and by Geminiani (1751) as in ex.50.
This method of fingering chromatics permits cleaner, faster
playing, and better intonation.

Ex.50

VIOLIN TECHNIQUE

Some of Flesch's preferences are illustrated in the fingerings he recommended for passages in works by Kreutzer and Paganini (ex.51). Despite his generally modern concept of fingerings, some of Flesch's suggestions are questionable in terms of, for example, 18th-century performing practice. Harmonics and

Ex.51 C. Flesch: *Alta scuola di diteggiatura violinistica*

(a) Kreutzer: Caprice no.23

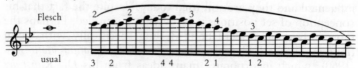

(b) Paganini: Concerto in D major

high positions on lower strings detract from the clarity we associate with Baroque and Classical styles (ex.52). Part four (pp.280–374) of Flesch's *Alta scuola* is devoted to fingering as a means of expression, a concept dealt with in other methods and treatises but too often neglected in modern playing.

Ex.52 ibid.
(a) J. S. Bach: Partita no.2 in D minor BWV 1004, Allemanda

(b) J. S. Bach: Sonata no.2 in A minor BWV 1003, Grave

Molto adagio

FINGERING – 20TH CENTURY

Among the many 20th-century methods and studies including fingering systems, Leopold Auer's *Graded Course of Violin Playing* (1926) has had enormous influence on left-hand technique. His method is largely for the highly gifted student, and the virtuoso repertory is thoroughly explored. The fingerings are often less modern than those of Flesch. Albert Jarosy, Sol Babitz and others have explored a new theory of fingering based on 'the natural fall of the fingers', which on the A string is represented by ex.53. According to Jarosy, fingering is not an

Ex.53

individual matter, and 'what is needed is a law of fingering, the fundamental rightness of which would dominate all personal methods' (Jarosy, 1921). His concepts are often contradictory and illogical, but they open up new possibilities. Babitz has explored them, sometimes to a point that many violinists would consider extremely unnatural (ex.54). Nevertheless, Jarosy's and Babitz's ideas about contraction, extension and relaxation of the hand are valuable, particularly when dealing with the often formidable difficulties of contemporary music.

Ex.54 S. Babitz: *Principles of Extensions*, p.8

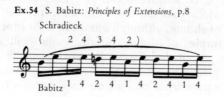

Yampol'sky (1933) did not take such an extreme position. His book is an intelligent and disciplined survey of both past and present fingering techniques. He set out various fingering principles with great clarity. He considered Kreisler's fingerings to be valuable as the expression of a unique musical personality, even if they were rooted in 19th-century conventions which have since fallen out of fashion. Joseph Szigeti also explored the subject in considerable depth in *A Violinist's Notebook* (1964) and *Szigeti on the Violin* (1969). His fingerings of examples from Bach to Bartók show his awareness of musical styles, as do also

97

VIOLIN TECHNIQUE

his various editions. His extension fingerings often seem impossible for those with hands smaller than his (ex.55). Ivan Galamian was important as the teacher of many outstanding violinists. His *Principles of Violin Playing and Teaching* (1962) embodies ideas about fingering which, while not new, have been widely adopted by players anxious to avoid unwanted slides.

Ex.55 J. Szigeti: *Szigeti on the Violin*, ex.5, p.66

(vi) Glissando

In the violin a sliding from one pitch to another is readily effected without distinguishing any of the intervening notes. This method of sliding is often called portamento. In practice, the terms 'glissando' and 'portamento' are often confused and used interchangeably whether the sliding is continuous (as in portamento) or whether it is effected by distinguishing each semitone (as in glissando). However, if, in the interest of clarity (which often entails some degree of arbitrariness), the distinctions made above are kept, it follows that while instruments which have fixed semitones can play glissando but not portamento, the violin (like the voice and the trombone) can produce either type of sliding, although glissando is far more difficult.

Two examples of sliding on the violin will illustrate the distinctions just made between the two terms. Ex.56 shows a chromatic glissando (from the fourth movement of Lalo's *Symphonie espagnole*), although no such term is used by Lalo. The passage shows clearly that Lalo wished every semitone to be distinguished in the downward slide from *e''''* to *e''*, even at the speed implied by the demisemiquavers. A slur over the passage directs the player to use a single bowstroke for the glissando, and the use of a single finger in sliding is implied (up to the last few notes).

In the second example (ex.57), taken from the second movement of Bartók's Fourth String Quartet, the composer indicated a sliding by a diagonal line – he used no terms. Obviously, at the *prestissimo* tempo of the movement, the slide must be a portamento, there being no time to distinguish any intervening notes. All four instruments of the quartet are directed to slide, as shown. These continuous slides of ex.57 are easier to execute than the chromatically articulated slide of ex.56.

Ex.56

VIOLIN SOLO

Ex.57

Vn 1

Vn 2

Va

Vc

(only notes involving glissando given here)

Flesch (*Die Kunst des Violin-Spiels*) proposed that glissando be used to mean a technically essential type of violin shift (the shift to be carried out quickly and unobtrusively) and that portamento be used for a type of shift (carried out either slowly or rapidly) intended to heighten the expression. These distinctions, however, have not been universally accepted. In Galamian's terminology (*Principles*, 1962), for instance, Flesch's portamento becomes 'expressive glissando'. Because of the variety and confusion of terms and meanings, Flesch used the term 'chromatic glissando' to describe the passage shown in ex.56 in order to make explicit the articulation of each individual semitone.

(vii) Vibrato

On instruments of the violin family, vibrato (an Italian term, from *vibrare*: 'to shake') is a fluctuation of the pitch of a note in performance produced by the oscillation or rocking of a finger which is stopping a string. On the violin and viola it is controlled by the finger, wrist or arm, and on the cello by the forearm. This slight alteration of pitch above and below the prescribed pitch is used as an expressive device and to add intensity to the tone. Many players now use a continuous vibrato of this type in all music, although such an approach was discouraged in most treatises before the 1920s. In the 18th and 19th centuries vibrato was applied selectively to some notes rather than others; it was generally considered to be an ornament, a means of expression most effective when used sparingly. Since a constant, wide vibrato tends to prevent clarity of intonation by obscuring the centre of pitch, it is possible that the overall texture in performances of earlier periods was more transparent, allowing inner parts, for example in string quartets, to be heard more clearly.

The use of vibrato is discussed as early as the 16th century by theorists such as Ganassi (1542–3) and Agricola (5/1545). Mersenne (1636–7), describing lute vibrato under the term 'verre cassé', comments that it was not used as much then as it had been in the past. Christopher Simpson (*The Division-Violist*, 1659), using the term 'close shake', Marin Marais (in his first collection of pieces for bass viol, 1686) and Jean Rousseau (*Traité de la viole*, 1687), describe a form of two-finger vibrato for the fretted viola da gamba in which a second finger makes a rapid shaking as close as possible to the stopped note – essentially a form of microtonal trill. In the late 17th century violinist-composers such as Johann Jakob Walther began to specify particular notes on which vibrato should be used (see ex.58, bars 3 and 4); by inference, vibrato should not be used on other notes. A symbol to indicate the use of vibrato is given in Daniel Merck's treatise (1695).

Ex.58 J. J. Walther: *Hortulus chelicus* (1688), no.1, Preludio

Throughout the 18th and 19th centuries there are numerous references to vibrato, many concerning performers who used it too frequently. It seems likely therefore that some players

already used a continuous or almost continuous vibrato, while more discerning players and commentators criticized them for it. Roger North (*c*1720; ed. Wilson, 1959, p.165, n.21) describes the 'wrist shake' as 'a great art, but as I think injured by overdoing'. Geminiani (1751) differed from most of his contemporaries in his statement that the close shake 'should be made use of as often as possible'. This statement however should not be read in isolation since his prescribed method of holding the violin 'below the Collar-bone' may itself have exercised a limiting factor on the use of a constant vibrato. In later editions of Geminiani's treatise, published after his death, the instruction to use vibrato as often as possible is deleted.

Leopold Mozart, discussing improvised embellishments (1756, chap.11), gives a detailed account of vibrato under the term 'tremolo'. He distinguishes three types: slow, accelerating and fast; gives examples for teaching vibrato; and shows where it might be used in a cadenza. He adds that 'it would be an error if every note were played with the tremolo. Performers there are who tremble consistently on each note as if they had the palsy'.

Spohr (1832) states that the deviation from the true pitch of the note should be scarcely perceptible to the ear and that vibrato should be noticeable only in passionate passages and for the strong accentuation of notes marked *fz* or >. His method includes studies and extracts from concertos by Rode and himself in which the sparing application of vibrato, notated by a wavy line, is well illustrated (see ex.59). Baillot (1834) points out that when vibrato is used the exact pure pitch should be heard without vibrato at the beginning and end of the note, in order

Ex.59 L. Spohr: *Violin-Schule*, p.198
P. Rode: Violin Concerto no.7, 1st movt, solo entry

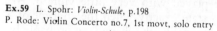

not to distress the ear. He adds that, above all, the player should avoid making a habit of vibrato. Baillot also discusses a vibrato (*ondulation*) produced by steadily varying the bow pressure on the string.

VIOLIN TECHNIQUE

Early in the 20th century Heinrich Dessauer, in the preface to his edition of Mendelssohn's Violin Concerto op.64, stated that his aim was to reflect the interpretation of artists such as Joachim who actually knew the composer. Concerning the lyrical passage shown in ex.60, he says that it is permissible to employ vibrato on a few and appropriate notes, but without exaggeration; above all, vibrato on every note, 'a fault which brings about a style of playing both affected and full of mannerism', must be positively avoided.

Ex.60 Mendelssohn: Violin Concerto in E minor, 1st movt, Allegro molto appassionato, bars 139–42

Leopold Auer (1921) complained that some violinists used vibrato as a 'convenient device for hiding bad intonation', while others, being 'pitifully misguided', used it habitually. He recommends that it should be considered as an embellishment and that 'only the most sparing use of vibrato is desirable'. Recordings made in the early 20th century reflect this different ideal and it is interesting to note the change of style between the recordings of Elgar's Violin Concerto made by Marie Hall in 1916 and Yehudi Menuhin in 1932, both directed by the composer. Similarly, in Elgar's own recordings of the Enigma Variations (1926) and the Second Symphony (1927) most passages for solo strings are played with very little vibrato. Although it is impossible to state exactly when the concept of a constant vibrato became fashionable, the change can probably be linked to the influence of performers such as Kreisler, Heifetz and Casals. Most soloists recorded after around 1930 seem to have adopted it.

In more recent music, where the composer has assumed that players will use vibrato as a matter of course, the terms 'non vibrato' and 'molto vibrato' have come into use. As a colouring device, vibrato may be exaggerated to produce as much as a quarter-tone pitch variance. Various notations have been devised to indicate a vibrato of varying width and/or speed (see

102

Ex.61

(a) fast vibrato   slow vibrato   wide, fast vibrato

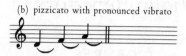

(b) pizzicato with pronounced vibrato

ex.61*a*). To notate a pronounced vibrato when playing pizzicato, a tie symbol is left incomplete, not joining the head of another note (see ex.61*b*). (See also Chapter Nine, §3.)

CHAPTER THREE

Violin Repertory

1. GENRES

Violin music evolved in five principal genres: the sonata with continuo; the sonata with obbligato keyboard; the sonata, suite, capriccio etc for unaccompanied violin; the violin concerto; and variations and short genre pieces for violin with orchestra or keyboard. Except for the solo concerto, all these genres developed during the 17th century, when composers began to provide an idiomatic repertory for the new violin; before its emergence as a solo instrument it had been used in the orchestra by Monteverdi and in the trio sonata by Salomone Rossi, as well as in dance music. The earliest known composition for violin and bass is a sonata for 'violino e violone' by G. B. Cima in his *Concerti ecclesiastici* (1610); the bass is not figured. In the Baroque sonata for violin and continuo, the violin is the soloist, supported by semi-improvised chords on the keyboard and a sustained bass part, which may be florid or imitative. Such works began to appear about 1620, reached an early peak with Corelli's op.5 (1700), full maturity with Tartini's op.1 (1734), and a late flowering with Porpora's sonatas of 1754. In the later 18th century some composers (for example Nardini and Viotti) began to omit the bass figures, implying the performance of sonatas as duos for violin and cello without keyboard participation.

The sonata with obbligato keyboard eventually superseded the sonata with continuo. The first important collection of sonatas for violin and obbligato harpsichord, by J. S. Bach (c1720), largely use a three-part texture, akin to the trio sonata: two upper parts played by the violin and the harpsichordist's right hand, and a bass by the harpsichordist's left hand. Bach's collection remained unpublished and little known, and the French composers who continued the trend in the 1730s were

almost certainly unaware of his sonatas. About 1734, Mondonville published his *Pièces de clavecin en sonates, avec accompagnement
de violon* op.3, in which the harpsichord part predominates and
the violin is relegated to a secondary role. In the third quarter of
the century a form developed that was essentially a keyboard
sonata with a simple (and often optional) violin accompaniment;
mostly the violin shadows the keyboard melody in 3rds or 6ths
below or plays accompanying figuration. This was the type of
sonata that the young Mozart inherited from Schobert and J. C.
Bach, but he gradually developed the balance between the two
instruments until they became more nearly equal partners.
Thereafter, a rich repertory of true duo sonatas was composed,
by Beethoven, Schumann, Brahms, Franck and others, and the
genre continued to flourish in the 20th century.

Violin music without accompaniment was well known in the
17th century; John Playford's *The Division Violin* (1684) contains
several examples. Probably the earliest extended work for violin
alone is the Passacaglia by H. I. F. von Biber (*c*1675). Of equal
historical importance was J. P. von Westhoff, whose Suite for
violin 'sans basse continue' (1682) and six partitas (1696) are
predecessors of J. S. Bach's sonatas and partitas of 1720. The
writing of large-scale works for unaccompanied violin was
revived by Reger in the 1900s and has found favour with several
20th-century composers (Hindemith, Bartók, Prokofiev).
Another type of unaccompanied piece was the caprice or capriccio, used by Locatelli and Tartini as cadenza-like insertions in
their violin concertos. The caprice was later developed as a study
piece (Gaviniès, Kreutzer, Rode) and was elevated to musical
significance by Paganini (1820).

The violin concerto addressed itself to the growing audiences
of public concerts, for whom the soloist had to display virtuosity and showmanship. From Vivaldi to Wieniawski, a long line
of violinist-composers contributed to the expansion of the
violin's technique and expressivity: the most prominent include
Tartini, Locatelli, Nardini and Viotti in the 18th century, and
Spohr, Paganini, de Bériot, Ernst and Vieuxtemps in the 19th.
Side by side with the virtuoso concerto the repertory was
enriched by concertos where musical values predominated, from
the great examples of Bach, Mozart, Beethoven, Mendelssohn
and Brahms to those of Sibelius, Elgar, Bartók, Berg, Stravinsky and Prokofiev.

Among shorter genres, the variation form remained a favourite vehicle for performers. As early as 1620 Biagio Marini published his variations on the romanesca (op.3), and the 17th-century repertory includes numerous examples. Important milestones are Corelli's 'Folia' Variations op.5 no.12 (1700) and Tartini's 50 Variations on a Gavotte by Corelli (sub-titled 'L'arte del arco'). Towards the end of the 18th century the 'thème varié' or 'air varié' (often on a popular operatic aria or national folktune) became increasingly popular. During the 19th century, with contributions by Rode, Kreutzer, de Bériot, Vieuxtemps, Ernst, Wieniawski and above all Paganini, it established itself as the favourite type of display piece. Another enrichment of the violin repertory was the short character-piece, such as the romance, elegy, ballade and legend, or national dances like the polonaise, mazurka or jota; there are charming examples, particularly by Slavonic and French composers (Smetana, Dvořák, Tchaikovsky; Chausson, Saint-Saëns). Adaptations or transcriptions became popular – Joachim's arrangements of Brahms's Hungarian Dances are exemplary – but there was soon a proliferation of mediocre pieces.

2. 17TH AND 18TH CENTURIES

(i) Italy

The first violinist-composer of importance was Marini. His *Affetti musicali* op.1 (1617) is for violin or cornett; his op.3 (1620) contains works conceived specifically for the violin (with continuo). His op.8 (written 1626, published 1629) requires double stops, higher positions and string-crossings as well as running passages. Carlo Farina (like Marini, active in Germany) composed a *Capriccio stravagante* (1627), remarkable for its technical innovation, with *col legno, sul ponticello,* pizzicato, tremolo, and other effects not found in works by such contemporaries as Dario Costello and G. B. Fontana. A more idiomatic violin style was developed by Marco Uccellini, who expanded systematically the higher register until the range encompassed three full octaves (in op.5 no.8, 1649). This proved sufficient for the next 50 years; even Corelli did not fully use it.

In the second half of the 17th century, such composers as Giovanni Legrenzi, Maurizio Cazzati and G. B. Vitali concentrated on developing the violin's expressive qualities, preferring to use it in chamber music rather than for solo exploits. Corelli's collection of six *sonate da chiesa* and six *sonate da camera* for violin and continuo (op.5, 1700) summarized and codified the achievements of the past century and influenced sonata writing for the next three decades (during which the distinction between church and chamber style gradually disappeared), until the Baroque style began to disintegrate. The form maintained its vitality through the increasingly complex works of Vivaldi (op.2, 1712), Geminiani (op.1, 1716), G. B. Somis (*c*1717), F. M. Veracini (op.1, 1720), Tartini (op.1, 1734) and Locatelli (op.6, 1737). The Baroque tradition was upheld by Veracini as late as 1744 (*Sonate accademiche* op.2), while Tartini and Locatelli embraced the *galant* style in their later works.

The concerto became an important virtuoso form in the early 18th century. The beginnings were modest: in Torelli's collection of concertos op.8 (published posthumously in 1708), the last six are entitled *Concerti con un violino, che concerta solo*; the solo violin is given extensive passages of modest difficulty. But it was Vivaldi who shaped the violin concerto for the next few decades, principally from about 1712 (*L'estro armonico* op.3) to about 1730 (op.12, *c*1728-32). He left about 225 solo concertos and many multiple violin concertos, in which he explored every aspect of technique and musical expressivity. He developed playing in the highest registers and used the bow in a great variety of strokes. From about 1730, Tartini, Locatelli and their contemporaries took over the creative leadership within the concerto form. Tartini began to attract attention as early as 1720. A number of his 125 violin concertos stressed virtuosity, and his clearcut concerto form remained the model until the 1770s, not only for the violin but also for the keyboard concerto. Bach's sons (particularly C.P.E. and J.C.) and Leopold Mozart had the highest regard for Tartini's accomplishments; in fact, Leopold Mozart's *Violinschule* (1756) contains examples drawn from Tartini's sonatas, including the 'Devil's Trill'.

Locatelli's influence was less far-reaching, but no less important: his 12 concertos *L'arte del violino* (op.3, 1733) contain 24 capriccios that represent the apex of violin technique up to Paganini (who acknowledged his indebtedness to Locatelli). While Locatelli showed no interest in teaching, Tartini formed a school of violin playing that carried his fame and his style from Padua all over Europe. His favourite student was Nardini, whose beautiful tone and expressive style were highly praised by

VIOLIN REPERTORY

Leopold Mozart, though he objected to the lack of technical bravura. As a concerto composer, Nardini lacked the incisiveness and brilliance of his teacher, but his sonatas, particularly the Seven Sonatas 'avec les adagios brodés', contain much beautiful music. Nardini took over the three-movement sequence of his teacher Tartini (slow–fast–fast) and expanded the first allegro to resemble Classical sonata form. But his best-known work, the Concerto in E minor, is a pasticcio by the editor, M. Hauser, of three sonata movements. A less objectionable editorial liberty is the 19th-century custom of adding a second Adagio to the three-movement sonatas of Nardini and Tartini to make them conform to the pattern of the old *sonata da chiesa*, as was done with the Sonata in D by Nardini, and Tartini's famous Sonata in G minor ('Didone abbandonata'). Gaetano Pugnani, who spent some time in London (1767–70) and was close to J. C. Bach, was a powerful performer and diligent composer. His sonatas (opp.3, 7, 8; c1760–74) use the modern sequence of movements (fast–slow–fast), and the first Allegro is close to Classical sonata form. He fused his Italian heritage with influences from the Mannheim school, and his works, which are competent though lacking a memorable profile, represent Italian pre-Classicism.

Viotti, who called himself with pride 'élève du célèbre Pugnani', can be considered the true classicist of violin music. His influence was enormous, not only on contemporary violinists but also on masters like Mozart, Beethoven and Spohr. His compositions (numbering close on 160), most of them composed before 1800, consist of sonatas, duos for two violins, trios and quartets, *symphonies concertantes*, and most importantly 29 violin concertos (some of which were transcribed for piano). The concertos can be subdivided into the 'Parisian' concertos nos.1–19 and the 'London' concertos (after 1792). The concerto type developed by Viotti became known as the 'French violin concerto' because it reflected Parisian taste of the 1780s, and spread its influence throughout Europe. Viotti had arrived at his style by fusing the tradition of the Italian violin school with the operatic brio of French music and the symphonic experience of German masters, notably Haydn. His French disciples, particularly Pierre Rode, Rodolphe Kreutzer and Pierre Baillot, moulded their concertos in the master's image but reinforced the typically French ingredients. Viotti's concertos have symphonic scope, particularly in the first movements, which have four orchestral tuttis framing three solo sections; the quality of orchestral writing was such that the public would applaud after the opening exposition as if it were a symphony. Beethoven's Violin Concerto shows traces of Viotti's influence; Spohr germanized the Viotti concerto type, and Brahms and Joachim were fervent admirers of Viotti's Concerto no.22 in A minor, which Brahms called a 'Prachtstück'. The last of Viotti's concertos hint at Romanticism; they were written in the first decade of the 19th century but published later.

(ii) England and Germany

Throughout the 17th century English string players, such as Thomas Simpson and William Brade, were held in high esteem on the Continent; they left England, often for political reasons, going to Germany, France, the Netherlands, Denmark and even Italy. They left behind a considerable prejudice against the violin and in favour of the old viols that were still used in England. In 1657 Anthony Wood reported that musical connoisseurs 'esteemed the violin to be an instrument only belonging to the common fiddler' and avoided it 'for fear of making these meetings to be vaine and fiddling'. That same year, however, Davis Mell, 'the most eminent violinist of London, and clock-maker', visited Oxford and was adjudged to 'have a prodigious hand on the violin'. Mell's fame was soon obscured by the arrival from Lübeck of Thomas Baltzer (d 1663), 'the most famous artist for the violin that the world [had] yet produced'. Baltzer was able to 'run up his fingers to the end of the fingerboard of the violin, and run them back insensibly, and all with great alacrity and in very good tune'. After the Restoration of Charles II, Baltzer became head of the king's new band of 24 violins. His successor was the English violinist John Banister, who established the first public concerts in London in 1672. Gradually a change of musical taste became noticeable, as Roger North reported: 'The decay of French music, and favour of the Italian, came on by degrees. Its beginning was accidental and occasioned by the arrival [in 1672] of Nicola Matteis [who excelled by] his *arcata* or manner of bowing, his shakes, divisions'. Matteis printed four books of *Ayres for the Violin* in the 1680s. With the publication in 1683 of the trio sonatas by Purcell (in which he 'faithfully endeavour'd a just imitation of the most fam'd Italian Masters'), Italian violin style was definitely established as superior.

VIOLIN REPERTORY

Italian violin music continued to dominate English taste throughout the 18th century: Corelli's concertos and sonatas were immensely popular, and Geminiani (mainly in London and Dublin from 1714 until his death in 1762) was widely regarded as a model: he had many pupils (including M. Dubourg and M. C. Festing), and his books on violin playing were highly influential. Later the playing of Felice Giardini took the Italian *galant* style to England.

The early development of German violin playing is indebted to foreign musicians. From Italy came Marini (1623) and Farina (1625), from England Simpson (1610), Walter Rowe (1614), and Brade (*c*1600), who founded the school of Hamburg, where he died in 1630. Brade's student Nicolas Bleyer composed a set of ostinato variations on *Est-ce Mars* (*c*1650), one of the earliest German pieces for violin and bass. In the second half of the 17th century, German violinists equalled and even surpassed the Italians in technical matters like double stop playing, reflected in such works as the Sonata for violin and basso continuo by P. F. Böddecker (1651) and the suites by Mathias Kelz (1658, 1669). Musically more rewarding are the *Sonatae unarum fidium, seu a violino solo* (1664), by the Viennese J. H. Schmelzer, the first German collection devoted entirely to sonatas for violin and continuo. A fusion of German and Italian elements, the works require the 6th position and demand a variety of bowstrokes, including bouncing bow.

H. I. F. von Biber (*d* 1704), an important Bohemian composer active in Austria, composed 15 'Rosary' Sonatas (also called 'The Mysteries') about 1675, which depict the 15 Mysteries of Jesus and the Virgin Mary. Though obviously conceived as church music, they include a number of dance movements, such as gavotte, gigue, courante and sarabande, counter-balanced by gravely beautiful movements in contrapuntal style. In them Biber made extensive use of scordatura tunings to facilitate playing unusual chords. The collection also includes a Passacaglia (for unaccompanied violin) on the descending tetrachord G–F–Eb–D, 65 variations of imaginative variety, alternating between fleet passage-work and rich chords, which could have served as a model for Bach's Chaconne four decades later. Biber made even more technical demands in his eight sonatas for violin and continuo (1681): passages into the 7th position, bowings such as staccato, ricochet and *bariolage*, double stops and three- and four-part imitations, all in a musically rewarding context.

Two works by the Dresden virtuoso J. J. Walther, *Scherzi da violino solo* with continuo (1676) and *Hortulus chelicus* (1688), represent the technical summit of German violin playing at that time, both in left- and right-hand technique: rapid runs reach the 7th position while the bow is used for groups of staccatos and bouncing arpeggios ('con arcate sciolte').

Walther's colleague in Dresden, J. P. von Westhoff, visited Paris in 1682, and England in 1684–5. His success at the court of Louis XIV was all the more astounding since Lully was still alive, but the technique of the German violinist (particularly his multiple stops) was clearly superior to anything the French performers could offer. Von Westhoff's works reveal an impressive technical competence and also a feeling for Italianate cantabile playing that many of his German colleagues lacked; his recently rediscovered partitas (1696/*R*1974) are important precursors of Bach's works for unaccompanied violin.

After 1700 the Italian influence on German violin playing was even stronger, as exemplified by J. G. Pisendel who studied with Vivaldi in 1716 and was active in Dresden until his death in 1755. Pisendel knew J. S. Bach, for whom (in Dresden in 1717) he may have played his own unaccompanied violin sonata. Bach may have written his famous six sonatas and partitas for violin solo with Pisendel's performance in mind. Clearly, he was following in them the German tradition of unaccompanied violin playing and the German predilection for polyphonic treatment of the violin. The three sonatas are arranged in the *sonata da chiesa* four-movement pattern with a fugal movement in second place. The partitas consist of suites of dances; the second Partita in D minor ends with the incomparable Chaconne. Bach's violin concertos, on the other hand, show the influence of Vivaldi. Yet Bach was restrained in the use of technical display and preferred to treat the solo violin as *primus inter pares*, with rich interplay between tutti and solo sections. He wrote the earliest collection of sonatas for violin and obbligato harpsichord ('a Cembalo concertato e Violino solo', *c*1720).

Handel took no particular interest in the solo violin, in spite of the fact that he was personally acquainted with Corelli and Geminiani. Among his 15 solos with basso continuo (op.1, *c*1722) are the famous six sonatas, beautifully wrought works in the Italian *sonata da chiesa* style. Telemann, who was a violinist, composed two collections of six sonatas each for violin and continuo (1715, 1718) and two dozen fantasies for violin 'senza basso' (i.e. unaccompanied). Two other collections of 12 solos each (*Sonate metodiche* op.13, 1732; *12 Solos*, 1734) use the violin interchangeably with the transverse flute; they are musically attractive but not idiomatic for the violin. Telemann did not care for the concerto genre – he hated 'difficulties and crooked jumps' – but he nevertheless composed some 180 concertos.

Pisendel's tradition was taken to Berlin by his pupils Johann Gottlieb Graun and Franz Benda, who were at the court of Frederick II of Prussia. Graun (a brother of the more famous opera composer Carl Heinrich Graun) published six sonatas in 1726 that show a fusion of German and Italian traditions. At the time Benda joined the court orchestra in 1733, Graun was leader and enjoyed a fine reputation, particularly for his interpretation of *adagio* movements. Benda studied with Graun and also became a master of the soulful cantabile, which he embellished with rich ornamentation. Benda's compositional style is comparable with that of his colleagues C. P. E. Bach and J. J. Quantz. Only a few of his works were published: six sonatas for violin and continuo op.1 (1763), two violin concertos op.2, and two collections of sonatas for violin with a written-out piano part. Benda's adagios, for which he indicated at least two versions, unadorned and richly ornamented, have been used as source material for 18th-century ornamentation. Benda's student, F. W. Rust, composed sonatas for unaccompanied violin (1795) but they were not published until 1853 in a version that appears to be heavily edited.

The Mannheim composers wrote comparatively little for the solo violin although most of them were professional violinists. Johann Stamitz wrote two collections of sonatas for violin and continuo (opp.4 and 6, 1760–61) and two imaginative divertimentos for unaccompanied violin 'en duo' (polyphonic pieces for one violin). When he appeared with his own concertos in Paris in 1754 he was widely acclaimed, but the works show Tartini's influence and lack a distinctive character. In succeeding years the Mannheim concerto became increasingly French in character (Carl and Anton Stamitz, Ignaz Fränzl, the brothers Eck) until, in 1800, Spohr (a pupil of Franz Eck) succeeded in fusing French and German influences into a masterful concerto genre.

(iii) France

France did not produce any violin solo music in the 17th century; all attention was focussed on the string orchestra and orchestral discipline, as exemplified by the 24 Violons du Roi (1626) and Lully's rival ensemble, the Petits Violons (1656). The Italian violin style came in slowly. François Couperin composed his first trio sonatas in 1692, and J.-F. Rebel published his *Pièces de violon avec la basse continue* in 1705. His rival, François Duval, published sonatas from 1704 to 1720. The violin technique of the early French composers is far simpler than that of their Italian and German contemporaries. Rebel tried to resist the Italian influence by keeping the traditional style of Lully, by using French titles for movements, and by following the order of movements of the French lute suite of the 1650s. After 1700 Italian violinists were settling in Paris, among them Michele Mascitti, a pupil of Corelli, G. A. Piani (known as 'Desplanes') and G. Ghignone (known as 'J.-P. Guignon'); with the founding of the Concert Spirituel in 1725 many more foreign virtuosos were attracted. At the same time French violinists went abroad to study, including J. B. Senaillé, J.-B. Anet (also known as 'Baptiste') and J.-M. Leclair; in their works they succeeded in combining their French heritage and Italian influences. François Francoeur, though not taught in Italy, revealed Italian influence in his sonatas in free chamber style. Mondonville systematically explored the use of harmonics in his sonatas *Les sons harmoniques* op.4 (c1738). He composed written-out keyboard parts for his *Pièces de clavecin en sonates, avec accompagnement de violon* op.3 (c1734) in which the relationship between the keyboard instrument and the obbligato violin is flexible and surprisingly modern, very different from the contrapuntal three-part texture of Bach's sonatas.

Ensemble music centred around the keyboard with accompanying strings became the French fashion, leading ultimately to the violin being designated optional. Representative of this trend is the music of Johann Schobert, a German living in France whose works were published in Paris during the 1760s. for a time, young Mozart was impressed by Schobert and he arranged some of his music.

The leading French violinist of his generation, Leclair, remained faithful to the old sonata for violin and continuo in his four superb collections (opp.1, 2, 5, 9: 1723–38). Schooled in Turin by Somis, Leclair surpassed his master in technical innovation and emotional depth and considerably raised the level of French violin playing. He retained the old four-movement pattern and added variety by the inclusion of movements like the

VIOLIN REPERTORY

vivacious *tambourin* and *chasse*, and the old majestic *tombeau*. He
was a formidable executant of double stops and bowing but he
avoided the highest positions. His workmanship was exemplary, and his bass line was figured with elaborate care and
audacious imagination. His concertos (op.7, 1737; op.10, 1744),
on the other hand, offer the soloist little opportunity for display.
He also composed duos for two unaccompanied violins (opp.3,
12) and trio sonatas (opp.4, 6, 8, 13) that match the sonatas in
excellence. Leclair's best pupil, L'abbé *le fils*, published a violin
method, *Principes du violon* (1761), which is a worthy French
counterpart to the methods of Geminiani (1751) and Leopold
Mozart (1756).

While the works of L.-G. Guillemain are technically outstanding, the most important violin composer and performer of the
second half of the 18th century was Pierre Gaviniès, affection-
ately called 'the French Tartini'. In his sonatas (opp.1, 3) and
concertos (op.4), all published in the 1760s, he simplified the
excessive ornamentation of the *style rocaille* and shaped his slow
movements with great, often melancholy expression and sensi-
bility, creating a French equivalent to the German *Empfind-
samkeit*. His 24 *matinées* (unaccompanied caprices) show a
technique unsurpassed until Paganini, and they have remained
an indispensable part of violin instruction. A younger generation
of exceptionally gifted performers and composers enlivened the
Parisian scene in the 1770s and 1780s: Simon le Duc, Saint-
Georges, M.-A. Guénin, Nicolas Capron, Abbé Robineau and
others. Their writing was pre-Classical, graceful and refined in
the sonatas, fiery and brilliant in the concertos. La Laurencie
spoke of a 'Mozartism before Mozart'; certainly the young
Mozart was impressed by the Parisian school, and French traits
are found in his violin music. Viotti's arrival in Paris in 1782 and
his overwhelming success obscured the merits of his French
predecessors; in fact, Viotti absorbed many of the achievements
of the French school and thus was able to influence the future
course of French violin playing without a noticeable break in
continuity.

(iv) Viennese Classical school

Haydn, Mozart, Beethoven and Schubert all wrote for the
violin, primarily sonatas and concertos. Some of their pieces are
limited by the fashion of the day, others are less inspired; but at
their best, these masters created standards that will remain valid

as long as the violin is played. For Haydn the violin was principally an ensemble instrument (quartets, symphonies). The combination of violin and keyboard did not interest him; the collection of Haydn's violin sonatas contains only one original work, no.1 in G, also published as a trio (H XV:32). Five others were originally keyboard sonatas (the violin part was added by someone else) and two are arrangements of string quartets (op.77 nos.1 and 2). Haydn's four published violin concertos (H VIIa, nos. 1–4) are attractive but not innovatory.

Mozart's relationship to the violin was far more personal; his father had trained him as a violinist and he had professional competence on the instrument. Of his five violin concertos, three have become an indispensable part of the repertory: no.3 in G (K216), no.4 in D (K218) and no.5 in A (K219). Two other concertos are of doubtful authenticity: no.6 in E♭ (K268), which aroused suspicions when it was first published in 1799, and no.7 in D (K27i), printed in 1907, which must have been retouched by another hand. The so-called 'Adelaide' Concerto is a falsification. There are also violin concerto sections within several of his serenades, notably the Haffner (K250/248b). In his own words, Mozart was 'no great lover of difficulties', and he kept the technical demands moderate in all his concertos. Written – except possibly for no.1, which may be earlier – within a span of six months in 1775, they show a process of maturing. The first two are still conventional in the framework of the Austro-German tradition, although the second betrays French influences. While the fourth is the most violinistic and brilliant of the set, the fifth is the most original, with its haunting slow introduction in the first movement, beautifully contrapuntal Adagio, and elaborate Tempo di Minuetto with sprightly 'alla turca' episode (for which the entire concerto is known as the 'Turkish'), all proof of the 19-year-old composer's consummate mastery.

The latest critical edition of Mozart's violin sonatas contains 26 works that demonstrate the evolution from the early type of keyboard sonata with accompanying violin to the mature works where the instruments are equal partners. They fall into three groups: the childhood sonatas (K6–9 and 26–31) composed in 1763–6, the sonatas of early maturity written in Mannheim and Paris in 1778 (K296, 301/293a, 302/293b, 303/293c, 304/300c, 305/293d, and 306), and the sonatas of mastery composed in Salzburg and Vienna in 1779–87 (K376/374d, 377/374e, 378/317d, 379/373a, 380/374f, 454, 481, 526, 547). While the earliest sonatas show dependence on Schobert and J. C. Bach in their complete subordination of the violin, the sonatas of the middle period represent a big step forward. Mozart described them in a letter of 14 February 1778 as 'keyboard duets with violin'. For a time Mozart retained the two-movement form (similar to J.C. Bach's) though his piano sonatas of the same period are in three movements. In terms of mood, the two genres are comparable: the *Sturm und Drang* is as evident in the Violin Sonata in E minor K304/300c as it is in the Piano Sonata in A minor K310/300d. The later violin sonatas are expanded to three movements and the two instruments are treated in a technically more brilliant fashion. Such a 'concert sonata' is the well-known Sonata in Bb (K454, 1784), composed for the violinist Regina Strinasacchi, or the one in A (K526), perhaps the most virtuoso of them all, particularly in the 'moto perpetuo' finale.

Mozart's works served as inspiration for the young Beethoven when he approached the combination of piano and violin in his set of three sonatas op.12. These appeared in 1799 and were criticized by the *Allgemeine musikalische Zeitung* for a certain 'contrariness' and artificiality. There followed the sonatas opp.23 and 24 in 1801, op.30 nos. 1–3 in 1803, op.47 in 1805 and op.96 (composed in 1812), altogether ten. Although Beethoven's violin playing was described as 'dreadful music' by his student Ferdinand Ries, his writing for the violin is nevertheless as idiomatic as his piano writing, despite a few awkward passages. Beethoven continued where Mozart left off: he stressed the partnership of the two instruments, the close interrelationship and artful balance, while making increasing demands on the technical ability of both players. While the Kreutzer Sonata op.47 exemplifies a trend towards concerto-like brilliance, in his last sonata (op.96) Beethoven reverted to a chamberlike intimacy, a lyricism that foreshadows his late works (he wrote the sonata for Rode, and added a few exposed passages to please the visiting French virtuoso).

Contemporary violinists showed little enthusiasm for Beethoven's violin compositions; even Spohr, who was acquainted with Beethoven, thought little of the concerto and the later quartets. The concerto, first played by Franz Clement in 1806, had few repeat performances: 1812 in Berlin (Luigi Tomasini), 1828 in Paris (Baillot), 1834 in Vienna (Vieuxtemps) and 1836 in Leipzig (Uhlrich). Only after the young Joachim played it in Leipzig in 1844 (with Mendelssohn conducting) did the work begin to find interpreters and admirers. In shaping it Beethoven had created a new type, a 'symphonic' concerto in which the soloist is part of a symphonic concept with few opportunities for virtuosity. Beethoven was certainly familiar with the French concerto and with Viotti's concertos; he had heard Viotti's disciples Kreutzer, Baillot and Rode and was not averse to imitating some of their technical devices; but he refused to make his concerto a display piece, and this explains its slow acceptance by the professional virtuosos. Two other Beethoven violin works deserve attention, the romances opp. 40 and 50 (with orchestral accompaniment). At first he could not find a publisher interested in these detached slow movements, too difficult for the amateur, too modest for the professional; they are now appreciated for their expressive purity.

Schubert turned to the violin in 1816 and composed three sonatas 'for piano with accompaniment of the violin' D384–5 and 408, now known as sonatinas. The diminutive indicates merely that they are comparatively easy to perform; otherwise they are fully developed sonatas, the first in three movements, the other two in four with a minuet in third place. Professionally more demanding is the four-movement Duo in A D574, composed in 1817 but not performed during Schubert's lifetime. The *Rondo brillant* D895 (composed 1826, published and performed the following year) was an immediate success, but although Schubert played both the piano and the violin the writing is strangely unidiomatic, even at times awkward. The same is true of the Fantasy in C D934, but it is a musical masterpiece. The complex form has four basic sections: a slow introduction (which returns before the Finale); a gypsy-like Allegro; a set of variations on the song *Sei mir gegrüsst* (with one variation held in reserve and interposed between the finale and the work's coda); and an energetic finale. The work bristles with unidiomatic difficulties for both instruments (some of the violin passages are in fact unplayable in the original version) but its overflowing Romanticism and tender imagination outweigh all technical problems. Almost forgotten among Schubert's violin compositions are the *Konzertstück* in D D345, the Adagio and Rondo in A D438 and the Polonaise in B♭ D580 (both with string orchestra); and the variations on the song *Trockne Blumen* D802 (originally for flute and piano). Because most of these works were published only after long delay, there was no possibility of their influencing the development of the violin.

VIOLIN REPERTORY

3. 19TH CENTURY

(i) Concerto

After Beethoven's great masterpiece, the violin concerto developed along several independent lines. Spohr, Mendelssohn, Schumann, Bruch, Brahms and Saint-Saëns among others stressed musical values; Paganini, de Bériot, Vieuxtemps, Wieniawski and Ernst followed the virtuoso path. Some composers introduced a new type of 'national' concerto (Joachim, *Hungarian Concerto*; Lalo, *Symphonie espagnole* and *Concerto russe*; Bruch, *Scottish Fantasy*; and works by Dvořák and Tchaikovsky).

Spohr's 15 concertos are a bridge between Beethoven and Mendelssohn. He composed his first in 1802–3, a few years before Beethoven's was written, and his last in 1844, the year that Mendelssohn completed his. Spohr inherited the Mannheim tradition from his teacher Eck but soon fell under the spell of the French school, in particular of Rode, whom he endeavoured to imitate. Out of this blend of German and French elements evolved his personal style: the drama and pomp of the French concerto combined with German sensitivity and a strong infusion of chromatic harmony which heightened the Romantic mood. In his Concerto no.8 (1816), known as 'Gesangszene', he combined elements of concerto and opera to make the work more readily understandable to Italians. He returned to Classical concepts in the Ninth Concerto (1820). He was both attracted and repelled by Paganini, rejecting his performing 'tricks' at a time when violinists all over Europe wished to acquire them. Spohr now seems a bulwark against the trivialization of musical taste, a man of the highest musical standards who salvaged the traditions of Corelli and Tartini and handed them over to Joachim.

Mendelssohn began to sketch his violin concerto in 1838, but the first performance was not until 1844, with Ferdinand David as soloist. The work, with its exquisite technical treatment of the violin, has become so familiar that one easily forgets the originality of form: the elimination of the lengthy double exposition in the first movement, the placing of the cadenza in the middle of the movement, the tying together of first and second movements, as well as the ingenious bridge between the Andante and the finale. Mendelssohn's brilliant concerto reflects contemporary Romanticism yet is shaped by musical values that transcend it.

Mendelssohn's protégé was a young violinist of Hungarian descent, Joseph Joachim, who became the greatest violinist-interpreter of the second half of the 19th century, and to whom many concertos and sonatas were dedicated (works by Schumann, Bruch, Brahms, Dvořák and others). In 1853, his last creative year, Schumann wrote two works for Joachim, the Fantasie op.131 and the posthumous Concerto in D minor. The Fantasie is a one-movement work for violin with orchestra, with a cadenza at the end; it has some inspired moments, but its themes are not memorable, and the relationship between violin and orchestra is ineffective. Schumann urged Joachim to tell him 'what was not practicable' in the violin part, but Joachim, at that time only 22 years old, hesitated to advise. The Fantasie was given its première by Joachim (with Schumann conducting) on 27 October 1853 in Düsseldorf and was repeated in January 1854 at Hanover. By that time Schumann had completed his D minor Concerto, which he tried out with Joachim while he was in Hanover. It was agreed that the new work needed some revision, but Schumann's suicide attempt a few weeks later made the project impossible. Joachim kept the manuscript in his possession, refusing permission to have it published 'in deference to the reputation of the beloved master'. Nor did Joachim agree to retouch it himself. In fact the concerto, rediscovered in the Berlin Library in 1937, has certain weaknesses, particularly in the finale, that explain Joachim's action. Also written for Joachim was Bruch's Concerto no.1 in G minor (1866), a sympathetic though scarcely profound work with warmly Romantic themes, a concise structure and an unusual first movement (called 'Vorspiel') with recurring recitatives for the soloist. Bruch was unable to duplicate the success of this early work; the Concerto no.2 in D minor is played far more rarely, the *Scottish Fantasy* (1880) is revived only occasionally, while the last two concertos (op.58, 1891), and the *Konzertstück* op.84, 1911) are completely forgotten.

Brahms's Violin Concerto op.77 (1878) grew out of the composer's friendship with Joachim, to whom he sent a few sketches of the last movement so that he could 'prohibit the awkward passages right away'. Joachim answered two days later: 'It is all playable, some of it even violinistically original – but whether it will be enjoyable to play in a hot concert hall is a different question'. Even after their joint first performance of the work on 1 January 1879 in Leipzig, Brahms urged his friend to make further changes in the violin part, but despite a considerable correspondence Brahms ultimately rejected as many suggestions as he accepted. Hence the unusual difficulty of the solo part is due not to an ignorance of the instrument but to broader musical factors. Brahms followed Beethoven's model to create a 'symphonic' concerto in deliberate opposition to the virtuoso trend of the Romantic concerto. While there are structural parallels between the concertos of Beethoven and Brahms, Brahms filled out the form with so much personal content that his concerto is now considered the worthy counterpart to Beethoven's. In 1887 Brahms composed his Double Concerto for violin and cello with orchestra, which Joachim is said to have preferred to the Violin Concerto.

In contrast to his deep involvement with the Brahms concerto, Joachim showed little interest in the Concerto in A minor by Dvořák. He received the manuscript late in 1879 but did nothing with it for two years and never played it publicly, though in a session with the composer in September 1882 he did make some suggestions concerning the solo part. The first performance was a year later, in October 1883 in Prague, with the Czech F. Ondříček as soloist. The themes of the concerto have a warm national colour, the technique is idiomatic, and the structure (with its finale episode) is original; yet it must be considered a lesser work than Dvořák's Cello Concerto. Other late 19th-century concertos, not in the forefront of the repertory, were written by Karl Goldmark, Richard Strauss and Busoni.

In France, Lalo's impassioned Concerto in F minor op.20 (1872) was followed by his famous *Symphonie espagnole* op.21 (1873), written for Sarasate. The latter is an ambitious work in five movements (the fourth, Intermezzo, is often omitted); despite the term 'symphony' it is a concerto for a virtuoso performer who dominates throughout. It is filled with Spanish-type themes, colourfully orchestrated, and written with unerring flair for the violin. Lalo's further exploitation of national idioms (*Concerto russe* op.29, 1889, and *Fantaisie norvégienne*, 1880) was of no particular consequence. Saint-Saëns wrote three violin concertos (in A, op.20, 1859; in C, op.58, 1879; in B minor, op.61, 1880) but only the last is played with any frequency. Chausson, a disciple of Franck, wrote an attractive double concerto (op.21) for piano, violin and string quartet in which the sonorities are balanced with great imagination, and the well-known *Poème* op.25 (1896) for violin and orchestra which was inspired by the playing of Ysaÿe (who is said to have contributed to the shaping of the solo part). The work is an artful mixture of Franckian concepts and impressionist colouring.

Among the Russian composers only Tchaikovsky seriously pursued the concerto genre. His Violin Concerto op.35 in D (1878) has a first movement of symphonic length, an ingratiating Canzonetta and a somewhat repetitive finale with a Russian episode. The orchestral tutti sections are symphonically powerful but the orchestra is thinned out in the solo sections so that the violin is easily audible. Despite a disastrous criticism by Hanslick after the première in Vienna, the Tchaikovsky concerto has become a standard repertory piece. Rimsky-Korsakov wrote a Fantasy on Russian folk themes for violin and orchestra (op.33, 1887), a rather awkward attempt at 'nationalizing' the concerto form. The Concerto op.54 (*c*1900) by Arensky and the Concerto in E minor by Jules Conus (1896) are of minor value.

The principal 19th-century virtuoso concertos include the following: the Concertos nos.1 and 2 by Paganini (the 1820s), the Concerto no.2 by de Bériot (1830), the Concertos nos.1, 4 and 5 (1840, 1850, 1860) by Vieuxtemps, the *Concerto pathétique* by H. W. Ernst (1844), and the Concertos nos.1 and 2 by Wieniawski (1853, 1862). Paganini wrote five, possibly six violin concertos, but only the first two were published, posthumously in 1851 (the others are partly in manuscript though recordings of all have been made). These two (the second with the famous 'Clochette' rondo) show him as a gifted melodist and a phenomenal technician. Paganini's playing became known to audiences outside Italy in 1828, and for the next six years he performed extensively in Austria, Germany, France, England and Belgium. There were few violinists who did not attempt to copy his technical innovations. The publication of his 24 Caprices in 1820 had already stimulated interest, and the result was a remarkable rise in the general level of violin playing.

De Bériot began with a mildly difficult First Concerto in the 1820s and followed it with a technically brilliant and adventurous Second Concerto; but he later reverted to a more graceful and less technical approach (he wrote ten concertos of which nos.7 and 9 are still used for teaching purposes). His best

VIOLIN REPERTORY

student, Vieuxtemps, heard Paganini in London in 1834 and was deeply impressed; the result was Vieuxtemps' First Concerto in E (1840), which combined technical display with a rejuvenation of the French concerto style. His Concerto no.4 in D minor (1850) was an attempt to 'reform' the concerto genre by re-grouping the movements into a declamatory first movement with cadenza, a slow second movement, a scherzo and a finale. Berlioz acclaimed the work as a 'magnificent symphony with a principal violin'; in truth, however, it was a disguised virtuoso concerto where the violin was embedded in an unusually rich orchestral background. The Concerto no.5 (1860) is a one-movement piece of noble sentiment and technical dexterity; it was originally written as a competition piece for the Brussels Conservatory but soon became a widely played repertory work.

Ernst's Concerto in F♯ minor (1844) came closest to the Paganini ideal. Ernst's technique is in some ways more difficult and intricate than Paganini's; but Ernst pursued musical ideals and was, in Joachim's view, the greatest violinist-musician of his generation. Ernst's Polyphonic Studies (each dedicated to one of his famous colleagues) show him at the summit of his mastery. Wieniawski was the youngest of the group of virtuosos influenced by Paganini. Of his two concertos, the first in F♯ minor (1853) is primarily a technical display piece, while the second in D minor (1862) maintains a high level of Romantic feeling, invention and violinistic writing. Wieniawski also enriched the repertory with shorter pieces in the Polish national idiom (mazurkas, polonaises). Even his Etudes (op.10, *L'école moderne*; op.18, *Etudes caprices*) are musically conceived (Kreisler and others provided them with piano accompaniments).

(ii) Sonata

Compared with the brilliant concerto, the sonata for violin and piano played a secondary role in the repertory of the post-Beethoven era. Often a virtuoso violinist and pianist would join forces in writing a *duo brillant* – usually a fantasy on some operatic aria – but the emphasis was on brilliance, alien to chamber music. Apart from Mendelssohn's youthful Sonata op.4 in F minor (1825), there were no significant contributions to the genre until Schumann's opp.105 and 121 (both composed in 1851). They are among his most mature chamber works; the two instruments are beautifully integrated, though the violin is occasionally in too low a register for effective contrast. With his three sonatas for violin and piano, Brahms continued the Beet-hovenian tradition. The first, in G, op.78 (1878-9) is a con-tinuous cantilena; the creative impulse came from two of his songs, *Regenlied* and *Nachklang* (op.59 nos.2 and 3). It was written almost simultaneously with the violin concerto; yet Brahms differentiated sensitively in his use of the instrument in solo and chamber music. The Second Sonata op.100 in A (1886) is also lyrical, but more concise and intimate. The Third Sonata in D minor op.108 (1886-8) is the most widely played; each of its four movements is shaped with a master's touch: the com-bination of drama and intimacy in the first movement (with a unique development section built on a pedal point, using the violin technique of *bariolage*), the broad repose of the second, the mysterious shuffle of the intermezzo, and the virile attack of the finale, all entrusted to two instruments that balance each other to perfection yet speak with a personal voice. A late flowering of German Romanticism is found in Richard Strauss's Sonata in E♭ op.18 (1887), youthful, exuberant, by turns sentimental and highly sophisticated. Busoni's Sonata in E minor op.38*a* (1898) is eclectic.

France rediscovered chamber music after the 1870–71 war with Prussia, and a society was formed for its cultivation. Sonatas for violin and piano were composed by Franck, Fauré, Saint-Saëns and d'Indy. Franck's Sonata in A, written in 1886 for Ysaÿe, is an undisputed masterpiece for its melodic inspira-tion, thematic integration, and balance of the two instruments, which are used with unsurpassed idiomatic finesse. More modest but equally engaging is the youthful Sonata no.1 op.13 (1876) by Fauré; his Second Sonata (op.108, 1917) receives very few performances. The two sonatas by Saint-Saëns (op.75, 1885; op.102, 1896) are polished vehicles for virtuoso display.

Grieg's three sonatas, though no longer subjects of much attention, have a freshness of melodic invention and a lyricism characteristic of Grieg's nationalist style (no.1, op.8, 1865; no.2, op.13, 1867; no.3, op.45, 1887). His compatriot Christian Sinding achieved more lasting success with his Suite op.10 in A minor for violin with piano accompaniment (*c*1890), while his three violin concertos and four sonatas have disappeared from the repertory. Dvořák's Sonata op.57 (1880) is not played often, but his charming Sonatina op.100 in G (1894), which reflects his American impressions, is more popular; its second movement was arranged by Kreisler as 'Indian Lament'.

(iii) Short genre pieces

The 19th century witnessed the birth and proliferation of the shorter piece for violin with orchestra or piano. Most were dedicated to sheer technical display and led to extensive trivialization of the repertory. Countless 'airs variés' were written, the best among them by de Bériot and Vieuxtemps. Paganini began the fashion of virtuoso variations (*Carnaval de Venise, Le streghe, I palpiti* etc), followed by Ernst and many minor imitators. The fantasy on operatic themes became an indispensable part of musical entertainment, often written by a pair of notable virtuosos such as Charles Lafont and Ignaz Moscheles, Vieuxtemps and Anton Rubinstein, H. W. Ernst and George Osborne. Some composers tried to give more dignity to the shorter pieces, among them Vieuxtemps with his *Fantasia appassionata* and *Ballade et Polonaise*, Berlioz (*Rêverie et Caprice*), Schumann (*Märchenbilder*), Joachim (Variations op.11), Ernst (*Elegie*), Smetana (*Aus der Heimat*), Dvořák (*Romantische Stücke*), Saint-Saëns (*Havanaise; Introduction et Rondo capriccioso*), Tchaikovsky (*Sérénade mélancolique; Souvenir d'un lieu cher*). Wieniawski's polonaises and mazurkas, and Sarasate's *Zigeunerweisen* and Spanish dances are well-made virtuoso pieces. The fashion for transcriptions began in the 19th century with such solid arrangements as the Brahms–Joachim Hungarian Dances, the *Ave Maria* by Schubert–Wilhelmj and the 'Air on the G String' by Bach–Wilhelmj, but by the 20th century had led to a flood of inferior arrangements and even falsifications.

4. 20TH CENTURY

In the period up to the end of World War I a number of significant concertos and sonatas were produced, many of which have become established in the repertory. The most important concertos are those of Sibelius (1903–5), Glazunov (1905), Reger (1908), Elgar (1910), Nielsen (1911), Delius (1916) and Szymanowski (no.1, 1917; also no.2, 1933). Szymanowski enriched the repertory with such shorter works as *Notturno e Tarantella* (1914) and *Mythes* (1915), which are written in a highly sophisticated neo-impressionist idiom. Reger contributed nine sonatas for violin and piano and 25 works in a neo-Baroque

20TH CENTURY

style for unaccompanied violin. Best known is his *Suite im alten Stil* for violin and piano (op.93, 1906).

Debussy's Sonata, one of his last and most mature works (1916–17), combines his impressionism with a rediscovered classicism and certain jazz influences. Leaning towards impressionism are the works by Cyril Scott (Sonata, 1910; *Suite Tallahassee*, 1911). Ives's four sonatas (1903–8, 1903–10, 1902–14, 1915) have lately received new attention. The period between the two wars was one of amazing vitality. Each country in Europe, as well as the USA, produced new personalities, new ideas. In Germany, Hindemith became the leading figure. A violinist and violist, he produced a wealth of idiomatic string music, dominated by his 'motoric' rhythmic sense. Four sonatas for violin and piano (op.11 nos.1 and 2, 1918; in E, 1935; in C, 1939) show the early influences of Brahms and Reger and indicate his return to tonality. There are also two sonatas for unaccompanied violin (op.31, 1924) based on linear counterpoint. The *Kammermusik* no.4 (op.36 no.3, 1925) creates a new relationship between the solo violin and orchestra, while the more conventional Violin Concerto (1939) returns to the cantabile tradition. Other German composers of the period were Ernst Toch (Sonatas opp.23, 44), Karol Rathaus (Sonatas opp.14, 43; Suite op.27), Ernst Krenek (Concerto, 1924, and Sonatas), Kurt Weill (Concerto op.12 for violin and wind), and Hans Pfitzner, a late Romantic (Concerto op.34, 1923). Schoenberg presented his Violin Concerto (1936), which he said required a 'six-fingered violinist', and Berg wrote a warmly appealing Violin Concerto (1935). Webern wrote four pieces for violin and piano (1910) in his individual pointillist style, and Schoenberg composed a late Fantasy for violin and piano (1949).

An important contribution to the violin repertory was made by Bartók: two sonatas for violin and piano (1921–2) and two rhapsodies for violin with piano or orchestra (1928) show his fusion of modernism and national heritage. His First Violin Concerto (1907–8, published 1959) is an early work, but his Second Concerto (1937–8) is recognized as one of the most important masterpieces of the century, and despite the novelty of its musical idiom and the unusual technical problems for the soloist, has been generally accepted into the standard repertory. Far more complex is the Sonata for unaccompanied violin (1944), commissioned by Yehudi Menuhin. Bloch's suite *Baal Shem* (1923) explores the Hebraic heritage, while the two sonatas

(1920, 1924) and the imposing Violin Concerto (1937–8) display a fiery temperament. A year before his death Bloch completed two suites for unaccompanied violin (1958).

In France after World War I impressionism yielded to a more sharply etched style, with influences of American jazz. Thus Ravel produced his (partly polytonal) Sonata for violin and piano (1922), with a stylized 'blues' as second movement. His *Tzigane* (1924) is a modernized virtuoso piece. Most productive was Milhaud: two sonatas (1911, 1917), two concertos (1927, 1946) and several shorter pieces are written with his customary elegant mastery. Honegger produced several sonatas for violin with or without piano (1918, 1919, 1940), and one for two violins (1920), but they did not become established, despite some interesting details. Roussel's Violin Sonata no.2 (op.28, 1924) is not as well known as it deserves to be. During the 1920s it was Stravinsky who dominated the Parisian scene. His original ideas on violin treatment were first displayed in *The Soldier's Tale* (1918). There followed the Suite (after Pergolesi) for violin and piano (1926), the Violin Concerto (1931) and the *Duo concertante* for violin and piano (1932). Stravinsky enlisted the help of several noted violinists (Pawel Kochański, Samuel Dushkin) in shaping the violin parts, but apparently his own ideas prevailed: the violin writing is craggy and not very idiomatic, but it challenges the soloist to find solutions to new technical problems.

Prokofiev wrote two violin concertos (1923, 1935) in which he mixed lyrical cantilena with his satirical style in a highly effective manner. His two sonatas for violin and piano were written after his return to the USSR: no.1 in F minor op.80 (1938–46) and no.2 in D op.94*bis* (1946); the latter is actually an arrangement of the flute sonata (same opus) made with the help of the violinist David Oistrakh. It is the custom among Soviet composers to work closely with performers; thus the concertos of Khachaturian (1940), N. Y. Myaskovsky (1938), Shostakovich (no.1, 1948) and Kabalevsky (1948) were composed for Oistrakh, the concertos by T. N. Khrennikov and Kara Karayev as well as the Concert Rhapsody by Khachaturian were written for Leonid Kogan. Khachaturian's engaging concerto uses Armenian folk material with rhythms influenced by Gershwin. The First Concerto by Shostakovich was completed in 1948 but withheld by the composer until 1955 because the political climate was thought to be unfavourable for a work of such modernity. It is indeed a highly original and intricate composition, cast in four movements of which the intense third, a passacaglia, is the high point. Kabalevsky's concerto was written for young performers and is comparatively simple though attractive in its thematic freshness.

English composers produced a number of significant violin compositions, including three sonatas (1905–15, 1924, 1930) by Delius, the *Concerto accademico* (1925) and the Sonata in A minor (1957) by Vaughan Williams, three sonatas and a Violin Concerto in E (1937) by Bax, and the violin concertos by Britten (1939, revised 1950) and Walton (1939).

Italian compositions of note are the intense, dark-hued Sonata in A minor by Pizzetti (1919), the *Concerto gregoriano* by Respighi (1921), concertos by Casella (1928) and Malipiero (1932) and several works by Vittorio Rieti (*Serenata*, 1932; *Rondo variato*, 1945; Concerto no.2, 1969). Other European contributions to the literature are by Martinů (two sonatas and a concerto, 1943), Frank Martin (Sonata, 1932; Concerto, 1951) and Henk Badings (sonatas and four concertos, 1928, 1933, 1944 and 1946, and the excellent Double Concerto for two violins and orchestra, 1954).

In the USA after 1918 a new orientation towards Paris produced an amalgam of French clarity, the home-grown jazz heritage and Austro-German dodecaphony. Closest to the French style is Virgil Thomson (Sonata, 1930; *Four Portraits*, 1931). Quincy Porter (Sonatas, 1926 and 1929) and Walter Piston (Concerto and Sonata, 1939) could be called neo-classicists, while the concertos by Samuel Barber (1939) and Menotti (1952) are lyrical and neo-Romantic. The American idiom is represented by Douglas Moore (*Suite Down East*, 1944; Sonata, 1929) and Roy Harris (Concerto, 1944). Leaning towards dodecaphony were Riegger (Sonatina, 1947) and Ross Lee Finney (Concerto, 1944). The leading composers are Copland (Sonata, 1943), Sessions (Concerto, 1935; Duo, 1942) and Elliott Carter (Duo, 1974).

American composers continued to be interested in the concerto; violin concertos were composed by William Schuman (1947), David Diamond (1937, 1948, 1976), Peter Mennin (1950), Ben Weber (1954), Piston (no.2, 1960) and Benjamin Lees (1963). The unaccompanied violin attracted George Perle (Sonatas, 1959 and 1963), Sessions (Sonata, 1953) and Lees (*Invenzione*, 1964–5). Leon Kirchner wrote a duo (1947) and a *Sonata concertante* (1952) for violin and piano, as well as a double concerto for violin and cello with ten wind instruments and percussion (1960). More experimental is Charles Wuorinen with his Concerto for amplified violin and orchestra (1972), Variations for solo violin (1973) and Fantasia for violin and piano (1975). Latin American composers began to turn their attention to the violin, among them the Mexican Carlos Chávez (two concertos, 1952 and 1965) and the Argentinian Alberto Ginastera (Concerto, 1963).

Dallapiccola's violin works include *Due studi* for violin and piano (1946–7), consisting of an atmospheric sarabande and a strongly dissonant, effective fugue, and two *Tartiniana* (1951, 1957) for violin and piano or orchestra, in which themes by Tartini provide a basis for sophisticated elaborations. Berio's *Due pezzi* for violin and piano (1951) and Nono's *Varianti* for violin solo, strings and woodwind (1957) represent extremely modern idioms.

German works include Blacher's Violin Concerto op.29 (1948) and the Solo Sonata op.40, Wilhelm Fortner's Sonata (1945) and Concerto (1951), Giselher Klebe's Two Sonatas for solo violin op.8 (1952) and a Sonata for violin and piano op.14 (1953), and Henze's Violin Sonata (1946) and Concerto (1947). The concerto by the British composer Alexander Goehr has been performed with success. French composers, on the other hand, seem to have lost interest in the violin as a solo instrument. Soviet composers are relaxing from their adherence to tradition and a few more adventurous works have appeared: the Sonata op.134 (1969) of Shostakovich, the Concertos of Karayev and Alfred Shnitke, and various chamber works for violin and piano by G. I. Ustvol'skaya, V. N. Salmanov, Arno Babajanian and Sergey Slonimsky. The Second Concerto op.129 (1967) of Shostakovich was received with considerable approval. Polish composers have been far more experimental, for example Tadeusz Baird in his *Espressioni varianti* for violin and orchestra (1959) and Penderecki in his *Capriccio* for violin and orchestra (1967) and Violin Concerto (1976).

CHAPTER FOUR

Extra–European and Folk Usage

1. EUROPE

F rom Praetorius's time the violin rapidly penetrated throughout Europe to all strata of society wherever there was
already a native tradition of bowed string-playing (rebecs,
fiddles, viols, bowed zithers etc); this was probably because of
its greater dynamic range and more flexible tone. It often
retained the name of the older instrument, and the term 'fiddle'
(for variants of it) is still used synonymously for the violin. The
instrument had been introduced into Finland and western
Norway by the early 17th century, and by the early 18th century
was in general use throughout most of Scandinavia, some Baltic
states and the British Isles. In these countries and in France and
the Low Countries the violin was often used solo, the playing
style making much use of the open strings as variable drones to
enrich the musical texture and help with rhythmic accentuation.
Until the middle of the 20th century, most Western European
folk musicians rarely played outside the 1st position; they used
the left hand to hold the fiddle along the arm and against the
chest rather than under the chin. Musicians in the Shetland Isles,
for example, have been reported rotating the instrument against
the chest in order to move the bow across the strings. Cheap
instruments were readily imported because they proved to
be ideal for dance music but numerous native variants also
appeared. One notable local refinement is the Hardanger fiddle
(*hardingfele*) of western and southern Norway, which has rich
inlaid and painted decoration and four or five extra sympathetic
strings.

In Wales, the fiddle (*ffidil*) superseded the bowed lyre (*crwth*)
during the 18th century as the principal bowed folk instrument
and was eventually to challenge the harp as the main accom-

26. Gypsy band with two violins, cimbalom (dulcimer) and double bass, north-east Hungary

panying instrument for popular dance (although both instruments frequently performed together in that capacity). From the 18th century onwards, however, dance was vigorously condemned by puritanical nonconformist religion; whereas during the 19th century the harp was retained as a symbol of nationality and granted a respectable place within the eisteddfod, the *ffidil* was doomed to be associated almost solely with taverns and wild celebrations. By the end of the century it was almost extinct, and played only by gypsy families until around World War I. More lately it has been revived by Welsh folk-dance and song groups.

In south-eastern Europe the violin displaced indigenous instruments, becoming a favoured instrument of gypsy musicians. Two violins, a string bass and a plucked instrument make a typical dance ensemble in central Europe and the Balkans, though in Romania and the Moldavian SSR the violin repertory also includes the virtuoso instrumental *doina*, a largely improvised genre in rhapsodic style and free metre.

The violin is the most popular folk instrument in Poland. The *skrzypce* is made by villagers themselves out of a single piece of wood, apart from the soundboard, and has three or four strings. The *skrzypce podwiązane* or *skrzypce przewiązane* is an ordinary violin with a match or small stick placed under the strings and then bound, so that it can be played as in the 1st position but in a higher register; in the 19th century this instrument began to replace the *mazanki*, a small fiddle with three strings that was played with the bagpipe (*dudy*). The *skrzypce* is played chiefly as the melody instrument in folk bands. In Czechoslovakia the *oktávka* (octave-violin) and the *shlopcoky* (scuttle-shaped violin) are used as well as the standard violin. Instruments are played solo, in combinations such as bagpipe and violin, or in diverse ensembles of bowed string instruments.

In Romania the *vioară* is known under several different local names. Players, particularly in Oltenia and Muntenia, use a wide range of scordatura to facilitate the playing of certain tunes, to obtain unusual sounds and to imitate other instruments, such as the bagpipes. The *contră* of Transylvania has only three strings (tuned *g–d'–a*), which are stretched over a notched bridge and bowed simultaneously to obtain chords. The violin in south-west Moldavia usually has seven sympathetic strings, probably a relic of the Turkish *kemençe*, with sympathetic strings. The

131

Stroh violin, called *vioră cu goarnă* ('bugle violin') or *làută cu tolcer* ('funnel violin'), became widespread between the two World Wars (it was invented in London for use in gramophone recording studios at the turn of the century). *Lăutari* (professional folk musicians) make the instrument themselves, replacing the soundbox with a metal bell and resting the strings on a small mica sheet.

The *smuikas* of Lithuania is also often made by the musicians themselves and accordingly is found in a great variety of sizes and forms, of varying quality. The back and sides are made of maple, apple or ash, the belly of fir or pine and the bridge and tuning-pegs of oak, hornbeam, beech or ash. The instrument may have three, four or more strings, usually tuned in 5ths, but in bands the tuning is adapted to suit the concertina and the clarinet. The player sometimes places a small piece of wood on the soundboard to muffle the timbre; experienced musicians adorn dance melodies with melismata and double or triple stopping. Similar traditions of violin playing are also found in neighbouring countries such as Estonia, where the instrument is known as the *viiul*, and Belorussia, Moldavia and the Ukraine, where the *skripka* has its own folk technique. The instrument is usually tuned in 5ths, but higher and lower tunings are used depending on the genre of music. Players use mainly the bottom two strings, more rarely the third. Fiddle playing has been an established profession in many Belorussian towns since the 17th century and the instrument maintains a strong role in rural musical life.

In Portugal the violin has kept the older name *viola*; indigenous bowed instruments are distinguished by the name *rebecca* (from 'rebec'). The Portuguese played a major role in the dispersal of the violin throughout the world; they took it with them to their trading posts and colonies in the East, for example Goa, India and the port of Melaka in Malaysia, as well as along the coast of Angola in Africa.

2. MIDDLE EAST AND SOUTH ASIA

The violin has been adopted into a wide range of traditional oriental art music, from North Africa to South India, and each culture has adapted the holding position to meet its own requirements. In many cases the first introduction of the instrument to these countries was in European-influenced, popular music contexts, such as café music of the Near East and 19th-century urban theatre music of the Indian cities. The violin has shown its flexibility and power as an accompanying instrument, especially where a voice sets the model in timbre and phrasing, as well as for solo playing. In Morocco, one or more violins take a leading part in the vocal–instrumental *nawbā* suites played by traditional orchestras. In North Africa and Turkey it is usually called *keman* (from the generic term *kemençe* or *kamānche*, the latter used for spike fiddles) and is played in an upright, gamba position, resting on the seated player's thigh. In Iran, the violin is the only Western instrument to be admitted without reservation into traditional music because it is possible to play the whole of the *kamānche* repertory on it when technique and articulation are suitably adapted. Its great success at the beginning of the 20th century threatened the existence of the *kamānche*, but its popularity has since been eclipsed by the traditional instrument.

In India, where it was introduced almost two centuries ago, the violin is especially prominent in the classical music of the south and is used to accompany vocal music as well as being an important solo instrument. It is usually played with the scroll resting on the right foot of the player, who sits cross-legged; the other end is wedged against his left shoulder (fig.27a, p.134). The player's left hand is thus free for the complex slides and graces of Indian art music. The strings are tuned to tonic and 5th of the lower and middle octaves (for example c–g–c'–g'). The violin is especially compatible with the tense, bright vocal timbre of the south Indian vocal style. In northern India, Pakistan and Bangladesh, where the classical vocal styles *dhrupad* and *khayāl* are more long-breathed and relaxed, the violin is much less common in vocal accompaniment; here it is in competition with the deeper-toned, indigenous *sārangī* fiddle. Alternative north Indian names are *behalā, bela* (Hindi) and *behālā* (Bengali), which probably derive from the Portuguese *viola*; in Goa, where the Portuguese ruled for over four centuries, the violin is called 'rebec'.

The violin was brought to Sri Lanka by Parsi theatrical troupes from Bombay during the 19th century. The *ravikiñña* is now used by the Tamils for playing Carnatic music and, less often, for *rukada* (string-puppet plays).

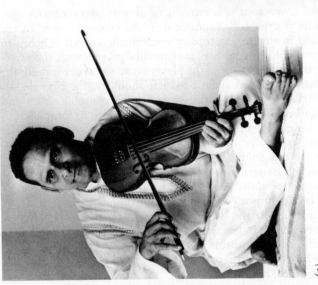

27. Playing position of the European violin as adopted in (a) India and (b) North America

FOLK USAGE IN THE AMERICAS

3. SOUTH-EAST ASIA

The violin was introduced into South-east Asia by the Portuguese during the 17th century, and became known as the *biola* from the Portuguese name. European instruments were played in European fashion in colonial houses by slaves of varied origin. In Djakarta in 1689, a bride who had 59 slaves referred in a letter to 'a slave orchestra which played the harp, viol and bassoon at meal-times' (Boxer, 1965, p.240). Ensembles combining Malay instruments and styles with European ones entered the Malay courts of the Riaulinggu archipelago, East Sumatra and the Malay peninsula. Old royal dances combining Portuguese movements with intricate Malay hand and finger movements are still practised in areas such as Bintan Island, Riau; these include the *tari makan sirih* ('betel-nut-eating dance'), accompanied by *biola*, accordion, *rebana* (frame drum) and gong, and the *tari joget jangkung* ('tall *joget* dance'), accompanied by *biola*, guitar, *rebana* and gong. In east Aceh, an ensemble accompanying local dances includes *biola, geundrang* (double-headed drum), *buloh meurindu* (bamboo clarinet) or *bangsi* (bamboo flute) and one or two *canang* (small bossed gong). *Biolas* are usually made locally by hand and are generally tuned like the European viola.

The Osinger people of East Java use the *biola* in their *gamelan gandrung*. It is played in several other ensembles, including the *orkes Abdul Muluk* (theatre ensemble) of South Sumatra and Jambi, the *orkes gambus* of northern Java, West Sumatra and Malaysia, and the *orkes Lampung* of Lampung, Sumatra.

Biyolin is the term used for the violin by many westernized groups in the Philippines. The instrument is used to play European-type songs in serenades or for entertainment in town feasts. String players for city symphony orchestras are sometimes recruited from the provinces where musical traditions date back to training by Spanish friars in the 17th century. More recently, the *biyolin* has been introduced among non-Western groups playing music based on native forms.

4. THE AMERICAS

The fiddle has been the most prominent folk instrument on the North American continent since the late 18th century, and has a repertory of over 1000 distinct tunes. Fiddlers with individual repertories of 300 to 500 tunes have been reported. The instrument is held against the chest as well as under the chin (fig.27b); little bow is used, and a player rarely uses more than 1st position. Scordatura is common, particularly in the south. Playing tradition is predominantly British–American (many British tunes have survived with remarkable tenacity); in the south, however, black, Afro-American fiddlers have contributed their own style, the use of syncopation being a notable characteristic. A typical mid-20th-century dance band consists of fiddle, banjo, guitar and mandolin (all of which play *fortissimo*).

Although the violin was never as popular in Spain as the guitar, it is used in many of the Hispano-American music cultures of the Americas. In Mexico, it appears in the *mariachi* ensemble, typically of two violins, a vihuela, a *jarana* (five-course guitar), a harp or *guitarrón* (large four-string bass guitar) and two trumpets. It also appears in the *huapango* ensemble (with a *huapanguera*, a large five-course guitar with eight or ten strings, and a *jarana*), where its lively style is reminiscent of fiddle playing in the southern USA. The violin has also been adopted by Mexican Indian groups; tunes heard on transistor radios or played by local mestizo groups are transformed as they are assimilated and so acquire an indigenous quality.

The standard European violin has replaced the *rabel* (three-string fiddle) in Panama and has been adopted by the Chané people in Argentina. It was brought by missionaries to Paraguay, where the Macá and Lengua Indians make their own rustic fiddles; it is used to perform creole pieces, particularly the *polca*. The Guatemalan Maya include a three- or four-string *rabel* in their *zarabanda* ensemble, and a similar instrument is played by the Quechua in Ecuador. In Peru, the Aguaruna Indians make a fiddle (*kitaj*) of balsa wood with two strings of plant fibre; the Guaycuru of Argentina play a single-string fiddle.

Violins are used throughout Jamaica, mainly for dance music; they are held against the left side of the rib cage and played in florid style. The 'bamboo violin', found in isolated areas (more properly a type of idiochord bowed zither), is made from a green bamboo plant and its four strings are fibres lifted off the main stem. A bridge is placed under the strings, cut in such a way that the tension of each string gives the required pitch. The bow, soaked in water before use, is also made of bamboo.

CHAPTER FIVE

The Viola

1. THE INSTRUMENT

The term 'viola' now refers to the alto (or, more properly, to the alto–tenor) member of the violin family (for earlier meanings, see §(ii) below). The viola came into being in northern Italy at about the same time (around 1535) as the violin and the cello.

(i) The modern viola

In general, the viola has the darker, warmer and richer tone qualities of the alto voice as opposed to the lighter, more brilliant soprano of the violin. Viola tone is less assertive, being more mellow, even subdued at times. Its highest string (a') generally produces something of a contrast in timbre to the other strings, being somewhat more nasal and piercing. The lowest string (c) of a fine viola is capable of a clear, beautiful, resonant and powerful tone that is eagerly sought by both makers and players. The strings are tuned to $c–g–d'–a'$, a 5th below the violin, and consequently the viola requires a larger and longer body. But its size has never been standardized as to depth of ribs, width of bouts or length of body. The body may be from 2.5 to over 10 cm longer than the violin's (which is standardized at an average 35.5 cm).

The basic problem of the viola is that physically it cannot achieve the perfect acoustical results of the violin and still be played at the shoulder. To produce optimum strength of tone and, especially, beauty and depth on its lower strings, the ideal viola would have to be too long for the player's arm. In the violin the virtually perfect relationship between size and pitch was achieved empirically, evidently with quick instinct, by such great makers of the 16th century as Andrea Amati and Gasparo da Salò. To duplicate this triumph in the same degree on the

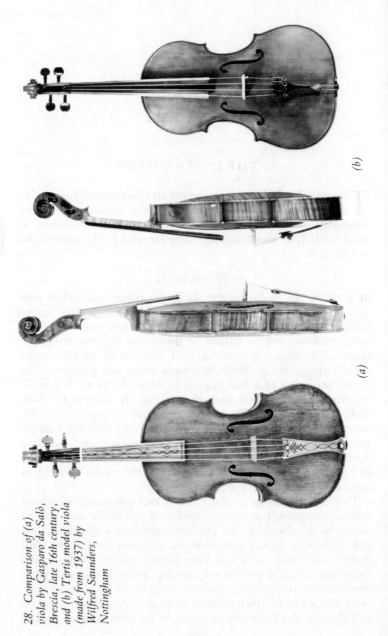

28. Comparison of (a) viola by Gasparo da Salò, Brescia, late 16th century, and (b) Tertis model viola (made from 1937) by Wilfred Saunders, Nottingham

138

viola was impossible because the viola, sounding a 5th below the
violin, would require acoustically a body half again as big as the
violin's (thus about 53 cm long). A body length much over
43 cm is difficult for the player of average reach to handle (a
contributing factor, of course, is the depth of the ribs). Differing
sizes are explained by the differing lengths of players' arms and
by whether the maker wants to produce an instrument basically
alto or tenor in tone quality (see §(iii) below), but it is hardly
possible to produce a truly powerful and resonant C-string
sound with a small-bodied viola. (For further discussion of the
acoustical properties of string instruments, see Chapter Nine.)

Just as the length of the viola varies from instrument to
instrument, so, naturally, does the sounding length of the
strings (i.e. the open string measured from inside the nut to the
inside of the top of the bridge). On the modern violin this length
is standardized at about 33 cm. On a typical modern viola with a
fairly substantial body length (for instance, 42.5 cm, as on the
'Tertis' viola; see §(iv) below), the corresponding open-string
length is about 38.5 cm (see fig.28b). An extant specimen of a
large viola of the late 16th century (made by Gasparo da Salò and
now in the Ashmolean Museum, Oxford; fig.28a) has a 44.5 cm
body, but the open-string length is only 36.2 cm because the
instrument still has its original short neck.

The strings of the viola were originally gut, but a wound C
string must have been used throughout the 18th century and a
wound G string by the late 18th century. In modern practice,
wound strings (i.e. with metal wound over gut, perlon or metal
cores) are often used for all four strings to aid their 'speaking'
capacity, to improve their evenness of tone and response from
string to string, and to reduce breakage. Sometimes a metal (not
wound) A string is used, but a gut A is now practically obsolete.
The fingering and bowing techniques of the viola are similar in
principle to the violin's, and many technical studies (e.g.
Kreutzer, Ševčík) are simply transposed down a 5th for the
viola. Differences in technique are related to the viola's larger
size. For one thing, its weight and size require that it be held
with its scroll generally a bit lower than it is on the violin; the
violin's typical horizontal position would be too tiring. Viola
fingering, while similar to the violin's, demands larger spacing
and sometimes greater left-hand strength; the viola is thus
somewhat more difficult to handle. The vibrato is generally
somewhat slower and less intense on the viola than on the violin.

VIOLA

Again, viola bowing is in principle the same as the violin's except that the viola's thicker strings respond more slowly than those of the violin, and the bow itself is generally a bit thicker, heavier and slightly shorter.

(ii) Earlier meanings of the term 'viola'

By 1535 the alto–tenor violin (our viola) was established as one of the three principal members of the new violin family, but it was not called 'viola' because at that time the term had a variety of meanings both general and specific. Around 1500 'viola', in the most general sense, might mean any string instrument, plucked as well as bowed. From this general sense, the Italian term *viola* (Fr. *vielle*; Ger. *Fidel*) was modified in various ways to describe a specific family or a specific instrument. Examples from the 16th and 17th centuries are the *viola da braccio* ('arm viola'; a member of the violin family), *soprano di viola da braccio* (violin), *viola da gamba* ('leg viola'; a member of the viol family) and *basso di viola da gamba* (bass viol). Later instances are the viola d'amore and viola pomposa.

When used before about 1550, 'viola' may also have the specific meaning of a Renaissance fiddle or a *lira da braccio* (but not generally rebec). Frequent statements to the contrary notwithstanding, the unqualified term 'viola', used alone, rarely if ever means violin. However, the converse is sometimes true: in Venetian usage around 1600, 'violino' may mean viola (alto violin) as well as violin proper (for example in L. Zacconi, *Prattica di musica*, 1592; G. Gabrieli, *Sonata pian e forte*, 1597).

In the 17th and 18th centuries 'viola' is often used with adjectives to denote different registers (but not change of tuning, which, whatever register was involved, was invariably upwards in 5ths from *c*). In Albinoni's *Sinfonie e concerti a cinque* op.2 (1700), for example, two of the partbooks are labelled 'Alto Viola' and 'Tenor Viola' for what are respectively viola I and viola II parts, one playing in the alto register and the other in the tenor; Handel's op.3 no.1 concerto has one part marked 'Alto Viola' and another 'Tenor' in the Walsh edition of 1734. Similarly, in the five-part French ensembles described by Mersenne (1636–7) the three 'parts of the middle' are all violas (all with the customary *c* tuning), but of differing sizes and playing in different registers. In the 24 Violons du Roi (the court ensemble established by Louis XIII in 1626) the viola parts were called *haute-contre* or *haute-contre taille* (contralto or contralto–

tenor: viola I), *taille* (tenor: viola II) and *quinte* or *cinquiesme* (fifth: viola III).

By the 18th century 'viola' (alto violin) was equated with *viola da brazzo* (*braz.*), from *viola da braccio* (see above); hence *Bratsche*, the modern German term for viola (alto violin). Sébastien de Brossard's *Dictionaire de musique* (Paris, 1703) ties the two sets of meanings together, equating *braz. I* with *haute-contre* (alto viola or viola I), *braz. II* with *taille* (tenor viola or viola II) and *braz. III* with viola III. Brossard also mentioned 'viola IV', but said it was not used in France. The term 'violetta', used in the 16th century to mean 'violin' or even 'viol' in certain contexts, often refers in the 18th century to the viola (alto violin). But adjectives may alter the meaning: *violetta marina*, for instance, is a species of viola d'amore.

(iii) 'Instruments of the middle'

Historically, the viola was 'the instrument of the middle', being used for both the alto and tenor registers: in the 16th and 17th centuries, a four-part ensemble might use two violas; and a five-part ensemble, three violas (see references to Mersenne in §(ii) above). This distribution accounts for the relatively large number of violas produced in these two centuries by makers of the time, including such famous ones as the various members of the Amati family in Cremona and, in Brescia, Gasparo da Salò and Maggini. The distribution of parts explains also why the sizes of violas varied from very large models, needed to play in the deep tenor register, to small models for playing in the higher alto register.

Some of these tenor violas are so large as to be barely playable on the arm. The huge Andrea Amati tenor viola (1574; fig.29, p.142), made for Charles IX at Paris and now at Oxford, has a body length of 47 cm. That of a Stradivari tenor of 1690 is virtually 48 cm according to the Hills. With regard to such very large violas, the viola virtuoso William Primrose once remarked: 'The viola is difficult enough without having to indulge in a wrestling match with it'. Few of these large tenors still exist. Besides the usual attrition over the years from breakage, fire and hard usage, a number of them were later altered and shortened to make them easier to hold and play for violists of a later time.

This was one reason why few violas were made in the first part of the 18th century; instruments were already in plentiful supply in varying sizes from the past. Also, violas were in less

29. Tenor viola ('Charles IX') by Andrea Amati, Cremona, 1574

demand for musical reasons. The typical ensemble texture of the early 18th century was four parts, the usual orchestral distribution now being two violin parts, one viola part and one cello–bass part, as opposed to as many as three viola parts in certain five-part ensembles in the 17th century. Moreover, two of the prevailing forms of chamber music, the solo violin sonata and the trio sonata, rarely used a viola part at all. (For usage of the viola in concertos of the early 18th century, see §2(i) below.) It is therefore not surprising that, although more than 500 genuine Stradivari violins are thought to exist, Doring could account for only 11 violas, some of which were 17th century instruments.

(iv) Construction: 19th and 20th centuries

With the perfecting of the modern (Tourte) bow around 1786, a new era in string playing began. Around 1800, the viola, like the violin, went through various alterations to increase string tension and carrying power and to facilitate technique, especially left-hand fingering and shifting (see Chapter One, §4). Involved in such changes were a lengthened and thrown-back neck and fingerboard, a longer and heavier bass-bar, somewhat heavier strings (the lowest being wound; see §1 above), and a rather higher bridge. New violas made in the 19th and 20th centuries conformed to these specifications, and earlier instruments were altered as needed to fit the new conditions. The new-model (Tourte) bow was ideally suited to drawing out the increased power and fuller tone inherent in the new-model viola.

Some 19th-century makers were possessed with the notion of improving the viola acoustically by lengthening or enlarging the body. In 1876, for example, Hermann Ritter introduced a *viola alta* (built by K. A. Hörlein), an exact enlargement of the violin; Wagner was interested enough to use this instrument in the orchestra at Bayreuth. Ritter's viola, however, was about 48 cm long on the body – acoustically desirable but effective only in proportion to the length of the player's arms. (For further such examples, see Berner.)

Beginning in 1937, the English viola virtuoso Lionel Tertis (1876–1975), after long experience and experiment, began collaborating with the violin maker Arthur Richardson to create a model viola intended to combine fullness, depth and beauty of tone in a full-size viola still manageable by the player. This 'Tertis' model (see fig.28b), first heard in concert in 1939, has since been produced by a number of craftsmen around the

143

world, and is illustrated and described in Tertis's autobiography (1953).

Another recent and novel approach, inspired partly by musical considerations and partly by new acoustical studies, is that of Carleen Hutchins, after earlier research by Frederick Saunders. Hutchins and her associates designed and built a whole new violin family of eight members, acoustically scaled to the violin as the ideal. Of the eight members of this new family (including two pitched above the present violin), four are new and three are re-scaled members. Among the latter is the 'viola' (alto), re-scaled to a body measurement of over 50 cm, and played like a cello, using an endpin.

2. REPERTORY

(i) To 1800

The best viola makers have often been successful in minimizing the inherent acoustical difficulties discussed above and a fine viola, played by a true artist, is therefore capable of a beauty and variety of tone and effects of virtuosity that are thrilling and moving in the alto–tenor register. However, the viola has always suffered as a solo instrument by comparison with the greater brilliance of the violin and the strength and depth of the cello. Both violin and cello can compete more successfully with the symphony orchestra in concertos, and this explains why, over the years, composers have written innumerable violin concertos, a fair number for cello and until recently comparatively few for viola. Before 1740 the viola was seldom treated as a soloist in any context, generally being banished to the decent obscurity of the accompaniment, realizing the harmony of the middle parts. At the low point of its fortunes the instrument was described by J. J. Quantz (*Versuch*, 1752):

> The viola is commonly regarded as of little importance in the musical establishment. The reason may well be that it is often played by persons who are either still beginners in the ensemble or have no particular gifts with which to distinguish themselves on the violin, or that the instrument yields all too few advantages to its players, so that able people are not easily persuaded to take it up. I maintain, however, that if the entire accompaniment is to be without defect, the violist must be just as able as the second violinist.

From such stuff are splendid inferiority complexes born and bred in violists! Yet it was true that before 1740 there were no known outstanding violists and virtually no repertory requiring them. (The Viola Concerto in B minor ascribed to Handel is a 20th-century forgery, 'realized' and 'orchestrated' by Henri Casadesus and probably written by him.) Virtuoso music composed before 1740 exists for 20th-century concert violists mostly in the form of arrangements or transcriptions – transposed down from the violin or up from the cello (for example the Bach solo violin sonatas and the cello suites), or transcribed from the viol, viola d'amore or other instruments. On the other hand, there is a fair amount of viola music in ensemble that is musically fascinating to play, especially in fugues and other pieces found in the concertos of such composers as Corelli, Bach, Handel and Vivaldi. Geminiani promoted the viola to the role of soloist in the concertino of his concerti grossi. There are viola parts of genuine musical interest in the 'orchestras' used in the sacred and secular works of Bach and Handel, especially when contrapuntal textures or descriptive effects (as in opera from Monteverdi to Gluck and Mozart) are involved. Sometimes a melody was given to the inside voices, as in the second passepied of Bach's Suite no.1 in C, where the melody is played by the second violins and violas in unison. Occasionally the viola was used for special colouristic or sonorous effects: for instance, as a true bass of an accompaniment (there being no bass part or figured continuo), as in Vivaldi's Violin Concerto in A minor op.3 no.6, whose slow movement features an aria-like violin solo accompanied by two violins and a viola. In Purcell's soprano aria 'See, even night herself is here' (from *The Fairy Queen*, 1692) the accompaniment is two muted violins and (evidently unmuted) a viola which acts as the true bass to an imitative-counterpoint trio. However, in spite of the many musical beauties discoverable in the ensemble use of the viola in early music, the viola part in the orchestra seldom exploited the technical potential of the instrument, even within the limits of 3rd position.

After about 1740 the viola began to enjoy a new lease of life, though less noticeably in its orchestral role than elsewhere. It was treated increasingly as a solo instrument in concertos. According to Ulrich Drünner (1981), the history of the viola concerto begins with that of Telemann (probably written shortly before 1740) and is represented by only three other concertos from the Baroque period, those of J. M. Dömming, A. H. Gehra and J. G. Graun. The early classical viola concerto is represented by Georg Benda and Zelter in Berlin, Vanhal in Vienna, and the Stamitz family in Mannheim. The Concerto in D by Carl Stamitz, one of the virtuoso violists of his day, is one of the standard works in the modern repertory. A description of the viola in J. N. Forkel's *Musikalischer Almanach für Deutschland* of 1782 concludes: 'But would anyone who has heard a Stamitz play the viola with a taste for majesty and tenderness, which appears to be peculiar only to him, not then declare himself for the viola, would he not then accept it among his favourite instruments'. In 1792 E. L. Gerber wrote of him: 'With what extraordinary art and facility he plays the viola'. Among the better known classical viola concertos are those of J. A. Amon, F. W. H. Benda, F. A. Hoffmeister, Roman Hofstetter, Ignace Pleyel, Josef Reicha, G. A. Schneider, Joseph Schubert and, above all, Alessandro Rolla.

During the lifetime of Haydn, Mozart and Beethoven a good many changes took place in the treatment of the viola in chamber music, especially in quartets and quintets and occasionally in string trios and duos (e.g. those of Mozart; his Trio for viola, clarinet and piano K498 should also be mentioned). The changes came about partly because a basic concept of late 18th-century chamber music was that a single player played each part (thus setting chamber music apart from the orchestra where each string part, at least, was played by several players). In this context a violist of any attainment would become increasingly impatient simply playing harmonic filler 'parts of the middle' while the first violin was playing the main melodies. Except for fugues, where the musical interest was equally distributed, composers of early quartets, like Haydn, saw that the inside parts of string quartets would have to be made more interesting by giving them thematic motifs or even, from time to time, main melodies, obbligato parts or virtuoso figuration (as in Haydn, op.33 and later). This factor in turn animated the solo player to greater mastery of the technique of his instrument.

A greater equality of part-writing and a notable advance of viola technique can be observed in the mature chamber music, especially string quartets, of Mozart and Beethoven. For instance, in Mozart's last string quartet (K590, 1790), the part-writing is equalized, solos are given to the viola, and a considerable degree of virtuosity is demanded of the instrument, especially in those chromatic passages which are assigned it. Similar remarks may be made about Beethoven's chamber music, which also makes additional use of special devices or colouristic effects. A melody might be emphasized or rein- forced, for example, by playing it in octaves, as in the viola and first violin parts in the first movement (bars 42ff) of op. 18 no. 4. More unusual at this time is the exploiting of the colour possibilities of the higher register of the C string in the fugal last movement of op. 59 no. 3, where from bar 160 the violist is required to play on the C string in the 5th position. Beethoven treated the viola in somewhat comparable fashion in the orches- tra, but not to the same degree. Even when the orchestral violas are heard playing melodic material they are often doubled with the second violins (as in the Ninth Symphony, slow movement, D major theme) or with the cellos.

Mozart, in his concerto for violin and viola (Sinfonia concert- ante K364/320d, 1779), treated the violin and viola as equal partners, even sharing the same degree of difficulty in the written-out cadenza. He thus made technical demands of the viola quite unprecedented at that time, requiring the player to reach the 7th position at the end of the last movement (bar 439; see ex. 62). Mozart was himself an excellent player on both

Ex.62 Mozart: *Sinfonia concertante*, K 364/320d, finale, bars 437–40
As written (sounds a semitone higher)

violin and viola, and in certain respects his double concerto is one of the most fascinating pieces ever written for viola – if played as he wrote it. For one thing, he provided subtle supports for the violist, the details of which might escape casual attention. He also scored the concerto so that the natural brilliance of the violin is somewhat muted, while the natural reticence of the viola is somewhat brightened and amplified. This was done by using the key of Eb for the concerto and by writing a scordatura part for the viola. The key of Eb is not a brilliant one for the violin (none of the open strings serves to reinforce the principal notes of this key). The same is normally true of the open strings of the viola, but Mozart followed the practice of writing the part

VIOLA

in D, with the strings tuned up a semitone. This 'transposition scordatura' means that the violist fingers the music as if it were in the key of D, but it sounds in E♭. This particular retuning has several important effects: it increases the tension on the strings, making the viola a bit more brilliant and slightly louder; three of the four viola strings – now tuned to what is enharmonically d♭, a♭, e♭' and b♭' – reinforce the tonic, subdominant and dominant notes of the main key of E♭; and finally, it is easier for the violist to play in D than in E♭. In short, by the choice of key and by this particular way of writing for the viola, Mozart managed to equalize the violin and viola physically, as well as musically, with respect to brilliance, carrying power and ease of execution. The technique of tuning the viola up a semitone or whole tone was used in several late 18th-century and early 19th-century pieces, including Vanhal's concerto in F (written in E♭ for the viola), Carl Stamitz's viola and piano sonata in B♭ (written in A for the viola) and his Sinfonia concertante for violin and viola, in which both solo instruments are tuned up a semitone. Two versions of the Sinfonia concertante exist in manuscript copies. In one (in the Library of Congress, Washington, DC) the orchestra is in E♭ and the soloists are in D; in the other (Fürstlich Bentheimsche Bibliothek, in the Universitätsbibliothek, Münster), both orchestra and soloists are in D.

Mozart's Quintet in G minor for two violins, two violas and cello (K516, 1787) amply demonstrates the potential of the viola as a chamber music instrument in the hands of a master. Particularly noteworthy is the practice, possibly learnt from Michael Haydn, of highlighting the first violin and first viola as soloists on an equal footing, while at the same time ensuring that each instrument in the ensemble has an interesting part to play. Also worthy of remark is the way that Mozart made the first viola serve as either a treble or a bass: that is, as a bass to the trio of the upper three instruments or – a marked contrast in tone-colour – as the treble to the lower three. The resulting dark–light colour contrast of trio combinations is illustrated by the opening bars of the work. Finally, in the slow movement, the contrasted key of E♭ is subdued still more by Mozart's direction to use mutes on all the instruments (mutes being rarely called for in 18th-century chamber music). The second subject is worked out in a glorious duet between violin I (bar 27) and viola I a few bars later. Even viola II has a moment or two of dramatic comment (e.g. bar 19) on the musical action.

148

Several viola methods, somewhat analogous to those for violin and cello, were published at the end of the 18th and the beginning of the 19th centuries; they include those by M. Corrette (1773), M. Woldemar (between 1795 and 1803), F. Cupis (c1801) and M. J. Gebauer (c1805).

(ii) From 1800

Early in the 19th century an outstanding method by A. B. Bruni (c1816) and viola studies by B. Campagnoli and J.-J.-B. Martinn were published. In the 20th century the viola began to share in the technical advances of the violin (most violists having begun their training as violinists). The trend towards virtuosity became much more pronounced in the 20th century, when, for instance, players were obliged to cultivate the highest positions on the lower three strings. The average orchestral violist around 1900 was still regarded as a cast-off from the violin section, but in the 20th century the viola was increasingly called upon, especially the viola soloist in chamber music, to perform special effects such as *col legno* bowings (e.g. Schoenberg), rebounding pizzicatos (Bartók), glissandos, harmonics and so on. Developments in fingering were similar to those for the violin (see Chapter Two, §2(v)) and are enshrined in the methods of Dolejši (1939) and Primrose (1960) as well as in the 20th-century repertory.

Berlioz had already shown (1834) how magical a *sul ponticello* could sound in an arpeggio passage for solo viola against muted orchestral strings (in 'Marche des pèlerins' from his *Harold en Italie*). These demands by composers meant that an efficient technique was slowly being acquired by violists in all types of instrumental music. After Beethoven, the string parts in the music of such composers as Berlioz, Brahms, Verdi and Tchaikovsky gradually increased in difficulty. In Wagner and Richard Strauss and later in Mahler and Ravel, and of course 12-note compositions, the demands made on violists are greater still, tending at times to equal those on the other strings. In much 20th-century chamber music, for instance, the technical demands on the viola are often as great as on the other parts, notably in Schoenberg's String Trio or Bartók's string quartets (particularly nos.3–6). In the case of modern concertos the viola soloist is normally called on for an imposing array of accomplishments of the left and right hand – in the relatively rare (though increasingly frequent) viola recital, one may occasionally hear such a tour de force as a transcription of a Paganini caprice.

While 19th-century composers seldom called on the viola soloist for the same degree of pyrotechnics as the violin, they became more appreciative of the viola's potential with respect to tone-colour and sonority. Brahms is a good example. In the Agitato movement of his String Quartet in Bb op.67, he assigned the opening solo to the viola accompanied by muted violins and cello – a remarkable essay in the colouristic use of the viola ranging over all four strings. In his Serenade op.16 Brahms omitted the violins, featuring the violas as a treble part, as he did also in the first movement of the *German Requiem*.

Treated mainly as a tenor in early times, the viola had also been used occasionally as an alto or even, for special effect, as a bass (see examples of Vivaldi and Purcell cited in §(i) above). The cultivation of tone-colour of different registers after 1800 led composers to use the viola as any voice-part of the ensemble for momentary effect. To increase power and sonority, special violas such as Hermann Ritter's *viola alta* were introduced into the orchestra. Since sonority and colour of the string section were important components of Romantic music in achieving its effect, some later composers who disliked this type of music – Stravinsky, for example – sought to use the strings more drily or even percussively rather than melodically or colouristically, or did not use them at all (his *Symphony of Psalms* is scored without violins or violas).

For reasons already suggested, there are dozens of violin concertos for every one for the viola (Drünner lists 141 between 1740 and 1840, knows of none between 1840 and 1870, and finds a gradually increasing number after 1870). Indeed, it would be difficult to call to mind more than one 'famous' viola concerto in the 19th century: namely, Berlioz's *Harold en Italie*, and that a viola concerto disguised as a programme symphony. Even this work originated through a special set of circumstances. Paganini, having acquired a fine Stradivari viola, commissioned Berlioz to write a viola concerto for him. *Harold en Italie* was the result, but Paganini declined to play it because, as he told Berlioz, 'I am not given enough to do'. Berlioz, however, was by no means uninterested in the viola. 'Of all the instruments in the orchestra', he stated, 'the viola is the one whose excellent qualities have been longest ignored'. In *Harold* (and elsewhere) Berlioz wrote marvellously for the instrument, not only for the solo part but also for the orchestral violas – consider the main 'Harold' melody, the cadenza at the end of the first adagio, or the whole of the 'Marche des pèlerins'.

In the 20th century compositions featuring the solo viola have become more numerous because, among other reasons, the presence of such outstanding players as Lionel Tertis, William Primrose and Paul Hindemith has encouraged composers. Tertis, in particular, inspired a number of pieces by British composers, including (though indirectly through Thomas Beecham) the Walton Viola Concerto, one of the best in modern times. (This work was offered to Tertis for its first performance but was actually first played with Hindemith as soloist, 3 October 1929.) The posthumous Bartók Viola Concerto ('prepared for publication by Tibor Serly') was commissioned by and written for Primrose, who first performed it. Hindemith, equally distinguished as composer and violist, wrote a number of solo works for viola, which, in the older tradition of the composer–performer like Mozart, he played himself. Among these are four viola concertos, six pieces for viola and piano and four for unaccompanied viola. Many other distinguished composers might be mentioned for their viola compositions, including Bloch, Henze, Milhaud, Piston and Shostakovich.

In spite of the relatively numerous 19th- and 20th-century pieces originally written for the viola as a soloist in one capacity or another, perhaps the instrument is most at home (and treated in the most congenial fashion by composers) in chamber music. Among the many chamber-music combinations, composers have evidently written for the viola the most frequently and with the greatest devotion in that most perfect of musical mediums, the string quartet, as a number of the finest works of the most celebrated composers attest: among them Beethoven, Schubert, Dvořák, Brahms, Debussy, Ravel, Bartók, Dohnányi, Shostakovich, Prokofiev, Schoenberg and Webern. The viola is common in quartets and quintets with piano, and has fared well in string quintets and sextets (two violas), some of which approach orchestral sonority (e.g. those of Brahms).

Composers tended, conversely, to shy away somewhat from the viola as a solo instrument in works involving fewer instruments, where each became more prominent to the whole. Thus the string trio of violin, viola and cello is much less commonly used by composers than the piano trio (violin, cello, piano).

VIOLA

Similarly, there are few sonatas in the 19th century originally written for viola and piano: even the two by Brahms (op.120, 1895), arranged by the composer from his clarinet and piano sonatas, do not have quite the verve and freshness of the original versions. The same might be said of several other Brahms chamber works in which he substituted viola for clarinet. The viola is, however, sometimes used with marked success in song accompaniments, as in Brahms's *Geistliches Wiegenlied*, where the singer is accompanied by piano and viola obbligato.

In any case, the literature available to the modern violist is very considerable, ranging from simple ensemble parts to concertos of great difficulty, and the instrument may be said to have progressed immensely since 1750 in realizing its potential of tone and technique. The viola is a stepchild no longer.

CHAPTER SIX

The Violoncello

The name 'violoncello' first became current in the mid-17th century, but bass violins of one kind or another are mentioned in several treatises of the 16th and early 17th centuries. Jambe de Fer (1556, p.61f) referred to the 'bas de violon', Zacconi (1592, p.218) to the 'basso di viola da braccio', Praetorius (ii, 2/1619, 'Tabella universalis', p.26) to the 'bass viol de braccio' and Mersenne (ii, 1637, p.185) to the 'basse de violon'. The term 'violone' is often found in Italian church archives of the same period (e.g. those of Santa Maria Maggiore, Bergamo) to refer to a bass violin rather than a bass (or double-bass) viola da gamba (see Bonta, 1978), and it is as a diminutive of this that the instrument now known as the violoncello is recognized. The term 'violoncino' for an instrument now indistinguishable from a violoncello is first encountered in a volume of sonatas by Giovanni Battista Fontana (Venice, 1641). The earliest known use of the term 'violoncello' is in Giulio Cesare Arresti's *Sonate* op.4 (Venice, 1665). While 'violoncino' and even 'violone' continued to be used for a violoncello until the early 18th century, the newer term was soon generally accepted in Italy and Germany; after 1700 it was common in France and England. The abbreviation 'cello' is commonly used in English and German.

1. EVOLUTION

The instrument originated in the early 16th century as a member of a whole family of instruments, of different sizes and with varying compasses, known as 'viole da braccio'. The earliest source, Agricola (1529), describes four instruments of the violin type with different ranges, including a bass instrument with

three strings tuned F–c–g. This range was soon extended by the addition of a string a 5th below. Instruments tuned Bb'–F–c–g are mentioned by Lanfranco (1533) and his Spanish translator Cerone (*El melopeo y maestro*, Naples, 1613), by Zacconi and by Jambe de Fer. The tuning, achieved by extending the 5ths of the violin downwards systematically, did not prove ideal for ensemble playing, however, and so the practice that had already been found successful with the viol family was adopted: the strict sequence of intervals was replaced by tuning two members of the family an octave apart. The bass instrument thus acquired its modern tuning of *C–G–d–a* (an octave below the viola), which had been described by H. Gerle (*Musica teusch*, Nuremberg, 1532). Praetorius listed *C–G–d–a* and *F–c–g–d'* for the bass instrument, as well as *F'–C–G–d–a* for a 'Gross-Quint-Bass'. An analysis of the tessitura used by Monteverdi shows that the tuning of *C–G–d–a* was current in Italy by about 1600. The lower tuning was retained in France and England until the 18th century; Corrette (*Méthode*, 1741) stated that the higher tuning was introduced into France around 1710, and J. F. de la Fond's *New System of Music*, published in London in 1725, proves that it was in use in England by that time.

The earliest known makers of instruments that would be recognized today as cellos were Andrea Amati (*d* before 1580) of Cremona, Gasparo da Salò (1540–1609) of Brescia and his pupil Giovanni Paolo Maggini (*c*1581–*c*1632). Their instruments were considerably larger than the standard modern cello, some having a body length of 80 cm or more (surviving examples have been reduced in size). The decisive move towards a smaller cello probably took place at Bologna in the 1600s with the introduction of a silver-covered bottom string (see Bonta, 1977). This facilitated the development of an advanced technique without sacrifice of the sonority which, with unwound gut strings, could have been obtained only with greater length (necessitating wider stretches for the fingers).

The dimensions of the cello nevertheless continued to fluctuate during the rest of the century, varying between 73 and 80 cm, with a preference for the larger model. This preference is to be observed in the instruments (now mostly cut down) of the Rugeri and Guarneri families of Cremona, the Rogeris of Brescia, the Grancinos and Testores of Milan, the Tononis of Bologna and the Gaglianos of Naples, all of whom were making cellos before the more famous Stradivari. Andrea Guarneri has often been credited with creating the smaller cello, and both Francesco Rugeri and G. B. Rogeri are said to have made some (see Hill, p.111f); but David Tecchler was still making fine examples of the larger model in Rome in the mid-18th century. Between about 1707 and 1710 Antonio Stradivari, who had previously made only large cellos, decided on a medium length of 75 to 76 cm, and this has been standard ever since. Even with the larger models of before 1700 the length of the vibrating part of the strings was about 2 or 3 cm shorter than it is today, and it did not arrive at the now normal length of about 69 cm until the necks of the whole violin family were lengthened during the 18th century.

In the late 17th and early 18th centuries the range of some cellos was extended upwards by a fifth string. Increasing musical demands also led to experiments with smaller instruments of the same compass as the cello, which could be played in the violin position. Several late 18th-century writers ascribed to Bach the invention of an instrument of this kind, with the tuning C–G–d–a–e', and although Bach composed nothing that specifies its use there are good reasons not to confuse it with the violoncello piccolo for which he wrote parts in nine of his Leipzig cantatas. Whether the five-string cello for which Bach wrote his sixth unaccompanied suite (BWV1012) was this same violoncello piccolo or simply a normal-sized cello with an extra e' string is difficult to determine. Subsequent variants of the standard instrument have included the 'violoncello d'amore', a small cello with sympathetic strings as on the viola d'amore, and the arpeggione, a six-string instrument with guitar-like frets, invented by J. G. Staufer of Vienna in 1824. Van der Straeten (1915, pp.638ff) mentioned three other instruments: the 'violoncello portatile' made by Johann Wilde (d 1770), a collapsible cello which, when assembled, had a box-like shape similar to that of the so-called 'porta cello' sometimes used by beginners today; the 'harmonicello', built by J. C. Bischoff in 1794, with five gut strings and ten sympathetic metal ones; and the curiously named 'cellone', a large cello tuned a 4th below the standard instrument, made by Alfred Stelzner of Dresden about 1890.

Experiments of this kind were not a success, and the earlier ones were in any case soon made redundant by the rapid development of playing techniques. Other modifications made to the violin family during the 18th century were due to changing concepts of the sound required. The neck and fingerboard were lengthened and curved more sharply, the bridge was raised, and thinner and tauter strings gave the cello a clearer and more responsive tone. With these developments the evolution of the instrument was essentially complete. Modifications since the late 18th century, including the introduction of the Tourte bow and of the endpin, resulted mainly from a desire for greater sonority and a more virtuoso technique.

2. TECHNIQUE AND PERFORMERS

The principal factors governing the development of cello playing technique were its structural and functional membership in the violin family and the size necessitated by its compass, which inevitably led to some approximation to viol technique; the cello could only be played upright, like the viola da gamba. By the last quarter of the 17th century viol players, especially in France, had developed highly flexible and refined left-hand and bowing techniques. The subtlety of the bowing technique was influential not only on string playing but also on wind playing and singing during the early years of the 18th century. Left-hand technique, with its emphasis on expanding and contracting the hand (see fig.33, p.162) and placing the thumb so as to balance the weight of the hand, also greatly influenced cello playing in the 18th century. At first the cello player sat with the instrument placed between his legs on the floor (see fig.31, p.158) or stood with it leant against his body or supported with a strap. Occasionally it was placed on a stool, and some pictures show it held in a horizontal position, perhaps to play pizzicato or merely to pose. The grip round the neck, with the fingers falling obliquely on to the strings, and the purely diatonic fingering, with four fingers filling in the intervals between the 5ths in which the instrument was tuned, both derived from violin playing. This technique was good enough for the simple demands made of the instrument in the 16th century, when the violin family occupied a musically and socially humble position, being used principally for dance music. However, as the rise of monody, thorough bass and concertante style around 1600 gave the violin an increasing importance, the cello, too, was called upon to perform a more complex role, demanding a technique more suited to the length of its strings and the position in which it was held. The instrument was from then held without the aid of the left hand, leaving it more free to execute fast passages and changes of position, while the fingers came down on the strings vertically, making double stopping possible.

Towards 1700 it became usual for the player to place the

31. Violoncello resting on the floor: detail of painting 'The Cello Player' (c1660) by Gabriel Metsu

instrument between his knees and support it with his calves (see fig.32, p.160), in the traditional posture of the bass viol player. This high position permitted him to draw back the neck towards himself, so that the left hand could approach the strings from the side instead of from behind and could thus reach the whole area of the fingerboard without difficulty. Since the place where the bow touched the strings (the 'point of contact') was also raised, the entire length of the bow could be used. This way of holding the cello made possible the introduction (*c*1720) of the practice of using the thumb as a movable saddle in the upper registers, thus making the entire compass of the instrument more accessible. Thumb position is first described in Michel Corrette's *Méthode* (1741; see p.164 below).

Because of the length of its strings, the purely diatonic fingering of the violin is not at all suitable for the cello, and this fingering was changed, after a transitional, still diatonic, stage (which used the first, second and fourth, or first, second and third fingers) to a system with regular semitone intervals between one finger and the next, with the option of extending the interval between the first and second fingers to a whole tone. The changes of position made necessary by this were at first executed only with the first and fourth fingers, but eventually the whole hand was used, moving through three diatonic steps, as appropriate. Through this principle specific fingerings for the lower positions were achieved. For higher positions, when the thumb was brought into play, the reduction of the effective length of the strings combined with the particular anatomical relationship of the thumb to the fingers altered the circumstances and the fingering system more closely resembled those of violin playing. While changes in ways of holding the instrument can be traced from iconographical sources, and extensions of its compass can readily be seen from an examination of the music composed for it, the chronology of advances in fingering techniques is less easy to ascertain. There are no instruction manuals from this period (the earliest dates from the mid-18th century, and such works, being designed for amateurs, are anyway rudimentary), and the researcher is forced to base any deductions on such evidence as can be gleaned from a detailed study of the demands made by the repertory.

Much of the same uncertainty applies to the study of bowing technique, though certain developments can be observed. Until the second half of the 18th century cello bowsticks were either

32. *Violoncello with no endpin, supported between the knees: portrait (c1764–7) of Luigi Boccherini by an unknown artist*

straight or convex, like those of the viol and the violin. The usual grip was 'overhand', with the palm of the hand turned downwards – the same grip as that used with smaller members of the violin family. An underhand grip was occasionally found (see fig.31) as viol players accustomed themselves to the newer instrument, but after 1750 the overhand grip replaced this completely in all countries. The bowing hand, at first placed near the middle of the bow (see fig.32), moved nearer to the nut as the length of the bow came to be more fully exploited, and the bow was held no longer with the fist, but with the fingertips (see fig.36, p. 171, and fig.37, p.172); this permitted greater tonal variation. Between about 1750 and 1786 the bow underwent a number of changes (see Chapter Eight, §2), resulting in the concave bowstick of pernambuco wood perfected by François Tourte. According to Fétis, Tourte fixed the length of the cello bow at 72 to 73 cm, with playing hair of 60 to 62 cm. Among his successors as bowmakers in France were Dominique Peccatte and F. N. Voirin; in England John Dodd was particularly well known for his cello bows. The concave bow helped to make possible a more intense and carrying tone, rendering the instrument suitable for playing in larger rooms. The greater tension and elasticity of the bow laid the foundations of brilliant, virtuoso bowing technique, and allowed the player to exercise an optimal influence on tone-colour and dynamics.

In Italy, where the viol had been completely replaced by the violin by the beginning of the 17th century, cello technique remained related to violin technique for an exceptionally long time; it was there that the cello first became a solo instrument. Before 1700 Petronio Franceschini, Domenico Gabrielli and Giuseppe Jacchini had all made reputations as solo cellists in and around Bologna; all three were cellists at the cathedral of S Petronio there. In France, on the other hand, the bass viol retained its dominant position as a solo instrument at least until the 1730s, and its cause there was championed by Hubert Le Blanc (1740). Thus, although the cello was restricted for a much longer period to being merely the lowest part in violin ensembles (e.g. the 24 Violons du Roi), its fingering technique developed along the lines of the viol. Development in Germany was governed by the large number of Italian musicians employed at the courts, and features of violin-influenced technique survived into the 19th century, for example in the highly individual playing style of Bernhard Romberg (1767–1841). England fol-

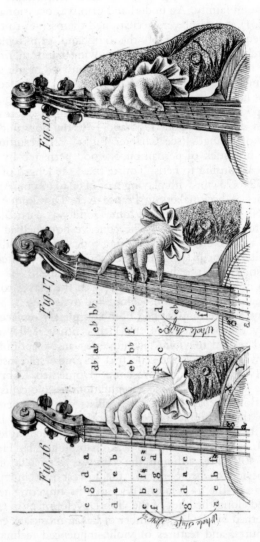

33. Violoncello hand positions from John Gunn's 'The Theory and Practice of Fingering the Violoncello' (1789): 1st position (left), extended position (centre), and the position described by Gunn as formerly much in use, and originating probably from the position of the hand on the violin' (right)

lowed the same course as France. The violin family first came to prominence after the Restoration (1660), when Charles II formed a violin orchestra modelled on that of the French court.

The discrepancies in technique in different countries gradually disappeared in the mid-18th century, not least because of the number of Italian soloists who played all over Europe. Francesco Alborea (widely known as Franciscello) from Naples and Giovanni Bononcini from Modena had already made reputations as cellists (and the latter as a composer, too) outside Italy during the first half of the 18th century. Following these, many other Italian cellists visited and in some cases settled in foreign capitals: Giacomo Bassevi Cervetto, Salvatore Lanzetti, Andrea Caporale and Giovanni Battista Cirri all went to London, Jean Baptiste Stuck (known as Batistin) and Carlo Ferrari to Paris, Bernardo Aliprandi and Evaristo Felice Dall'Abaco to Munich, the latter's son Joseph-Marie-Clément Dall'Abaco to Bonn, Carlo Graziani to Berlin, Antonio Vandini to Prague with Tartini, and Giuseppe Dall'Oglio to St Petersburg. These were all overshadowed by Luigi Boccherini, who worked mainly in Paris and Madrid, and who made a feature of playing in the higher register, extending the instrument's range to bb'''. The first English cellists in London to make names for themselves in the second half of the 18th century after the Italians were William Paxton, John Crosdill, James Cervetto (son of Giacomo Bassevi Cervetto), Joseph Reinagle and John Gunn. In Germany Johann Baptist Baumgartner, Anton Filtz, Joseph Franz Weigl, Johann Georg Christoph Schetky, Johann Jacob Kriegck, Philipp Schindlöker, Franz Xaver Hammer, Johann Conrad Schlick, Johann Rudolf Zumsteeg and Peter Ritter became known at the same period. Bohemia, too, produced some remarkable cellists, many of whom sought employment in Germany and Austria: Wenzel Himmelbauer, Antonín Tadeáš Stamitz, Anton Kraft, J. B. Mara, Bernard and Jan Šťastný and Josef Reicha. Musical life in France was concentrated in Paris, where the Concert Spirituel provided an important venue for French cellists (Jean Barrière, the Duports, Emmanuel Guérin, the Jansons, Pierre François Levasseur, François Martin and Jean Balthasar Tricklir) as well as foreign ones (Boccherini, Francesco Brunetti, Crosdill, Ferrari, Lanzetti, Mara, Romberg, Anton Schwarz, Luigi Zandonati and Mikołaj Zygmuntowski). The circle of pupils of Martin Berteau (*d* 1765) created the first major centre of cello playing: well-known members of that circle included Louis Charles Joseph Rey, Joseph Bonaventure Tillière, Jean-Baptiste Cupis, Jean-Baptiste-Aimé Joseph Janson and Jean-Pierre Duport, and among their pupils were Levasseur, Tricklir, Jean-Baptiste Bréval, Dominique Bideau, Pierre-François-Olivier Aubert, Jacques-Michel Hurel de Lamare and Pierre Louis Hus-Desforges. Apart from Boccherini, the outstanding player at the turn of the century was Jean-Louis Duport, the pupil of his elder brother, with whom he spent many years in Berlin at the court of Friedrich Wilhelm II, an amateur cellist.

The teaching activities of the Paris circle of cellists must have been partly responsible for the number of instruction manuals for the instrument published at a relatively early date. Michel Corrette's *Méthode théorique et pratique* (1741) is generally thought to be the earliest cello method in any language, but it may have been preceded by the undated manuscript (in the Conservatorio di Musica S Pietro a Majella, Naples) *Principii da imparare a suonare il violoncello* by Francesco Scipriani (1678–1753). Corrette's fingerings are derived from violin technique, with slight consideration of the vertical position of the cello or of its size. Corrette did say, however, that if the neck is gripped too firmly by the hand, the fingers cannot move freely, nor can the thumb move to thumb position. This is the earliest mention of the thumb for playing beyond the 3rd position, though Klaus Marx (1963) was of the opinion that in view of the fact that new techniques are published in instruction manuals only after they have been known for some time, its use must have been established rather earlier. Corrette gave fingerings for scales in the 1st position, beginning on the C string (0124), and chromatic fingerings with slides. He also gave examples of half-position (1234) and said that violinists 'ne peuvent point s'accoutumer à cette position'. (It is difficult to understand why violinists could not get used to the half-position; perhaps Corrette thought that it would cramp the violinist's hand.) In a chapter on shifting, fingerings are given up to the 4th position, with some extension and thumb-position fingerings, the thumb being indicated by the word 'pouce'. Chapter 15 is for viol players who wish to learn the cello; comparative fingerings are given (fig.34).

Among the French manuals following Corrette's were those of Tillière (1764), F. Cupis (1772), Joseph Muntzberger (1800), Bideau (1802) and Bréval (1804), as well as the *Méthode* of the Paris Conservatoire (1804), on the compilation of which Jean

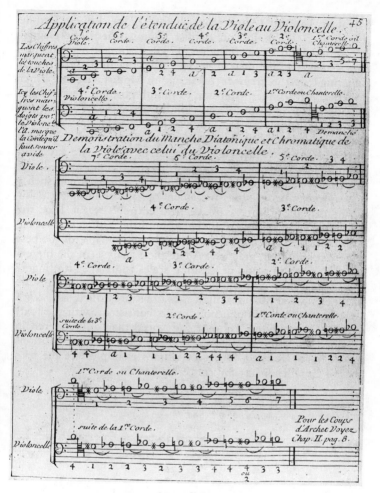

34. Comparative fingerings for viol and cello from Michel Corrette's 'Méthode théorique et pratique' (1741; Chapter XV, p.45)

Henri Levasseur and Charles-Nicolas Baudiot collaborated with the violinist Pierre Baillot and the composer Charles-Simon Catel. (Baudiot's own *Méthode de violoncelle* was published in two parts, in 1826 and 1828.) Olivier Aubert's cello method was first published in Offenbach in 1805, in London in 1811, and in Paris two years later. Other tutors of this period are those by

VIOLONCELLO

Salvatore Lanzetti (Amsterdam, before 1770), Robert Crome (London, 2/c1765), Johann Baptist Baumgartner (The Hague, c1774) and John Gunn (London, 1789). Baumgartner's *Instructions de musique, théorique et pratique* gave practical and musical fingerings in the manner of Leopold Mozart. Baumgartner preferred third-finger extension to thumb position, retained the oblique finger position of the violinist and advised against the playing of double stops. Gunn's *The Theory and Practice of Fingering the Violoncello* is of particular interest since it includes the first serious attempt to write a history of the cello and cello playing. It was also more forward-looking. Gunn argued that neither the hand nor the thumb should grip the neck in such a way as to hamper the free movement of hand and fingers. (This meant that the cello was to be held entirely by the legs; the adjustable endpin was not invented until the 19th century.) He claimed that his method encompassed 'the principle of the best fingering known in practice'. A complete analysis of the fingerboard in ascending and descending scales is given, with fingerings that accord with modern cello technique. Difficult scale passages and shifts into high positions are called for, with fingerings which (though not always consistent with the text) represent a technique far more advanced than any covered in previous methods. Double stops and the use of high positions are taken for granted. Many of Gunn's examples are the bass lines of Corelli sonatas and concertos (ex.63).

Ex.63 J. Gunn: *The Theory and Practice of Fingering the Violoncello*
(a) Corelli: *Sonata da camera a tre*, op.2 no.10, Allegro allemanda, bars 8–9

(b) Corelli: Violin Sonata op.5 no.9, Tempo di Gavotta, bar 1

The first comprehensive account of cello playing technique, reflecting the stage it had reached at the beginning of the 19th century, was in Jean-Louis Duport's *Essai sur le doigté du violon-*

celle, et sur la conduite de l'archet (Paris, *c*1813). Duport covers fingering systematically and includes specific instructions for holding the cello so that the left hand is free to shift uninhibitedly. Until this time, the neck of the instrument was held by the hand, and the fingers placed in positions analogous to those of violinists. There are lengthy discourses (with exercises) on thumb positions and double stops, alternative fingerings for scale passages, and advice on how to avoid playing successive notes with the same finger (ex.64). Regarding this practice

Ex.64 J.-L. Duport: *Essai sur le doigté du violoncelle*, Gamme de La mineur

Duport wrote: 'One will perhaps find it extraordinary that in the scales I carefully avoid playing two notes with the same finger, as one finds in all the principal books which have been published until now. My opinion is that this manner is vicious, and it produces a bad effect' (p.17). Duport deals thoroughly with the first four positions and all the double stops, including 2nds, 4ths and tritones, are carefully fingered – something rare in cello and violin methods of any period. Even 7ths, as suspensions to 6ths, are treated carefully, as are arpeggiated figures that include extensions. The material presented in the *Essai* formed an excellent starting-point for the virtuoso playing heard later in the 19th century, which for the most part developed and perfected techniques described by Duport.

In *Die Violoncellschulen von J. J. F. Dotzauer, F. A. Kummer und B. Romberg* (1968), Josef Eckhardt makes detailed comparisons of their methods (1832, 1839 and 1840 respectively). Anachronistically, Romberg advocated a violin-oriented left-hand position, whereas Dotzauer and Kummer adopted the modern position: that is, fingers more squarely away from the neck. All of them emphasized that the hand must be free to move quickly over the fingerboard. According to Eckhardt, Kummer's finger-

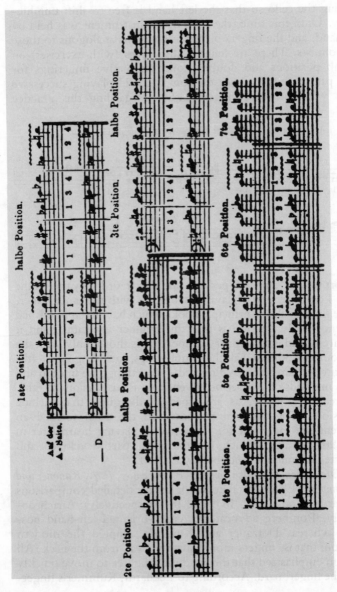

35. Fingering system for the cello, from Friedrich August Kummer's 'Violoncellschule' op.60 (1839); this system may have been the basis of the modern system (see Eckhardt, 1968)

ing system (fig.35) formed the basis of our present system. A nice example of portamento from Dotzauer's method (ex.65) is cited by Eckhardt. None of them, however, used the adjustable endpin, which allowed for even greater stability of the instrument, freeing the left hand completely (a service rendered to violin playing by the chin rest, which Spohr claimed to have invented *c*1820).

Ex.65 J. J. F. Dotzauer (1832)

The adjustable endpin was apparently first adopted about 1846 by the Belgian cellist A. F. Servais, but some kind of fixed endpin was known and used long before this. Robert Crome, in the second edition of his method, *The Compleat Tutor, for the Violoncello* (*c*1765), recommended beginners 'to have a hole made in the Tail-pin and a Wooden Peg to screw into it to rest on the Floor which may be taken out when he Pleases' (see Cowling, 1975, p.47f). The endpin made for greater security and improved resonance. The thumb gained greater independence as a playing finger, both in fast passages and even in melody playing when required; position-change technique was refined; and double stopping, harmonics, and virtuoso spiccato and staccato bowing were all developed to their limits. The participation of the upper arm and the shoulder was essential in all this, and resulted in an increase in the possible volume. Attempts were made at the same time to create a livelier tone: vibrato effects made by the bow, or by fingers lightly and rhythmically touching unbowed strings (called 'Pochen' by Dotzauer), and finally finger and wrist vibrato, all served to enrich the expressive range. The whole process of development borrowed extensively from violin technique but always lagged behind it, notably in tone production, which was neglected while players concentrated on virtuoso techniques. The result was that the quality of tone, particularly in higher registers, remained unsatisfactory. Notation for the instrument was originally some-

what unorganized, employing a large number of clefs, but by
c1800 it had been reduced to the bass, tenor and treble clefs,
although isolated instances of music written in the treble clef, to
be transposed down an octave, continued to occur for quite a
long time, such passages being written by Bruckner and Dvořák.

From Italy in the 19th century there came only one great
cellist, Alfredo Piatti, who settled in London. Other London
players included Robert Lindley and Piatti's pupils, William
Edward Whitehouse and Leo Stern. The Paris school also
waned; the only worthy successors to Jean Henri Levasseur,
Charles-Nicolas Baudiot and Louis Pierre Martin Norblin were
Auguste Joseph Franchomme and Pierre Alexandre François
Chevillard. A new centre in Brussels was founded by Duport's
pupil Nicolas Joseph Platel; there Adrien François Servais and
Jules de Swert came to the fore. Germany became the main area
of development. The phenomenon of the peripatetic cello virtuoso began with Bernhard Romberg before 1800, but his technique
was too old-fashioned to be influential later; although Sebastian
Lee and Georg Goltermann were taught by the Prell brothers,
who in turn were taught by Romberg, they cannot be regarded
as Romberg's lineal descendants. The Dresden school had the
greatest and most widespread influence. Direct pupil-teacher
lines reach from Justus Johann Friedrich Dotzauer, who was
probably influenced by Duport through Kriegck, down to the
present day, through Friedrich August Kummer, Karl Dreschler
and Carl Schuberth. The outstanding figures in this succession
are Bernard Cossmann, Julius Goltermann, Friedrich Grützmacher, Karl Davïdov, David Popper, Wilhelm Fitzenhagen,
Julius Klengel, Hugo Becker, Paul Grümmer, Emanuel Feuer-
mann, Gregor Piatigorsky and Enrico Mainardi. The Russian
Karl Davïdov (a pupil of Schuberth) revolutionized cello fingering by adopting the ideas of the violinist Ivan Khandoshkin,
who advocated the complete mobility of the hand over the entire
fingerboard without regard to set positions. The Austrian
Joseph Merk was important as both player and teacher in Vienna
during the first half of the 19th century.

The difficulty for women of holding a cello in what fashionable society considered a ladylike way may have contributed to
the paucity of women cellists before the 20th century. Van der
Straeten (1898, 3/1915) described various 'side-saddle' postures
used by women cellists, but reported that the normal way of
holding the instrument, between the knees, had by then been

36. The cellist Guilhermina Suggia: portrait (1923) by Augustus John

almost universally adopted. There were other and more powerful social conventions which militated against women as
instrumentalists in earlier centuries, but in spite of these some
women did succeed in making careers as concert cellists. Among
them was Lisa Cristiani (1827–1853), followed in the early 20th
century by May Mukle, Beatrice Harrison, Guilhermina Suggia
(see fig.36) and Raya Garbousova.

171

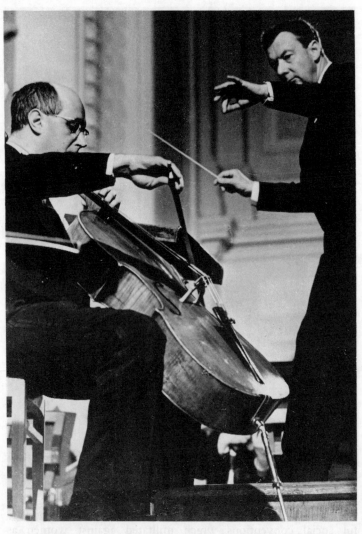

37. *Violoncello with bent endpin: Mstislav Rostropovich with Benjamin Britten in 1964*

Since 1900, players have had a steadily increasing success in bringing the tone of the cello in its higher registers closer to the more intense and lighter tone of the violin; in this way they have given the whole tonal range of the instrument a more persuasive sound quality. The use of longer or even bent endpins (used by Paul Tortelier and Mstislav Rostropovich; see fig.37) has helped, because the raising of the point at which the bow touches the strings and the greater inclination of the strings towards the horizontal both improve sound production and make it easier for the left hand to negotiate the upper part of the fingerboard; and technique has developed to the point that everything seems possible for the left hand. The use of steel-covered strings was another important development. Increasing preoccupation with chamber music, orchestral playing and teaching had even in the 19th century begun to prepare the ground for the change of emphasis from the virtuoso to the interpreter. Instrumental virtuosity is no longer regarded as an end in itself, and technique is now the servant of musical interpretation. The major role in this change of emphasis was played by Pablo Casals in whose hands the cello became at last the equal of the violin as a solo instrument. Casals brought the Bach unaccompanied suites into the regular recital repertory and helped to make known a great deal of the chamber music repertory. He made many innovations in both bowing and left-hand technique and combined all the previous ideas to form what many consider the most definitive cello school. His principles were explained in the influential, if controversial, *Traité théorique et pratique du violoncelle* (1922) by his colleague Diran Alexanian. Casals spoke of half-step shifts with the same finger, of shifting in repeated finger patterns, of as little shifting as possible within slurred articulations, and of contractions and extensions. An interesting point of technique, which he shared with Joseph Szigeti, was the plucking of the string with the left hand in order to ensure precise articulation in downward-moving slurred passages.

Casals's pupil Maurice Eisenberg gave what must be the fullest exposition of Casals's left-hand technique in his *Cello Playing of Today* (1957). Before Eisenberg worked with Casals he studied with Klengel and Alexanian in Europe and W. Willeke in America. In his preface he says that his working with cellists of different 'schools' enabled him 'to see the changing outlook of our epoch in a clear perspective. Above all I could appreciate how the former awkwardness in handling the cello had been replaced by a more "natural" technique, formulated to serve interpretative ends'. Included in the manual are thumb-position drills, studies of unisons and 10ths, fingered octaves, and fingerings for major and minor scales and arpeggios on all strings, and for double stops, chords and harmonics. Eisenberg devoted a good portion of his book to the posture of the player *vis-à-vis* the instrument and the position of the hand and arm in specific situations. He gave many examples from the cello literature, much as Carl Flesch did in *Alta scuola di diteggiatura violinistica* and Szigeti in *Szigeti on the Violin*. Eisenberg spoke about 'vocalization' and the 'living hand': the hand 'must be trained to be so vital and flexible that as soon as a finger strikes its note, the preparation for the following note begins'. Ex.66 shows Eisenberg's fingerings for the beginning of the second subject of the first movement of Beethoven's Sonata op.69.

Ex.66 M. Eisenberg: *Cello Playing of Today*, ex.11, p.12

According to Eisenberg, 'the hand shifting must never be audible. When the hand moves backwards across the strings to a lower position, the thumb should act as a pivot over which the extended fingers are shifted swiftly and smoothly'.

Other notable 20th-century cellists include Gaspar Cassadó, Pierre Fournier, André Navarra, Paul Tortelier, Christopher Bunting, Leonard Rose, Antonio Janigro, Zara Nelsova, Maurice Gendron, Janos Starker, Mstislav Rostropovich, Siegfried Palm, Lynn Harrell, Jacqueline du Pré and Julian Lloyd Webber; Nikolaus Harnoncourt was the leading figure among those involved in the revival of Baroque cello technique.

Starker's *Violoncello Exercises for the Left Hand* (1961) is a short but well-organized guide to playing in positions, shifting etc, with examples from the repertory. More comprehensive is the second part of Bunting's *Essay on the Craft of 'Cello-playing* (1982).

In a general way the development of the cello's technical resources has followed that of the violin, and many of the techniques available to the modern string player are common to both instruments (see Chapter Two, §§1 and 2). These include vibrato, glissando, right- and left-hand pizzicato, natural and artificial harmonics, *sul ponticello* and *col legno* bowing and the use of the mute (see also Chapter Nine, §2). Particularly effective on the cello, because of its compass and sonority, is a combination of pizzicato and glissando, used to good effect by Bartók, for example in his later string quartets.

3. REPERTORY

The cello escaped from its purely bass function during the last decades of the 17th century; while its continuo role was impor- tant during the whole of the 18th century, the Baroque sonata gave the instrument an increasingly independent voice, and eventually it achieved an equal status with other instruments in chamber music. The earliest works for solo cello were by instrumentalists in the *cappella* of S Petronio, Bologna; they include G. B. degli Antoni's *Ricercare* op.1 (Bologna, 1687) and Domenico Gabrielli's *Ricercari* (Biblioteca Estense, Modena, dated 1689). Both these collections may have influenced the Modenese composer Domenico Galli in the composition of his *Trattenimento musicale* (1691), consisting of 12 sonatas for solo cello. The first sonatas with continuo to appear in print were those in Jacchini's op.1 (Bologna, n.d.) and op.3 (Modena, 1697). Other works for solo cello are included in Luigi Talietti's *Suonate* op.1 (1697) and Angelo Maria Fiore's *Trattenimenti da camera* (1698), but earlier ones exist in manuscript. The genre flowered in the first half of the 18th century in works by Giorgio Antoniotti, P. G. Boni, Lanzetti, Benedetto Marcello, Platti, Porpora, Vivaldi and others. Cello sonatas of this period usually call for a compass of *C* to *d″* and use broken chords, string- crossing figuration, double stops and pedals; thumb position and harmonics are sometimes required as well. In France the cello sonata was cultivated by Italians living in Paris (J.-P. Guignon and Giuseppe Fedeli, for example) as well as by native French-

VIOLONCELLO

men, including Barrière, Boismortier, Corrette, François Martin and Patouart. Later in the century J.-P. Duport published four sets of cello sonatas, three of which are lost; the surviving ones use a compass of C to a''', epitomizing a French virtuoso's conception of the instrument's capabilities. In Germany the 18th-century continuo sonata reached its highest point of development in the works of Anton Kraft.

In Italy Jacchini made early experiments with the cello as a concertante instrument in small ensembles (as in his op.4, 1701), and Dall'Abaco at the Bavarian court embodied a more conventional relationship between cellist and orchestra in the 11th of his *Concerti a quattro* op.2 (1712). But the earliest solo concertos for cello and orchestra were the work of Vivaldi, who wrote 27 (rv398–424) for the young women cellists of the Conservatorio dell'Ospedale della Pietà in Venice, as well as one for two cellos (rv531). He was followed by Tartini, Porpora and Leonardo Leo, who all made important contributions to the cello concerto repertory; during the same period Carlo and Giovanni Perroni, Pietro Paolo Canavasso, Antonio Vandini and Giovanni Platti each wrote a concerto worthy of notice. Leo's six concertos (1737–8) make relatively few technical demands, exploiting the instrument's expressive and cantabile potential, doubtless a result of Leo's experience as an opera composer. A tradition of using the solo cello to accompany a singing voice began with Domenico Gabrielli, was developed by Giovanni Bononcini and then fully established in Handel's oratorios (notably in *Alexander's Feast, Ode for St Cecilia's Day, L'allegro, il penseroso ed il moderato* and *Judas Maccabaeus*) and Bach's cantatas. Bach's six suites (bwv1007–12), dating from his time in Cöthen, are the first solo works written by a non-cellist and are outstanding for their musical and technical demands. The fifth suite requires scordatura (relatively uncommon in German cello music) and the sixth is written for a five-string instrument (see §1 above).

While solo chamber works were less prominent in the Classical period, concertos in the Italian style continued to be written: in Durham by John Garth (op.1, 1760), in Berlin by C. P. E. Bach (wq170–72, 1750–53), in Vienna by Georg Christoph Wagenseil, Georg Mathias Monn (Concerto in G minor, c1745) and Anton and Nikolaus Kraft, and in various European cities by Italian expatriates such as Luigi Borghi, G. B. Cirri, Carlo Graziani and Domenico Lanzetti. The Mannheim school produced solo works and concertos by Ignaz Holzbauer, Anton

176

Filtz, Carl Stamitz, Franz Danzi, Peter Ritter and Johann Rudolf Zumsteeg. In the second half of the 18th century a primarily virtuoso repertory began to emerge in France, of no intrinsic musical interest apart from a few works by Jean-Baptiste Bréval and Jean-Louis Duport; mention must however be made of the four concertos (now lost) of Martin Berteau and of those by J.-B. Cupis *le jeune*, Jean-Baptiste Janson, J.-P. Duport and Daniel-François-Esprit Auber, whose four concertos were published under the name of the cellist Jacques-Michel Lamare.

It was Luigi Boccherini who, as both composer and virtuoso cellist, did most to raise the status of the cello as a chamber and concerto instrument in the late 18th century. In his string quartets and notably in his quintets with two cellos he often gave the instrument a concertante role. His elegant, pleasing melodies and brilliant writing for the instrument made his concertos among the most popular of their day. His Concerto in B♭ is still performed, although, until recently, most often in the edition of 1895 by Friedrich Grützmacher who, besides taking the second movement from another concerto, made substantial alterations to both solo and orchestral parts (but see Scott, 1984). Boccherini's other ten concertos await the recognition among modern performers and audiences that Haydn's have come to enjoy. Haydn's beguiling Concerto in D (H VII*b*:2, 1783) is a work in which virtuosity always serves musical ends and there is a perfect balance between soloist and orchestra. The work's authenticity was for a long time doubted because of its high technical demands; apparently Haydn was influenced by his pupil Anton Kraft (for whom the cello part of Beethoven's Triple Concerto op.56, 1814, was written). Haydn is now believed to have written five cello concertos, one of which (in C, H VII*b*:1) was rediscovered in Prague in 1961.

After the transition to the Classical style the cello was called upon to play a role nearer to that of the other string instruments in chamber and orchestral music as well. From Haydn's op.17 string quartets (1771) onwards the cello part was involved first in thematic development and finally in the actual statement of themes. In response to Friedrich Wilhelm II's love of the instrument, Mozart wrote three quartets with particularly satisfying cello parts (K575, 589 and 590, 1789–90, which he dedicated to the king, to whom Haydn also dedicated his op.50 quartets), Boccherini many works and Beethoven his first cello sonatas (op.5, 1796). In Beethoven's late quartets the absolute priority of the musical intention over instrumental exigencies created cello parts of unusual difficulty. In orchestral music the development was slower. Haydn still gave to a solo cello a special part incorporating particular features of the sinfonia concertante tradition (e.g. in symphonies nos.6, 7, 8, 13, 31, 36, 95 and the Sinfonia concertante in B♭) whereas Beethoven was the first composer to give the cello a melodic line above the bass in orchestral writing, often in unison with the violas (examples may be seen in the opening of the Third Symphony, the Andante of the Fifth and the Allegretto of the Seventh). This separation of the cello and bass parts came first in music for larger chamber ensembles; in Beethoven's Septet (op.20, 1800), and later in music by Spohr and Schubert (the 'Trout' Quintet D667 and the Octet D803). Schubert was particularly fond of using the cello for cantabile melodies in the upper middle position (e.g. in the Quintet with two cellos D956, or in the Eighth Symphony), and this preference can be observed in the whole Romantic chamber and symphonic repertory up to Brahms, Dvořák and Bruckner. Melodic passages for divided cellos are found chiefly in opera, from Rossini (*Guillaume Tell*) to Verdi (*Nabucco, Aida, Otello*), Wagner (*Die Walküre*) and Puccini (*Tosca*). The cello's potential in orchestral music reached its culmination in the work of Richard Strauss, most conspicuously in the symphonic poem *Don Quixote*, in which the cello is given a solo part to represent Don Quixote himself.

Most 19th-century solo works for the instrument were composed by cellists, who were strongly influenced, particularly at the beginning of the century, by the violin repertory. Travelling virtuosos wrote for their own use and also to meet the rapidly growing demands of flourishing middle-class audiences; their aim was both to satisfy the public's taste and to entertain. The artist's concern to demonstrate his technical capabilities and emotional eloquence was the most prominent feature of a large number of concertos, concert pieces and smaller forms with orchestral or piano accompaniment, down to salon pieces. There was also a torrent of arrangements of well-known themes, mostly taken from opera; fantasies, variations or potpourris of widely differing musical quality. The appeal of all these works was short-lived, and even the best works of Duport, Romberg, Servais, Franchomme, Piatti, Goltermann, Grützmacher, Davïdov, Popper, Fitzenhagen, Klengel and Becker are now used only as studies. Although the players wished for a more worthwhile repertory (this is demonstrated by the innumerable transcriptions made of Classical and Romantic works for the violin), music for the solo cello was only a peripheral interest for the greater 19th-century composers. In some cases this neglect may have resulted from ignorance of the instrument's capabilities, but another reason was no doubt the difficulty of balancing the cello, with its tenor range, against a Romantic orchestra or the developing grand piano.

Neither Haydn nor Mozart left any examples of the cello sonata with piano, and their piano trios (Haydn's especially) show the cello still very much tied to the bass of the piano part. As precedents for his two cello sonatas op.5, therefore, Beethoven could turn only to such isolated works as the Chevalier de Leaumont's *Duo concertant* (1787). In the op.5 sonatas the piano plays the dominant role, but after this Beethoven treated the cello as an equal; in the sets of variations on themes from Handel's *Judas Maccabaeus* and Mozart's *Die Zauberflöte* (both 1796) and the two op.102 sonatas (1815), and above all in the A major Sonata op.69 (1807–8), he composed works of classic equilibrium, using the appropriate registers to set the cello off to its best advantage. Other important examples of the grand duo repertory are to be found among the works of Bonifazio Asioli, J. N. Hummel (op.104), Georges Onslow (op.16), Ferdinand Ries (opp.20, 21, 125 and woo2) and Joseph Wölf (op.31). (Schubert did not contribute to the repertory, though his Sonata D821 for arpeggione is often played on the cello.)

In several later compositions the piano again asserted the superiority which it naturally possessed as the composers' own expressive instrumental medium; this is illustrated in compositions by Mendelssohn (*Variations concertantes* op.17, 1829, and the two sonatas, op.45, 1838, and op.58, 1842), Chopin (*Introduction et polonaise brillante* op.3, 1829, the sonata op.65, 1846), Schumann (*Fünf Stücke im Volkston* op.102, 1849) and Brahms (the two sonatas op.38, 1865, and op.99, 1886, and the composer's own arrangement of the Violin Sonata op.78). The cello part in Chopin's sonata is in fact quite demanding, and shows the stimulus of his friendship with Franchomme. Brahms's masterly sonatas are written more as chamber music. The dense piano part of each needs careful playing if it is not to obscure the melodic passages for the cello, especially in the second sonata which is more dramatic than the lyrical first

VIOLONCELLO

sonata. The sonorous melodic pizzicato passages, similar to those in Mendelssohn's earlier op.58, are notable in the second sonata; in the fourth movement (bars 128ff) Brahms asked for a slurred pizzicato, which is achieved by stopping a string firmly with the left-hand finger, or leaving it open, plucking that string with the right hand and then removing or putting down another finger on the same string – the two notes are thus successively produced. From the last decades of the century onwards sonatas were written by such composers as Grieg (op.36, 1883), Saint-Saëns (op.32, 1872, and op.123, 1905), Richard Strauss (op.6, 1882), Pfitzner (op.1, 1890), Reger (opp.5, 28, 78, 116; 1892–1910), Rakhmaninov (op.19, 1901) and Fauré (op.109, 1917, and op.117, 1921). Fauré and Saint-Saëns still cultivated the genre piece, a tradition carried on in the charming miniatures of Jean Françaix.

The concerto, being the more virtuoso form, began to receive the attention of major composers only after 1850. The character of the first two movements of Schumann's concerto (op.129, 1850) is governed by their expressive, cantabile thematic material, and the cello part is most satisfying for the player, but the finale betrays its pianistic origins and presents considerable technical difficulties, particularly of tone production. Tchaikovsky's *Variations on a Rococo Theme* (op.33, 1876) are by contrast a typical example of collaboration between composer and player. Both the brilliant solo part and the formal layout of the final version demonstrate Wilhelm Fitzenhagen's close involvement in the composition of this elegant, graceful work. In Dvořák's concerto (op.104, 1895) the cello was for the first time confronted with a pronounced symphonic orchestral part. Dvořák succeeded brilliantly both in incorporating his solo instrument into the ensemble and in giving it its full virtuoso due. Brahms admired it greatly, and his Concerto in A minor for violin and cello (op.102, 1887) is a noteworthy contribution to the concerto literature of the period. Among others are the concertos of Robert Volkmann (op.33, 1858), Johan Svendsen (op.7, 1870), Saint-Saëns (op.33, 1873, and op.119, 1902), Lalo (1877), Bruch (*Kol nidrei* op.47, 1881), Boëllmann (op.23, ?1893), d'Albert (op.20, 1899) and Dohnányi (*Konzertstück*, op.12, 1903–4).

19th-century compositions for solo cello were written almost exclusively as technical exercises. It was only after 1900, stimulated by Casals's rediscovery of Bach's suites as recital works, that new works in the genre began to be written for public performance by, among others, Reger (three suites, op.131c, 1915), Kodály (op.8, 1915), Hindemith (op.25 no.3, 1923), Krenek (Suite op.84, 1939), Dallapiccola (*Ciaccona, Intermezzo e Adagio*, 1945), Henze (Serenade, 1949), George Crumb (Sonata, 1955), Bloch (three suites, 1956–7), Bernd Alois Zimmermann (Sonata, 1960), Britten (Suites op.72, 1964, op.80, 1968, and op.87, 1972), Xenakis (*Nomos alpha*, 1966) and Penderecki (*Capriccio per Siegfried Palm*, 1968).

While the cello has never been as well provided for as the violin and the piano, there has been a welcome increase in the number of worthwhile chamber and concertante works for solo cello in the 20th century. Some of the many composers who have contributed to the chamber repertory are the following (works referred to are sonatas with piano, unless otherwise indicated): Kodály (op.4, 1909–10), Bridge (1913–17), Webern (*Drei kleine Stücke* op.11, 1914), Debussy (1915), Villa-Lobos (1915, 1916; *Bachianas brasileiras* for eight or more cellos, no.1, 1930, no.5 (with soprano), 1938–45), Delius (1916), Hindemith (op.11 no.3, 1919; *Kammermusik* op.36 no.2, 1925; 1948), Honegger (1920), Ravel (Sonata for violin and cello, 1922), Bax (1923), Ireland (1923), d'Indy (op.84, 1924–5), Kabalevsky (op.2, 1927, and op.71, 1962), Barber (1932), Shostakovich (op.40, 1934), Martinů (1939, 1941 and 1952), Blacher (1940), Rubbra (op.60, 1946), Elliott Carter (1948), Fortner (1948; *Zyklus*, 1964), Poulenc (1948), Prokofiev (op.119, 1951), Milhaud (op.377, 1959) and Britten (op.65, 1961).

During the same period the repertory for cello and orchestra has been enriched by many important works, including the following (concertos, unless otherwise indicated): Bloch (*Schelomo*, 1916), Elgar (op.85, 1919), Delius (1921), Ibert (1925), Martinů (no.1, 1930, rev. 1955; no.2, 1944–5), Glazunov (*Concerto-Ballata* op.108, 1931), Bax (1932), Prokofiev (op.58, 1933–8; op.125, 1950–52), Milhaud (op.136, 1934; op.255, 1945), Pizzetti (1933–4), Honegger (1934), Roussel (Concertino op.57, 1936), Pfitzner (op.42, 1935; op.52, 1943), Hindemith (1940), Barber (op.22, 1945), Khachaturian (1946; Concerto-Rhapsody, 1963), Kabalevsky (op.49, 1948; op.77, 1964), Rodrigo (1949 and 1982), Virgil Thomson (1950), Finzi (op.40, 1951–5), Henze (*Ode to the Westwind*, 1953), Krenek (1953), Walton (1956), Shostakovich (op.107, 1959, and op.126,

VIOLONCELLO

1966), Schuman (*A Song of Orpheus*, 1961), Jolivet (1962 and 1966), Britten (Cello Symphony op.68, 1964), Zimmermann (1965–6), Ligeti (1966), Ginastera (1968), Hugh Wood (op.12, 1969), Lutosławski (1970) and Penderecki (1972).

Many composers have found that the cello's combination of generous sonority and virtuoso capabilities make it better suited than other string instruments to the exploration of avant-garde techniques. Kenneth Heller's *Labyrinth* and Mario Davidovsky's *Synchronisms* no.3 (1964) are examples of works that have combined a solo cello with recorded electronic sounds. Morton Feldman's *Durations II* (1960) for cello and piano applies aleatory techniques to the duration of notes, and in Mauricio Kagel's *Match* (1964) two cellists dressed as table-tennis players perform 'against' each other, with a drummer as referee. The cellist Siegfried Palm (*b* 1927) has been a protagonist of cello technique among the avant-garde, and as well as giving numerous first performances he has inspired many new works.

CHAPTER SEVEN

The Double bass

The double bass is the largest and lowest-pitched instrument of the violin family. It has four or (less often) five strings tuned in 4ths and sounds an octave lower than the cello. It is best known for its contribution to the orchestra, where it supplies not only the power and weight but also the basic rhythmic foundation, and it has also been used as a continuo instrument. More rarely the bass is heard as a soloist, in which field its surprisingly large repertory includes over 200 concertos. The instrument, played pizzicato, is an essential member of jazz and dance bands; in many countries it is used in military and concert bands.

1. STRUCTURE AND TUNING

Double basses vary in shape and size more than almost any other instrument. There are two basic designs: one is shaped like a viola da gamba, the other like a violin. There are also a few examples of other shapes (e.g. guitar-like). Viol-shaped basses usually have a flat back, of which the top part slopes towards the neck; the two holes in the belly are sometimes C-shaped, and very occasionally there is a third hole in the form of a rose. Other instruments are more closely modelled on the violin, although for convenience of playing their backs also are some-times flat, and their shoulders less square.

Of the smallest basses (*bassetti* and chamber basses) some are little bigger than a cello, while some of the larger (full-size) instruments can have a body of anything up to about 140 cm in length. The normal (three-quarter) size found in orchestras is about 115 cm. One of the largest is 4.8 metres high and was built by Paul de Wit for the Cincinnati music festival of 1889. A great three-string 'octobass' was built in 1851 by J.-B. Vuillaume, who was so proud of it that he incorporated its design in a crest on his headed notepaper. The instrument is tuned $C'-G'-C$ and is now in the museum of the Paris Conservatoire. Berlioz thought highly of it, but it can be regarded as little more than a curiosity. Another large instrument (which belonged to Dragonetti) is in the Victoria and Albert Museum, London. The 'piccolo bass', a rare small double bass used in jazz, is fitted with thin strings and tuned an octave higher than the standard bass.

Normal four-string instruments are tuned $E'-A'-D-G$. On five-string basses the additional bottom string is most commonly tuned to B' (sometimes C'). Occasionally a mechanical attachment with levers serves instead of a fifth string. This device enables the player to extend the length of the fourth string, thus lowering its pitch to C': although useful in the orchestra it is impractical for playing rapid passages or glissandos. Much of the solo repertory requires the use of scordatura, the most common being $F\sharp'-B'-E-A$. Since aluminium-covered steel or nylon core strings have replaced their thick gut predecessors it is arguable whether the practice of scordatura tuning is still necessary. Strings are tuned by means of brass machines with steel worm-screws, but early basses had large wooden pegs. As with the size of the instrument itself there is no standard length of playing stop. Many orchestral instruments have a stop of about 105 cm, but variations from 100 to 110 cm are not uncommon. Orchestral music for the instrument is notated an octave higher than the actual pitch. Much of the solo repertory used to be notated at pitch, but this practice is now almost exclusively confined to Italy and is sometimes even referred to as the 'old Italian system of notation'.

2. HISTORY

Research into the evolution of the double bass reveals a tangled web of several hundred years of changes in design and fashion in the dimensions of the instrument and consequently in its stringing and tuning. The picture is further complicated by the simultaneous use during any one period of different forms of bass in different countries. The earliest known illustration of a double bass type of instrument dates from 1516 (fig.38) but in

38. *Possibly the earliest known illustration of a double bass: detail from 'Herod's Feast' (1570–80), probably a copy by a Tyrolean artist after a German painting of 1516*

DOUBLE BASS

1493 Prospero wrote of 'viols as big as myself'. Planyavsky (1970) pointed out that it is more important to look for an early double bass tuning rather than for any particular instrument by shape or name. A deep (double- or contra-) bass voice is first found among the viols. There existed simultaneously two methods of tuning – one using 4ths alone, the other using a combination of 3rds and 4ths ('3rd–4th' tuning). Agricola wrote of the *contrabasso di viola* as being the deepest voice available. He was referring to an instrument comparable with that made by Hanns Vogel in 1563 and now in the Germanisches Nationalmuseum, Nuremberg (fig.39). This ornately and beautifully decorated bass is fitted with gut frets like other viols and tuned *G'–C–F–A–d–g*. This high '3rd–4th' tuning was given by Praetorius (*Syntagma musicum*, 2/1619) for a six-string violone (a name also confusingly used in the 16th century to denote the bass of the viol family). He listed several other tunings, both high and low, for five- and six-string *violoni*. Most interesting of all is the low tuning *D'–E'–A'–D–G*, only one step removed from the modern *E'–A'–D–G* instrument. Orlando Gibbons scored for the 'great dooble base' in two viol fantasias. Whether a low '3rd–4th' tuning was used or a higher one cannot be certain.

Some fine basses, many of which were probably converted from their original form into three- or later four-string instruments, date from the late 16th century and early 17th. A notable three-string bass, originally built as such, is that by Gasparo da Salò, owned by Dragonetti and now in the museum of St Mark's, Venice. A beautiful six-string violone of much lighter construction by Da Salò's apprentice Giovanni Paolo Màggini is in the Horniman Museum, London (see fig.40a, p.188). This is of violin shape, with a flat back, and makes interesting comparison with the viol-shaped violone by Ventura Linarol (Padua, 1585) in the Kunsthistorisches Museum, Vienna (fig.40b).

During the early 17th century the five-string bass was most commonly used in Austria and Germany. Leopold Mozart referred in the 1787 edition of his *Violinschule* to having heard concertos, trios and solos played with great beauty on instruments of this kind. The earliest known playing instructions, by Johann Jacob Prinner (*Musicalischer Schlissl*, 1677, autograph in Library of Congress, Washington, DC), are for an instrument tuned *F'–A'–D–F♯–B*. Much more usual, however, is the tuning *F'–A'–D–F♯–A* cited in 1790 by Albrechtsberger, for

*39. Double-bass viol by Hanns
Vogel, Nuremberg, 1563*

(a)

40. *(a) Six-string violone by Gio(vanni) Paolo Maggini, Brescia, early 17th century; (b) viol-shaped violone by Ventura Linarol, Padua, 1585*

(b)

a violone or contrabass with thick strings and frets tied at every semitone round the fingerboard. Michel Corrette's 1773 *Méthode* throws much light on the bass techniques and tunings in use during the 18th and early 19th centuries when the bass was enjoying some popularity as a solo instrument. Many of the virtuoso pieces from the Viennese school of that period and later abound with passages of double stopping and, in view of the tunings required, were thought by early 20th-century authorities not to have been written for the bass at all. Later research revealed that the instrument has in the past been tuned in some 40 or 50 different ways; although the repertory is quite practical with the tunings the composers envisaged (e.g. one of the '3rd–4th' tunings), much is unplayable on the modern conventionally tuned instruments. There are in fact numerous solo concertos from this period.

In Italy an early tuning (cited by Planyavsky, 1970) is Adriano Banchieri's of 1609 for his 'Violone contrabasso', $D'–G'–C–E–A–d$. Later the number of strings was reduced, and three-string instruments were preferred. Even during the early 18th century a three-string bass tuned $A'–D–G$ or $G'–D–G$ was normal. It had no frets, and with the growth of the symphony orchestra it was logical that this more powerful instrument should supersede earlier models. Not until the 1920s was the additional E' string expected of most professional players. Until then any passages going below A' were transposed up an octave, resulting in the temporary disappearance of the 16′ line.

Apart from those of the Italian makers already mentioned, basses by Amati, Bergonzi, Grancino and Testore are particularly prized. Among the good English makers are Forster, Kennedy, Lott and Tarr (fig.41). In Austria fine basses were made by Jacob Stainer. Others have come from the schools of Mittenwald and Mirecourt.

3. BOWS

The double bass bow is sometimes constructed like a modern cello bow and sometimes like a combination of a cello and a viol bow. The cello-type bow, played 'overhand', is called the 'French' or 'Bottesini' bow (after a renowned player). It has the concave curvature, modern frog and 'hatchet' head of the cello

41. *Double bass by William Tarr, Manchester,*
1847

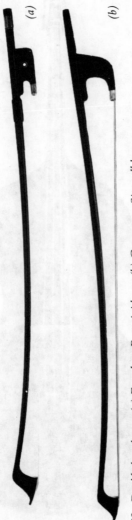

(a)

(b)

42. Double bass bows: (a) French or Bottesini bow; (b) German or Simandl bow

TECHNIQUE

bow, although the stick is thicker, heavier, somewhat shorter and more sharply curved inwards (see fig.42a).

The other type of bow is called the 'German' or 'Simandl' bow (after a famous Viennese teacher; see fig.42b). A combination of the French bow and the early viol-type bow (the 'Dragonetti', now obsolete), the 'Simandl' uses the modern 'hatchet' head and the incurve of the French bow but with a greater space between hair and stick at the frog, which is also somewhat different. The 'Simandl' bow and its predecessor the 'Dragonetti' were never played underhand like the early viol bow, but were grasped endways, almost like a saw, the palm enclosing the frog so that the two middle fingers went round the frog parallel to the stick, the little finger below the slide, the forefinger below the stick, and the thumb resting above and exerting pressure on the stick (see fig.43, p.194).

The French bow is used almost exclusively in France and England and to a large extent in the USA. The German bow, however, is used by almost all players in Germany, Austria and central Europe, and by a number in the USA. The French and German double bass bows were both introduced relatively late in the 19th century.

4. TECHNIQUE

Because of the instrument's size, double bass fingering has been subject to much experimentation, and a great variety of systems have been used. Modern methods have only partly standardized earlier systems and there are still many different fingering systems in use. Not only do these vary considerably but there is also no consistent method of identifying the positions. For instance, 'half-position' in one method may be called 'first position' in another and 'first degree' elsewhere.

Two systems are most commonly found. One, probably the most widespread, springs from bass methods published in Germany and Austria during the 19th century and is known as 'Simandl fingering'. The hand is positioned in such a way that a semitone lies between 1 and 2 and another between 2 and 4. The third finger is used only as a support for 4 until the higher positions are reached, when it is used instead of 4, which no longer reaches the fingerboard. Hindle in his *Der Contrabass-*

43. The Simandl bow grip as used on the double bass

Lehrer (*c*1850) fingered semitones 124 but brought 3 into use slightly sooner than the methods of Labro, Josef Hrabě, Simandl, Nanny and White, which are largely the same in their approach.

Bottesini in his *Metodo completo per contrabbasso* (n.d., before 1870) fingered semitones 134, and some modern Italian methods retain this use of 3 in place of 2 (Billè, Petracchi). Sometimes Bottesini fingered a semitone 14 in the lower positions (the old Lombardy school). The use of 4 in high positions is also not uncommon, in which event the wrist and hand are brought further forward to compensate for the short little finger.

The other main system has its origins in gamba or cello technique, and is frequently called 'extended fingering'. The hand is placed so that semitones lie between each of the fingers in all positions, thus avoiding many changes of position during playing. Advocates of the Simandl system say that extended fingering leads to poor intonation because of the stretching required. But as only two major diatonic scales (B♭ and F) are playable on a conventionally tuned bass without shifting, the advantages of extensions become obvious. Extended systems have been widely used on modern instruments with thinner

194

strings and lower bridges to increase facility. In addition, the weight of the hand is placed with a rolling action over the playing finger, thus reducing the need to stretch. Studies by Billè, Möchel, Rühm, Hegner and Gullbrandsson all include various types of extension.

Thumb positions and double stops on the double bass are required less frequently in the orchestral than in the solo repertory. Most systems use the thumb from half-way up the string, although some advocate its use much earlier. Natural harmonics can be produced at either end of the strings but, like artificial harmonics, they are seldom called for in everyday playing.

5. REPERTORY AND PERFORMERS

The earliest known works for a solo double bass instrument are the sonatas composed by or for Giovannino del Violone in the Bodleian Library, Oxford. Their origin is by no means certain, but they probably date from about 1690. No solo music is known from the 18th century (Stamitz's concerto, for example, is a transcription of a viola work) until the solo parts in Haydn's symphonies (e.g. nos.6–8) of the early 1760s; then, in the ten years from 1765, no fewer than 28 concertos appeared (by Vanhal, Zimmermann, Haydn, Franz Hoffmeister, Johannes Sperger and Dittersdorf).

In 1791 Mozart wrote his aria *Per questa bella mano* (K612) for bass and double bass to be performed by the singer Gerl with the bassist Friedrich Pischelberger (1741–1813); both were engaged in the production of *Die Zauberflöte* under Schikaneder. This work was published in 1822 – one of the first virtuoso double bass works to appear in print. Pischelberger and Johannes Sperger were the most outstanding virtuosos of the Austrian school at that time and it is unlikely that solo bass playing had ever before reached such a peak. Sperger's works include 18 concertos, three concert arias with soprano and a number of cassations and quartets. He played a five-string bass which he tuned in a number of different ways. Josef Kämpfer (1735–88), a Hungarian virtuoso, toured Europe towards the end of the 18th century and is said to have greatly impressed Haydn. Although he travelled as widely as St Petersburg, Copenhagen,

Hamburg and London, it was not until Domenico Dragonetti settled in London that the bass gained popularity in England.

Dragonetti's success was unique in that for over 50 years no musical gathering was considered complete without him. Not only did his fine performances win him recognition throughout Europe, but his kind, amiable personality endeared him to the British public. He counted among his friends Haydn, Beethoven, Hummel, Spohr, Liszt and many other composers. Rossini thought highly of him, and in 1824 composed a duet for him to play with the banker Sir David Salomons, an amateur cellist. At Rossini's insistence Dragonetti had a copy of his bow made for Cherubini, who had begun a double bass class at the Paris Conservatoire. The bass players there used the French overhand bowing, which some thought to lack the power of Dragonetti's endways-held bow. Rossini delivered the bow himself but the introduction was not a success. The British Library contains a large collection of Dragonetti manuscripts, and most British players are still taught in a tradition directly descended from his pupils.

The later Italian virtuoso Giovanni Bottesini had a different approach to the bass. While some critics praised Dragonetti's powerful tone and his ability to play in tune, others scorned his loud and rasping style. For Bottesini there was little but praise; his delicate tone and agile technique stunned audiences and his ability to 'dart from one end of the instrument to the other' was remarkable (H. R. Haweis: *My Musical Life*, London, 1888). The second half of his *Metodo completo per contrabbasso* explains how he extended the technique of the instrument by the use of arpeggios and very high harmonics. Bottesini was not only an internationally famous virtuoso but also a highly respected composer, conductor and musical director. On occasions he directed and conducted his own operas and even performed solos on the double bass during the intervals between the acts. He studied composition with Verdi, whose works he knew well – his numerous virtuoso solos have a close affinity with the style of popular 19th-century Italian opera. Among his lesser-known works are some concertos for two double basses.

In 1874 Franz Simandl published his *Neueste Methode des Contrabass-Spiels*, reprinted many times and still widely used. Simandl studied in Prague under Josef Hrabě and worked most of his life in Vienna. In France the *Méthode complète* (c1920–25) of Edouard Nanny has been more popular than Simandl's method. The early 20th century saw the rise of Sergey Koussevitzky, another virtuoso who conducted. The recordings he made in 1929 of his *Chanson triste* and *Valse miniature* and Láska's *Wiegenlied* show the perfect command he had of his instrument. Koussevitzky wrote comparatively little for the bass, his recital programmes consisting largely of transcriptions (notably the Cello Sonata by Strauss, Bruch's *Kol Nidrei*, Mozart's Bassoon Concerto and many Baroque works).

Since Koussevitzky many virtuosos have made recordings, and traditional bass technique has been greatly developed since the 1950s. Gary Karr has a repertory of more than 30 concertos, many of which he commissioned. The American Bertram Turetzky has commissioned over 200 works and has developed his own particular style of playing, centred on pizzicato and non-traditional bow techniques. In England Barry Guy has explored new avenues of sound by coupling the bass to electronic apparatus controlled during performance at the player's discretion. Other noted double bassists are the Czech player František Pošta, the Berliner Klaus Stoll and the ›Viennese Ludwig Streicher; another Viennese, Alfred Planyavsky, is an eminent historian of the instrument.

It is hard to be certain when the double bass obtained a regular place in the orchestra. Many 17th-century orchestras did not use 16′ tone; there was no double bass in the Paris Opéra orchestra, for example, until the early years of the 18th century. But court orchestras of the mid-18th century included double basses; usually they were more numerous than the cellos. A modern symphony orchestra generally has at least eight.

Any principal orchestral player must attain a standard equal to that of the virtuoso soloist; advanced technique is required for most of the works of, for example, Schoenberg, Strauss and Stravinsky. Some of the more exposed passages occur in Britten's *Young Person's Guide to the Orchestra* and *A Midsummer Night's Dream*, Ginastera's *Variaciones concertantes*, Mahler's First Symphony, Musorgsky's *Pictures at an Exhibition* (orchestrated by Ravel, 1922), Prokofiev's suite *Lieutenant Kijé*, Rossini's six early string sonatas, Saint-Saëns' *Le carnaval des animaux* and Stravinsky's suite *Pulcinella*. Chamber music with double bass includes several works by Mozart of a divertimento character (attesting the use of the instrument in such contexts in 18th-century Austria), Beethoven's Septet, Schubert's 'Trout' Quintet and Octet, Spohr's Octet and Nonet, and many works

DOUBLE BASS

by Hummel, Onslow and others. Dvořák used it in a string quintet (op.77). 20th-century composers have turned their attention to the instrument in their search for less familiar tone colours, for example Prokofiev's Quintet and works by Henze, many of which use artificial harmonics. In jazz a considerable level of virtuosity in pizzicato technique is required, particularly since the arrival of amplification.

CHAPTER EIGHT

The Bow

1. ORIGINS TO c1750

The use of the bow to draw sound from string instruments can be traced back to the 10th century, when the bow was known throughout Islam and in the Byzantine empire. The bow was introduced into Europe in the 11th century.

In the early centuries, from its origins up to about 1600, the bow had certain characteristics common to all specimens, notwithstanding the great variety of forms. Bows were always convex, like drawn hunting-bows. The hair, which was horsehair or a 'string-like material', was strung on a shaft of elastic wood or bamboo, bent in an arc. The bowstick was much weaker than on modern bows, so the hair gripped the strings less firmly. The hair was affixed directly to the stick, not to an adjustable frog (nut) which would have permitted alterations to the tension. Iconographic sources have yielded a great variety of bow shapes from around the end of the 10th century, ranging from the large, strongly arched, almost semicircular bow, held in the middle of the stick as in fig.44 (p.200), to the flat bow, hardly curved at all, with its hair almost touching the wood (fig.45, p.201). Illustrations of the bow being held with the fingertips, rather than in the clenched fist, occur as isolated instances at first, and become more frequent only in the late Middle Ages (see fig.46, p.202). Certain norms developed at an early date in the method of holding the instrument and in the technique of bowing. Generally, when the player held the instrument slanting upwards or sideways from his body the bow was held in an overhand grip and when the instrument was supported on the knee (*a gamba*) the bow was held in an underhand grip (see fig.47, p.203).

During the 17th century the bowstick remained generally convex, but was sometimes straight. The ribbon of white bow

44. *Strongly arched bow, held at the centre: detail of illumination from a Mozarabic MS, 'S Beati de liebana explanatio in apokalypsis S Johannis', c920–30*

45. *Long flat bow held by a boy playing a ?rebec: detail of a relief on a Byzantine ivory casket, 10th or early 11th century*

46. *Bow held with the fingertips by an angel playing a fiddle: detail from a panel of an Aragonese reliquary triptych, 1390*

47. *Musicians with (left) a rebec, holding the bow with an overhand grip, and (right) a viol with the bow held with an underhand grip: detail of a miniature from the York (or Hunterian) Psalter, English, c1170*

hair was narrow – perhaps 6 mm wide. During most of the 17th century the hair was strung at fixed tension from an immovable frog at the lower end of the stick to the point of the bow at the other end (see fig.48, p.204). The length of these bows varied considerably, the typical dance bow being short and the sonata bow substantially longer. For instance, the playing hair of the violin bow shown in Mersenne (1636–7) is only about 35 cm long (approximately the same length as the body of the violin), whereas the corresponding measurement of the so-called 'Stradivari' bow (c1700) at the University of California at Berkeley is 61 cm (the total bow length nearly 72 cm; fig.49a, p.205). In 17th-century examples in which there was no distinct 'head' (the hair and stick meeting in a point), the effective playing length of the bow hair was further reduced. Individual bowsticks varied also in weight, degree of tapering from frog to point, balance, and type of wood. The latter was commonly

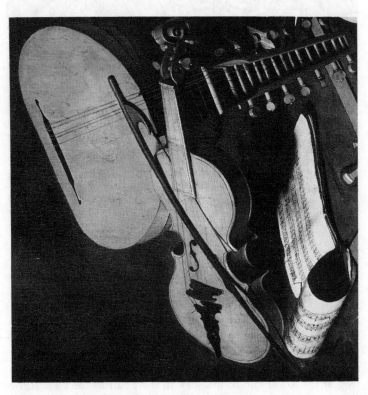

48. *Violin and convex bow with immovable (horn-shaped) frog: detail from the painting 'Love as Conqueror' (c1603) by Michelangelo Merisi da Caravaggio*

49. (a) Bow with 'pike's' head and movable frog by ? Antonio Stradivari, c1700; (b) bow (maker unknown) with 'swan-bill' head and immovable clip-in frog, c1700; (c) bow with 'hatchet' head and movable frog by François Tourte, c1790; (d) bow with 'battle-axe' head and movable frog, stamped 'Forster', c1775

Sinfonia

Leop: Mozart

Direct

CONVENIT IGITUR---IN GESTU NEC
VENUSTATEM CONSPICUAM, NEC TURPI-
DINEM ESSE, NE AUT HISTRIONES,
AUT OPERARII VIDEAMUR ESSE.

Vegel.Rhet.ad.her.
Lib. 3. XV.

G. Eichler delin.

Jac. Andr. Fridrich Sc. A.V.

50. *Leopold Mozart holding a violin and a convex bow: frontispiece from his
'Violinschule' (1756)*

snakewood ('specklewood'), sometimes brazilwood and occasionally pernambuco, a superior variety of brazilwood used in a few of the best early bows and almost exclusively in good modern ones. A number of bowsticks were fluted in all or part of their length, suggesting an ideal of combining lightness with strength.

During the late 17th and early 18th centuries – at the time of Corelli – the bow was gradually lengthened and straightened, especially in Italy and, after about 1720, in France. However, the distinctly convex bow persisted for a long time in Germany (as seen in Leopold Mozart's *Violinschule* of 1756; see fig.50). A few makers fashioned an occasional bowstick which curved inwards towards the hair (i.e. concave), an anticipation of the shape that was to prevail later. According to John Hawkins (*A General History of the Science and Practice of Music*, 1776), the 'sonata' bow in 1720 had been about 24 inches (61 cm) in length, the 'common' bow shorter, and the French (dance) bow 'must have been shorter still'. However, some bows (as shown in various 18th-century sources, e.g. Geminiani; see fig.8*b*, p.14) were as long as or even longer than the modern bow, which measures about 75 cm with a playing length of nearly 65 cm.

Bow makers devoted considerable attention to fastening and tightening the bow hair at the point and the frog. To hold the hair away from the point they developed after about 1650 the so-called 'pike's' head (see fig.49*a*), sometimes with a 'swan-bill' (fig.49*b*). The frog, which held the hair away from the bowstick at the lower end, was at first shaped like a horn, a type that continued in use from the 16th century to at least the early 17th (see fig.48). This frog was immovable, and held the hair at fixed tension. In another fixed-tension type the frog itself could be removed, being really a wedge inserted to tighten the hair by being clipped into a notched position in the bow (fig.51*a*, p.208). These 'clip-in' or 'slot-notch' bows apparently became obsolete after 1700. On a dentated bow (Fr. *crémaillère*) the hair tension could be regulated by a movable frog adjusted to one of several positions by an attached iron catch or loop that engaged one of several teeth fixed on the top of the bowstick (see fig.51*b*). In the modern bow the movable frog is tightened or loosened by means of a screw mechanism regulated by a screw button (or cap) at the lower end of the stick (fig.51*c*); a bow with a similar screw mechanism is extant with '1694' stamped on its movable (and original) frog.

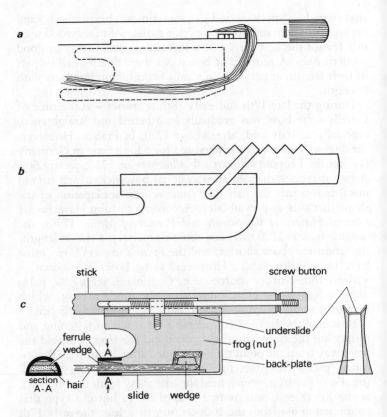

stick

screw button

underslide

ferrule
wedge

frog (nut)

section
A-A

hair

slide   wedge

back-plate

*51. Three types of frog: (a) clip-in or slot-notch; (b) dentated; (c) the modern
frog, showing the screw mechanism*

The best bows before 1750 were generally flexible, lighter
than the modern bow (which averages 56 grams) and balanced
nearer to the player's hand. While a number of early bows were
clumsy and inept, the best were marvels of elegance and musical
efficiency. To judge by contemporary illustrations, there was
little difference in basic design between the viol bow and the
violin bow in the 17th century (see Mersenne, 1636–7) or early
18th. However, some 20th-century investigators (e.g. van
Leeuwen Boomkamp and Van der Meer, 1971) believe but have
not proved that the viol bow was generally longer and a bit

heavier, and had a somewhat greater distance between hair and stick at the frog.

For a discussion of the so-called 'Bach' bow, an invention of the 20th century, see Chapter Two, p.50, and fig.17 (p.51).

2. SINCE *c*1750

The bow underwent a number of changes from about 1750 to about 1786, when it was standardized by François Tourte. During the transitional stage the stick gradually became concave and, on average, longer. Various designs of head were tried, leading to the modern 'hatchet' head. A stronger design for the movable frog was developed and a wider ribbon of hair was adopted. The result was a stronger bow, better suited to sustained and cantabile playing and to more varied strokes. This transitional bow was created for those who played the music of the Mannheim School and the late works of Tartini as well as the earlier works of such composers as Haydn and Mozart. The names most closely associated with this change were Tartini, Wilhelm Cramer, Tourte *père*, the Dodd family, and, most important, François Tourte (*le jeune*), considered the 'Stradivari of the bow'. Tartini and Cramer were famous violinists, not bow makers: few of the latter stamped their names on their work until the end of the 18th century.

According to Fétis (1856), Tartini designed a bow about 1730, using lighter wood, straightening the bowstick, shortening the head and grooving ('fluting') the lower part of the stick for a better grip. From Fétis's information it is clear that this was a late stage in the development of the 'old' bow, not a real step towards the modern bow. However, Tartini lived until 1770, and doubtless used a transitional bow at a later stage in his life.

The crucial step towards the modern bow was taken when makers abandoned the convex or fairly straight bowstick in favour of a concave one, a change that affected the bow's fundamental action. This change probably occurred in the 'Cramer' bow, named after Wilhelm Cramer (1745–99), a virtuoso violinist from Mannheim who went to London in 1772 and was there considered unrivalled as a violinist until the advent of Viotti in 1792. The Cramer bow, a transitional type, had a 'battle-axe' head (see below), an elegant and delicate frog, and a

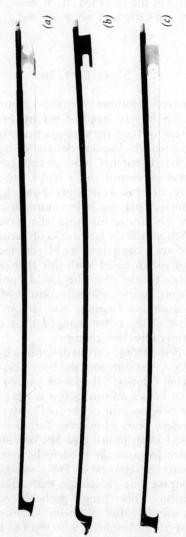

52. Three transitional violin bows, all with screw frogs: (a) Cramer-type, with 'battle-axe' head, slightly concave stick and cut-away frog, c1775; (b) by Tourte père, with modified 'pike's' head and concave stick, c1770; (c) by Edward Dodd, with 'battle-axe' head and concave stick, c1775

(a)

(b)

(c)

bowstick that was slightly concave and of moderate length (see fig.52a). Woldemar (2/c1800), a Parisian violinist, describing events a few years after their occurrence, evidently believed that the Cramer bow was the one in greatest favour immediately before the François Tourte bow (which he called the 'Viotti' bow). If Cramer-model bows were in great vogue between 1772 and 1792 they were doubtless crafted by a number of makers: in Paris, for example, by Tourte *père* (who stamped 'Tourte L.' on some of his bows; one extant specimen is actually a modified 'Cramer'), Lafleur, or the mysterious Meauchand; in London by Edward Dodd (see fig.52c) or John Dodd, or someone in the employ of the firm of Forster or Norris & Barnes. Some of the bows of Tourte *père*, however, are more graceful and advanced in design than the Cramer model; and in view of the great variety of heads, sticks and frogs of these 'transitional' bows it is difficult to evaluate Woldemar's claim that 'the Cramer bow was adopted in his [Cramer's] time by the majority of artists and amateurs'.

The concave bowstick favours a high, 'modern' head, because the earlier 'pike's' head is too low to afford sufficient clearance between the hair and the concave stick in the middle of the bow. A species of modern head was the 'battle-axe' head of the Cramer bow (a unique feature of its head was a peak in front matched by a peak in the back of the head proper: see fig.52a), which was supplanted by the modern 'hatchet' head of the Tourte bow (see fig.49c).

The distinctive and delicate frog of the Cramer bow, typically cut away at both ends and fashioned of ivory, must have been too lightly constructed; its lifespan was short, and few such frogs are extant.

About 1786 François Tourte (1747–1835) succeeded in producing in Paris a bow so remarkably satisfactory (see fig.49c) that it became the model in his own time and, with a few changes of detail, has continued as such. The superiority of Tourte's bows was acclaimed by Louis Spohr (*Violin-Schule*, 1832), who spoke of 'the trifling weight with sufficient elasticity of stick', of 'the beautiful and uniform bending, by which the nearest approach to the hair is exactly in the middle between the head and the frog' and of 'the extremely accurate and neat workmanship'. In effect Tourte combined the significant innovations of the transitional bows – including the concave bowstick and the higher, more massive head – in a final form that joined supreme playing qualities to incomparable grace. Although a legend in his own lifetime, he never stamped his bows; in a few cases he inscribed his name and age and the date on a piece of paper inserted in the slot holding the frog.

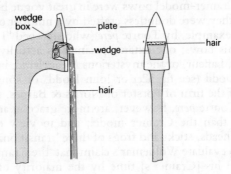

53. *Features of the head of the modern bow*

According to Fétis, Tourte fixed the length of the violin bow at 74 to 75 cm, the playing hair at 65 cm and the balance point at 19 cm above the frog. The viola bow was slightly shorter (74 cm); and the cello bow shorter still: overall length 72 to 73 cm, playing hair 60 to 62 cm and balance point 17.5 to 18 cm above the frog. The weight of a violin bow averaged about 56 grams, and the viola and cello bows correspondingly more. Tourte's bowsticks, invariably of pernambuco wood and finished as round or octagonal, tapered slightly from frog to head, being slimmer at the head end (for a mathematical formulation see Fétis, 1856, pp.125ff). He achieved the concave curvature by heating the stick completely through and then bending it, rather than by cutting at once to the desired bend. The band of hair was widened to about 1 cm and comprised 150 to 200 hairs from white horses. To prevent it from bunching into a round mass Tourte (according to Fétis, at Viotti's suggestion) spread the hair into a uniform ribbon by means of a ferrule, generally of silver (see fig.54c); he covered the surface from the ferrule to the end of the frog with a mother-of-pearl slide (Fr. *recouvrement*). Though claimed as Tourte's innovation, the ferrule and slide had probably been introduced earlier. (The details of the modern frog and its mechanical action of tightening the hair are shown in fig.51c, from which may be noted the rectangular form of the frog – generally made of ebony – and the squared-off screw button.)

Tourte selected a hatchet form of head, facing it with a protective plate, generally of ivory. The 'hatchet' head was heavier than the earlier 'pike's' head or even than most transitional designs; balance was restored at the frog end by the extra weight of the metal ferrule and by the added weights of the inlay ('eye') of the frog (see fig.49c), the back-plate (see fig.54c) and the screw button. Even so, the balance of the Tourte bow was farther towards the centre of the bow than in earlier examples. Tourte and his followers also adorned their best bows by using such precious materials as tortoise-shell for the frogs, gold for the ferrule, back-plate and screw button, and occasionally mother-of-pearl for the face of the head.

It is possible that John Dodd (1752–1839), Tourte's con-

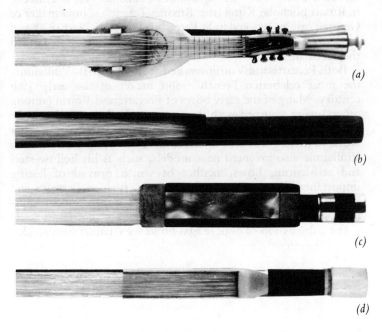

(a)

(b)

(c)

(d)

54. Comparison between the hair widths of the bows in fig.49: (a) 'Stradi-vari', c1700; (b) clip-in frog, c1700; (c) François Tourte, c1790; (d) 'Forster', c1775

temporary in London, perfected the bow about the same time as Tourte, arriving at very similar solutions. Dodd's bows, however, are not of such uniformly high quality, and a number of them are slightly shorter. To judge by the text and the bows illustrated in Baillot (1834), Viotti may have used a Dodd bow about 2.5 cm shorter than the Tourte model.

Only one later addition to the Tourte bow proved of functional importance: the underslide (Fr. *coulisse*), a piece of metal affixed to the part of the frog that comes in sliding contact with the bowstick, its purpose being to minimize wear from friction. Tourte had left this surface of the wooden frog without protection; the invention of the underslide is generally attributed to François Lupot (1774–1837).

The 19th century produced a vast number of distinguished bow makers, especially in France and England; among the most celebrated were Dominique Peccatte and F. N. Voirin (the 'modern Tourte') in Paris, and James Tubbs (*d* 1919) in London. In Russia Nicholas Kittel (the 'Russian Tourte'), a bow maker of German origin, worked in St Petersburg from 1839 to 1870; and in Germany Ludwig Bausch attained sufficient fame to be called the 'German Tourte'.

Both Peccatte and Voirin worked at first for J.-B. Vuillaume, the most celebrated French violin maker of the early 19th century. Many of the early bows of Peccatte and Voirin (among others) were stamped with the name of Vuillaume, who while not a bow maker himself spent much time studying Tourte's work so that he was able to direct the work of his own makers. Vuillaume also invented new models, such as his hollow-steel and self-hairing bows, neither of which proved of lasting importance. Bow makers after Tourte (such as Peccatte and Voirin), while otherwise adhering to the Tourte model faithfully, tended to make the bowstick about 1 cm shorter.

For a discussion of double bass bows see Chapter Seven, §3.

CHAPTER NINE

Acoustics

1. FOUNDATIONS

The acoustic centre of any string instrument is the string. Its action under the fingers or the bow, its responsiveness, and even the problems it forces the player to solve are major factors in establishing the musical identity of a family of instruments. The essence of the string families is in each case a set of strings mounted on a wooden box containing an almost enclosed air space. Some energy from the vibrations of the strings is communicated through the bridge to the box and air space, in which are set up corresponding vibrations. The loudness and nature of the sound, putting aside the acoustics of the room and the skill of the player, depend on the transfer of vibration from the strings to sounding box to air.

The sounding box, or body, of a string instrument is like a bell in one important respect. When it is tapped or struck lightly a multitude of notes, covering many octaves, is set into vibration, though of course this is more obvious with the bell than with the sounding box. The luthier is deeply concerned with the frequencies of these 'tap tones', or resonances, and with the patterns of their amplitudes over the surface of the instrument; the old masters were certainly aware of these facts, even though they tested them with their hands and ears rather than electronically. The body of a good instrument, therefore, has to be tuned to the frequency range in which it is to be used, the many resonances being suitably spaced within that range. A superb one must also have the best possible distribution of activity over its surface. The combination of the vibrating string as generator, providing a wide range of harmonics, and the sounding box as resonator, responding selectively according to its pattern of resonances, is the basis of a string instrument.

A vibrating string by itself produces almost no sound for two

215

reasons: it is so thin that almost no air is disturbed; and two diametrically opposite sides of the string are so close together that though the air on one side is compressed at a given moment and on the other rarefied, the two effects are so close that they arrive at the listener almost exactly together, thus cancelling each other. In order to avoid cancellation, one vibration must arrive earlier than the other by a substantial fraction of its vibration period.

The design of a musical sounding board or instrument box must circumvent these pitfalls. In the piano, the single sound-board is effective because its dimensions exceed, or at least are not negligible by comparison with, the wavelengths of the pitches throughout much of its compass. The upper and lower sides radiate with sufficient independence that their radiations do not cancel each other, even though the two surfaces of the single board move in identical patterns and to the same degree. When a single soundboard is smaller than the wavelengths of sounds coming from it, the radiations from the two sides tend to cancel each other when heard from a distance. This is why bowed and plucked string instruments use a box in which the two surfaces possess different patterns and amplitudes of vibration which support each other within an important range of frequencies. Unlike the single soundboard, the top and back, under favour-able conditions, can move inward or outward at a given moment so that almost the entire surface of an instrument cooperates to change the volume of displaced air, thus acting as a 'Nullstrahler' or 'simple source', at least in the lower frequency range (see Cremer, 1971).

In bowed string instruments this volume change in the body, so important to the sounds in the lower octaves, is made possible by the asymmetrical interior arrangement of the soundpost and bass-bar (see fig.2, p.4). When the bow is pulled across the string parallel to the top of the instrument, a rocking motion is set up in the bridge so that the forces that the two feet of the bridge exert downward are in 'push–pull' relationship with one pressing down and the other up in opposite phase. If the box had complete bilateral symmetry there would be no volume change, for the motion of one foot would completely offset the effect of the other. As it is, however, the soundpost beneath the right foot of the bridge (as the violinist sees it), firmly coupling the top to the more rigid back, tends to immobilize the right foot, while at the same time enhancing the motion of the left foot (see

Schelleng, 1971), so causing important changes in the body to occur in step with the left foot of the bridge. This creation of asymmetry is the chief acoustical function of the soundpost, called in French 'l'âme': its position, shape, wood quality and fitting can be highly critical to the performance of an instrument.

The bass-bar, running the length of the top plate approximately under the string of lowest tuning, tends to keep the vibrations of the upper and lower areas of the top plate in step with the left foot of the bridge. It is glued in such a way as to lend static strength to the thin wood of the top plate, which together with the soundpost must support a downward force from the strings of 7–9 kg in the violin itself. The final shaping of the bass-bar is one of the most critical tasks in the proper thinning, or 'tuning', of the top plate (see Hutchins, 1981).

The soundholes, f-shaped in the violin family, have two chief acoustical purposes: first to reduce the stiffness of the floor on which the bridge stands; and second to form a Helmholtz resonator. The rocking motion of the bridge, in addition to being affected by the bass-bar and soundpost, is limited by the stiffness of the wood between the soundholes (see Minnaert and Vlam, and Reinicke). In the violin family the thickness and width of the wood between the upper ends of the holes are particularly important. This reduction in stiffness provides a suitably tapered transition between the bridge and radiating areas of the top plate (see Hutchins, 1962, and Schelleng, 1963). The second function of the soundholes is to strengthen the sound in the lowest octave of the instrument. They are not simply openings to 'let the sound out of the box' generally over the frequency range; together with the walls of the box, the soundholes, or ports, form a Helmholtz resonator. The frequency of the Helmholtz resonance depends on the volume of air enclosed and the equivalent area of the soundholes, as well as on the flexibility or compliance of the walls. Félix Savart reported in 1819 an effect often overlooked, that the insertion of the soundpost causes an increase in the frequency of both the air and the wood vibrations of the violin; this Helmholtz resonance is usually the lowest fundamental resonance in the spectrum of the instrument. Reinforcement of sounds below this comes from the effect of strong resonances higher up. For example, the strong resonance characteristically near a' in the violin acts as the second harmonic reinforcing a on the G string (see Hutchins:

ACOUSTICS

'Instrumentation and Methods for Violin Testing', 1973).

Some unknown inventor discovered the usefulness of holes in the bodies of string instruments long before the invention of the somewhat similar 'reflex bass' of loudspeakers. The air in and about the ports swings rapidly in and out against the compression and rarefaction of the air within, thus providing the mass and stiffness necessary to a simple harmonic vibrator. Within a considerable range about the frequency of resonance, radiation due to the motion of air in the soundholes reinforces that arising directly at the outside surface of the box. According to simple acoustic theory this enhancement becomes zero at half an octave below resonance, a theoretical justification for the common practice in violin making of placing the Helmholtz air resonance of the violin near C♯–D on the G string (see Hutchins, 1962, and Schelleng, 1963).

Fig.55a, which shows the distribution and intensity of sounds produced by an excellent violin when the force exerted by the bow on the bridge is simulated electronically, using a sine-wave sweeping from 20 Hz to 20,000 Hz, illustrates the abundance of resonances encountered (see Meyer). The peak near 275 Hz is the Helmholtz air resonance already described. The others, with possible exceptions, are resonances in the wood. Fig.55b shows a 'loudness curve' made by bowing each semitone for an octave on each string as loudly as possible and measuring the intensity levels in decibels with a sound-level meter. Note that there is a resonance near g (196 Hz) not found with a sine-wave input. This occurs because the resonance peak near g represents not a fundamental but a 'subharmonic' (see Hutchins, Hopping and Saunders, 1960), which is strong in the wide-band input from the bowed string where the resonance at 392 Hz acts as the second partial, reinforcing the lower octave.

2. BOWING

When a bow is drawn across the string, the string appears to widen in a smooth ribbon of a lenticular shape; but this is an optical illusion. To a first approximation, the string under the bow takes the form of a sharply bent straight line, a phenomenon noted by Helmholtz. A slow-motion camera would show this bend, or discontinuity, moving around the lenticular path

218

extending between the ends of the string as in fig.56 (p.220). The 'stick–slip' action of the bow on the string, though somewhat similar to the chattering of a piece of chalk on a blackboard or the squeaking of a chair leg across the floor, is more complicated. As the discontinuity, or kink, moving from nut to bridge, passes the bow it dislodges the string from the hair to which it has been clinging and reverses the string's motion. When the

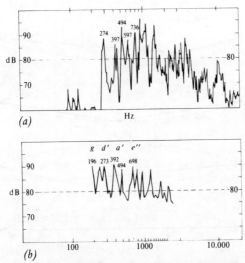

55. (a) *Response curve showing the distribution and intensity of sounds produced by a violin when the force exerted on the bridge is simulated electronically; (b) loudness curve obtained on the same violin by bowing each semitone for an octave on each string as loudly as possible*

discontinuity returns from the bridge it restores the forward motion of the string, which again sticks to the hairs. The bow is thus freed from the string not as a result of the gradual increase in stress between the rosined hair and the rosined string, but because the kink has arrived to set it loose. During the time of sticking, motion is in one direction followed by a quick snap back in the other on release, thus giving the saw-tooth wave-

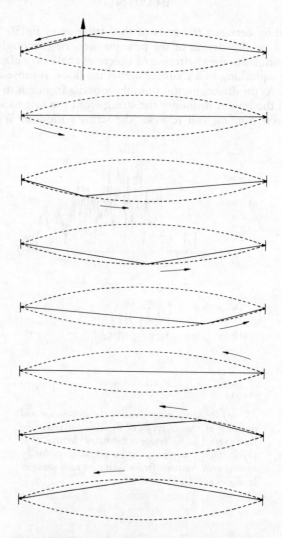

56. Shapes taken by a bowed string at a series of discrete points in time (solid lines) as the kink created at the point of bowing travels to the fixed end of the string and back once in every vibration, causing the optical illusion of a lenticular curve (dotted lines) (after Schelleng, 1974)

form of fig.57. If the motion of fig.57a is produced by a down-bow, the entire pattern will be reversed by an up-bow as in fig.57b. A vivid experiment to illustrate the change in direction as the kink moves around the lenticular path is shown in fig.58 (p.222).

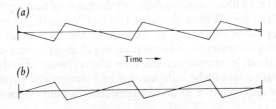

57. *Saw-tooth wave-forms of string displacement produced by the alternate sticking and release of the rosined string by the rosined bow hair: (a) when bowed with a down-bow; (b) with an up-bow*

Under the repetitive action of the bow the many partials, all simultaneously present, are kept in simple multiple relationship to the fundamental frequency even though the string may have a little stiffness. Stiffness in a string causes the partials to be somewhat higher in frequency than harmonic partials would be. In present-day strings the amount of stiffness is of little consequence, but when gut was the only material available for the heavier strings it was largely stiffness that made the G string of the violin family unsatisfactory. Metal and gut strings differ in tone quality when played open string because the relative absence of internal friction in metal permits greater response at higher harmonics. This difference is reduced in the fingered string by the soft, inelastic nature of the fingertip. The rubber dampers used with metal strings help to control this effect. Also, the higher harmonics are reduced by the practice of making wound metal strings with a core of several thin wires, sometimes braided, covered with two or three layers of wrapping.

It may not be obvious to some players that the bowed string is tolerant to a wide range of bow 'pressures' (technically 'bow force'), and that this is indeed a condition without which playing would be all but impossible. For any given bow velocity and location with respect to the bridge there is a minimum and a maximum tolerable pressure. Below the minimum the friction between hair and string becomes insufficient for proper sticking. Above the maximum it is too great to allow the string to detach itself when it should. In the first case the fundamental vibration gives place to a higher mode (at first to the octave); in the second a simple periodic vibration gives way to one of raucous irregularity. Fig.59 illustrates the different domains of bowing for one particular case. Within the area labelled 'normal', as pressure increases from minimum to maximum the content of higher harmonics increases with corresponding changes in tone-colour. If Helmholtz's approximation (see above) were strictly true, tone quality would be independent of location and pressure of the bow and, relative to usual experience, would be considered

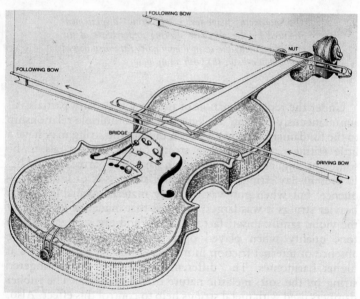

58. 'Following bow' experiment to demonstrate the action of a bowed string: a light (following) bow is suspended at its heavy end, with the point resting on a string near the bridge; a second (driving) bow sets the string in motion, and after a short period of slipping the suspended bow begins to follow in the same direction as the driving bow, thus indicating the direction of string motion during the longer interval of each vibration (when the suspended bow is placed at the opposite end of the string it moves in the opposite direction from the driving bow) (after Schelleng, 1974)

222

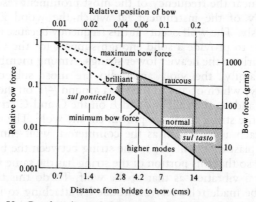

59. Graph indicating the normal playing range for a bowed string instrument at constant bow velocity: the maximum and minimum bow force tend towards equality when the bow is very close to the bridge and diverge when it is further away (after Schelleng, 1974)

brilliant because of the strong harmonic content of the sawtooth wave of fig.57a. Reduction of pressure lengthens the duration of slipping (to as much as doubling that indicated by Helmholtz) and smooths the corners of fig.57a, thus reducing high harmonics. This decrease is most noticeable when the bow is furthest from the bridge and pressure is near the minimum, that is, when one plays *sul tasto*. A similar increase in brilliance occurs as the bow approaches the bridge. Increase in velocity (bow speed) with corresponding increase in pressure is the common way of increasing loudness without change in tone-colour. Within limits, loudness is affected by any one of these parameters alone (velocity, position, pressure). Normally the player must have all three of these in mind in order to produce the proper combination of volume and tone quality. For further information on the acoustics of bowing, see Cremer (1972–3) and Schelleng (1973, 1974).

Bowed string instruments frequently display a disconcerting phenomenon known as the 'wolf' note, a narrow range of frequency within which response tends to stutter in a raucous manner (see Schelleng, 1963; Firth and Buchanan, 1973; and McIntyre and Woodhouse, 1978). In most cases this occurs at

ACOUSTICS

or very near the frequency of the most prominent resonance of the body of the instrument, at which the wood is moving vigorously. The wolf occurs at this frequency because the bridge is unable to provide a solid enough support for the vibrations, particularly of the heavier lower strings. Among members of the violin family, the viola and cello are most subject to this difficulty, which occurs in the viola around *f*–*f*♯ on the G and C strings, and on the cello around *E* on the G and C strings. The heavier the string the more prominent the wolf. The usual cure is to attach a mass such as the commercial wolf-eliminator (a blob of plasticene will do) to the string between the bridge and tailpiece so that this portion of the string has the same frequency of natural vibration as that of the wolf. To do this the bridge should be made relatively immobile by attaching to it a heavy mute or weight, and the mass and position of the eliminator adjusted until the frequency of the wolf is matched, as judged by plucking the string lightly and listening.

3. THE MUTE AND VIBRATO

The mute, which consists merely of a suitable mass attached to the top of the bridge (or pushed up against it), changes both the volume and the quality of the sound (see fig.12, p.24). Its tendency to immobilize the top of the bridge increases with frequency, so that higher tones are reduced and timbre becomes softer and less brilliant; the loudness of sound is correspondingly reduced. The low partial notes of the instrument are not greatly affected, but the loudness of the low notes is indirectly reduced by virtue of the 'residue effect'. According to this, the subjective sensation of fundamental pitch produced by the higher harmonics is somewhat reduced.

Of vibrato, much has been written from a musical point of view. Here only the physical characteristics will be considered, namely the changes in frequency level (recognized by the ear as pitch changes), intensity level (loudness), and variations in harmonic structure of the sound. The changes in pitch as the finger moves back and forth on the string are quite familiar. This motion causes all the harmonics to have the same rate of pitch variation as the vibrato rate, typically four to six per second. The intensity level of each harmonic also varies at this rate, but is different for each harmonic, some having a high intensity level and some a very low. Also, for some of the harmonics the intensity level is increasing, while at the same time it is decreasing for others. These variations cause the aurally pleasing changes in the quality of the sound of notes played with vibrato. (For further details see Fletcher and Sanders; see also Chapter Two, §2(vii).)

4. DEVELOPMENT, STRING TENSION, VARNISH

Few changes were made in the structure of classical violins until the early 19th century, when there was a demand for increased power. To achieve this violin makers lengthened the neck by slightly more than a centimetre and increased its angle to the plane of the violin body (see fig.13, p.26), while at the same time enlarging the bass-bar to provide appropriate stiffness and support. The resultant increase in string tension and the more acute angle of the strings at the bridge provided greater force from the strings through the bridge to the top of the violin. These changes gave the desired increase in power and dynamic range in modern violins. The thin-wooded, highly arched instruments (e.g. those of the Amati family and Jacob Stainer) apparently have not responded as well to these changes as those having thicker wood and flatter archings. With the increase of interest in early music many of the former are now being restored to their original condition to play the music – for more modest-scale performances – for which they were intended.

In spite of their frail structure, the instruments of the violin family are able to withstand the large tension of the strings; that in the violin is around 25 kg weight and that in the cello over 45 kg weight. In the violin this tension exerts a downward force through the bridge on the top plate of 7–9 kg weight, and on the cello there is a correspondingly larger force. In any given case the string tension is determined uniquely by the length, mass and frequency of the vibrating section of the string, and is independent of other factors. If a gut string and one of steel have the same mass per unit length, the tensions will be identical. The idea that a steel string is inherently harder on an instrument than a gut one is true only to the extent that heavier strings are used, or that the instrument is left unused with strings up to pitch for long periods during which changes in moisture in the body tend to increase the tension.

Much has been written about the beneficial effects on tone of the early varnishes, particularly of the beautiful finishes of the 'Cremona period' used on violins until the late 18th century. Until recently, however, there has been little documentation based on physical measurements of the changes in the violin sound or in the vibrating properties of spruce and maple caused by various coatings. These coatings are of two basic types: the undercoat (sealer or filler) applied to the clear wood; and the varnish or protective coating of greater or lesser thickness depending on the methods of the violin maker.

There is little documentation of the acoustical effects of the undercoatings, although work is now in progress. Many violin makers report that they believe this is an important element in tone production as well as in the preservation of the wood. However, experimental evidence provides information on the acoustical effects of the varnish itself. Meinel found that 'varnishing increases the damping . . . and that a hard varnish increases the damping at higher frequencies less than does a soft varnish'. Schelleng's measurements (1968) show that there is a decrease of motion in radiating plates, more or less uniformly throughout the spectrum, of about 1 dB due to added impedance of the varnish layer. Also, the increase in damping, as well as loss from internal friction caused by the addition of varnish, superposes additional reductions at resonance peaks. This reduction can amount to as much as 4 dB, an amount not to be ignored when 5 dB (see Lottermoser and Meyer) can be the measure of difference between an instrument of extraordinary power and one that is too weak.

In addition to overall changes, tests show that the spruce wood of the violin top and the maple used in the back respond differently to the coatings, especially with respect to cross-grain stiffness and damping. This means that the careful tuning of the plates, especially the top with the bass-bar, is altered markedly by the addition of filler and varnish. Violin makers are accustomed to compensating as far as possible for this effect, but many of them report that a violin 'in the white' sounds better than after it is varnished. Evidence indicates that the 'secret of varnish' may well be a method of providing adequate protection and acceptable appearance with the least possible material.

PLUCKED STRING

5. THE PLUCKED STRING

When the string is plucked, the pull of the finger creates a kink, or discontinuity, that divides the string into two straight sections. On release, a dynamic condition is set up in which two discontinuities travel in opposite directions, one towards the bridge and one towards the nut. These are identical to the modes of motion described for the up-bow and down-bow action in the bowed string. Since they are now both present at the same time, however, the wave shape of the force exerted on the bridge is radically different from that of the bowed string. In the bowed string, the Helmholtz approximation indicates a saw-tooth wave in which reversal is instantaneous regardless of the position of the bow on the string (fig.60a). This differs from fig.57a, which shows displacement at the bow where the shape of the curve depends on bow position. With the plucked string, on the other hand, the force at the bridge has a rectangular shape that depends entirely on the point of plucking. If plucking occurs at the middle of the string, the shape is that of a square wave with a minimal content of the higher overtones (fig.60b). If the pluck is

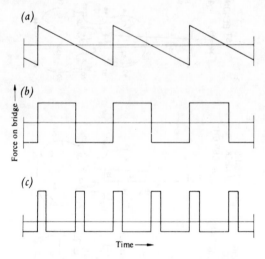

60. *Wave shapes of forces (not to be confused with those of displacement shown in fig.57) of a vibrating string on the bridge: (a) a bowed string; (b) a string plucked at its centre; (c) a string plucked near the bridge*

227

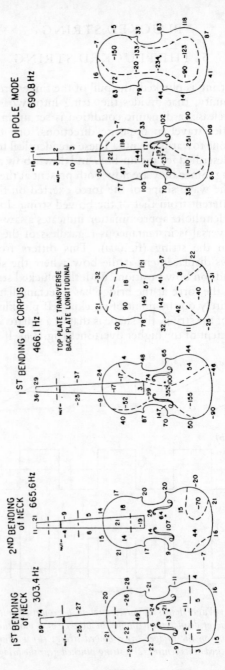

1ST BENDING of NECK 303.4 Hz

2ND BENDING of NECK 665.6 Hz

1ST BENDING of CORPUS 466.1 Hz
TOP PLATE TRANSVERSE
BACK PLATE LONGITUDINAL

DIPOLE MODE 690.8 Hz

228

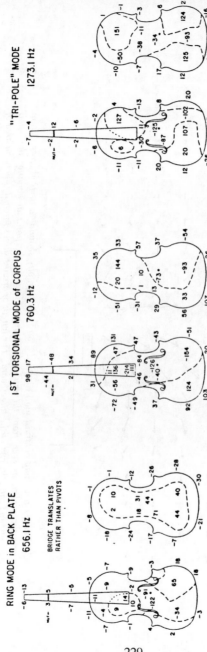

61. *A few selected resonance frequencies showing the mode-mapping of a violin done by modal analysis (the top plate is viewed from above the violin and the back plate is viewed as though the top plate were transparent): the unmarked numbers represent upward motion, the minus numbers represent downward motion, giving relative amplitudes; modal lines are dotted; the black dot (·) designates the position of the soundpost*

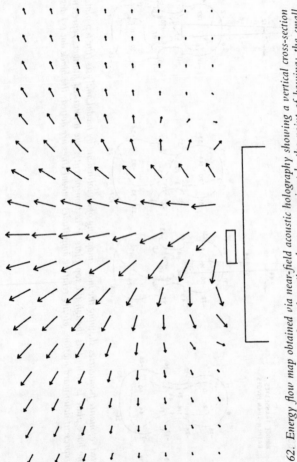

62. Energy flow map obtained via near-field acoustic holography showing a vertical cross-section above the violin, as seen from the tail end, at approximately the point of bowing; the small rectangle indicates the end of the fingerboard. The length of arrows shows intensity; note an area of strong positive intensity just to the right of centre. An energy sink to the left indicates that instead of all the energy being radiated at this frequency, some is being drawn back and absorbed by the instrument

near the bridge or nut, a sharp rectangular wave is produced which is exceedingly rich in high-frequency components (fig.60c). Thus a wider range of timbre is possible by changing the point of plucking than by changing the point of bowing. The actual change, however, is less than expected on ideal assumptions, because, in plucking, the high-frequency components die out more rapidly than in bowing, where they are maintained by the repetitive stick–slip action.

6. CURRENT RESEARCH

It is apparent that, in respect to quantitative analysis and the predetermining of the effects of structure, wind instruments possess two important advantages over string instruments: their shapes are amenable to simpler mathematical description, and the resonating material, air, is homogeneous, with the same elasticity in all directions. By contrast, the shapes of string instruments, while a delight to the connoisseur, are forbidding to the mathematician, and the resonating material, wood, is neither homogeneous nor isotropic, and cannot be standardized. This uncertain property of wood is not a serious difficulty in woodwind instruments because their massive walls do not share vitally in the resonance of the instrument. The result has been that designers of wind instruments have had the possibility, which they have brilliantly used, of forecasting the effects of changes in design, while the scientific luthier has been far more dependent on a series of steps in carving the plates of his instruments, each step guided by the best means at his disposal.

(i) Modal analysis

Modal analysis is now enabling us to observe the details of the motions of the entire violin (including neck, scroll, fingerboard and fittings) at their discrete resonance frequencies. For example, a small lightweight accelerometer is waxed to the surface of the instrument at a given point. The vibration modes are excited by taps from a small, light, weighted hammer containing another accelerometer. The freely suspended violin is tapped at 190 points on its surface. By means of signal processing the resulting data can show the motion of the entire instrument at each of its resonance frequencies (Marshall, 1985; see fig.61).

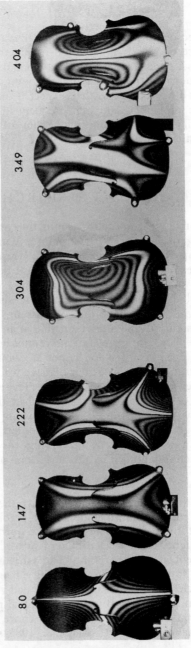

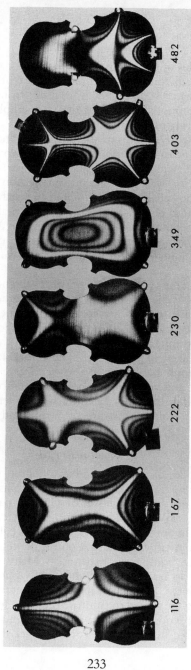

116   167   222   230   349   403   482

(b)

63. Vibration patterns of a pair of unattached top and back violin plates (the top complete with f-holes and bass-bar) as visualized by hologram interferometry: row (a) shows the mode shapes and the frequencies at which they occur in this top plate and row (b) those in this back plate; many other resonance modes occur at higher frequencies. This same configuration sequence for the lower resonance modes is found in the free plates of all instruments of the violin family, but the frequencies are different for each instrument. (Mode 4 in the top plate was not recorded)

233

ACOUSTICS

(ii) The sound radiation field

Not all the modes of the violin observed by modal analysis are efficient sound radiators. Two methods are currently being used to study the radiated sound field. Both differ from the impact-excited system of modal analysis in that they employ acoustical activation of the instrument.

One comprehensive study of the radiated sound field uses a motor-driven mechanical boom system with two microphones – one sweeping parallels of latitude, the other meridians of longitude in such a way as to get information on the spherical radiation of a sinusoidally driven violin in an anechoic chamber. By elegant methods of signal processing and digital analysis, the coefficients of incoming and outgoing waves are obtained so as to compute the acoustic pressure or any desired component of velocity of the sound radiation field (Arnold and Weinreich, 1980).

Acoustic holography is another powerful method for studying the radiation from the surface of a vibrating body. A violin (or guitar) is soft-mounted horizontally in the near-field of an open plane array of over 200 electret microphones (or of a robotic scanning microphone) and electronically vibrated at its discrete frequencies of resonance. The information obtained from each microphone can be processed to give the pressure, particle velocity and vector intensity in the half-space above the violin, making it possible to trace the acoustic energy as it flows around and away from the instrument (Strong and Torick, 1982; see fig.62).

(iii) Free violin-plate modes

The normal modes of free top and back violin plates have been visualized by hologram interferometry (Hutchins, Stetson and Taylor, 1971) and by the sinusoidal Chladni pattern method (Hutchins, 1981). By controlling certain parameters of modes 1, 2 and 5 (fig.63) in both top and back free plates before assembly, it is possible, to a large extent, to control the tone and playing qualities of each completed instrument. Many violin makers around the world have reported successful application of this method (Hutchins, 1987). Computerized finite element techniques are being employed to simulate these modes and to show the influence of wood properties, arching heights and thickness variations on free-free vibration (or tap tone) states (Rodgers;

MODAL ANALYSIS

Richardson, Roberts and Walker; and Rubin and Farrar). The exact acoustical relation of these free-plate modes to those of the assembled instrument is not yet known. Current thinking is, however, that the free-free mode characteristics provide desirable distributions of the plate stiffnesses which are effective in producing instruments with fine tone and playing qualities.

With the newer technologies and computer potentials that are developing today, whole new vistas are opening for discovering the mechanisms by which instruments of the violin family can produce musically effective and beautiful sounds in the hands of trained players.

APPENDIX ONE

Glossary of Terms

Cross-references within this appendix are distinguished by the use of small capitals, with a large capital for the initial letter of the entry referred to, for example:

See BRIDGE.

Ponticello (It.). BRIDGE.

Adjuster. *See* TUNER.

Alto. The modern French and Italian term for the viola; its usage derives from the instrument's range relative to other members of the violin family. 'Alto' or 'contralto' was also applied earlier to the smaller violas that were used for the higher viola range in ensembles that included the TENOR VIOLIN.

Ame (Fr.: 'soul'). French term for the SOUNDPOST. In some French sources it can also mean the bow.

Archet (Fr.). Bow.

Arco (It.). Bow.

Arpeggione [guitar violoncello, bowed guitar]. A bowed string instrument invented by J. G. Staufer of Vienna, 1823–4, and in existence briefly in the 19th century. Essentially a bass viol with a guitar-type tuning, its body was smooth-waisted in imitation of the guitar; it had 24 frets. Schubert wrote the sonata D821 for it.

Bach bow. A violin bow of very high arch invented in the 20th century for the performance of Bach's solo sonatas. It has a mechanical lever which, when operated by the thumb, allows the player to alter the tension of the hair and to play on individual strings or sustain multiple-stopped passages (see fig. 17).

Back [back plate]. The underside of the body of a string instrument. Made of hardwood, in the violin it is usually of maple and may be in one piece, or two pieces joined lengthways. The grain runs along the length of the instrument, but the wood usually shows figured patterns that run across the width (see figs. 2–4).

Back-plate. The strip of metal on the bow that runs down the back of the frog, ending on the underside next to the slide (see fig. 51c).

APPENDIX ONE

Bas de violon (Fr.). *See* BASSE DE VIOLON.

Bass. A term for the Double bass.

Bass-bar (Fr. *barre*; Ger. *Bassbalken*; It. *catena*). A strip of wood glued to the underside of the belly, running under the left foot of the bridge (the side carrying the lowest-sounding string). It serves to transmit the sound vibrations to the belly and helps support it (see fig. 2 and Chapter 9,§1). The modern bass-bar is usually about 265 mm long, 5 mm wide and 10 mm deep at the centre, tapering at both ends.

Basse de violon [bas de violon, basse d'orquestre] (Fr.). A bass member of the violin family, tuned Bb-F-c-g. It was used in the French opera orchestra until the early 18th century, when it was probably superseded by the cello. *Basses de violon* made $c1700$ are larger than 18th-century cellos and were probably played with the lower end resting on the ground. The term 'bas de violon' was first mentioned by P. Jambe de Fer (*Epitome musical*, 1556).

Bassetto (It.). A small type of double bass.

Belly [table, soundtable, top, top plate] (Fr. *table*; Ger. *Decke*; It. *tavola*). The upper surface of the body of a string instrument. It is made of softwood of fairly fine and even grain, which runs along the length of the instrument. In bowed instruments it is arched (see fig.2).

Block. A piece of softwood that is glued inside the instrument against the ribs where their ends meet. It supports the ribs and holds them in shape. The top-block also strengthens the neck and the bottom-block relieves the tensions exerted on the belly by the strings. Corner-blocks are placed where the C curves meet the upper and lower bouts (see fig.2).

Bogen (Ger.). Bow.

Bottesini bow. A type of double bass bow named after Giovanni Bottesini (1821–89); *see* FRENCH BOW.

Bottom-block. *See* BLOCK.

Bouts (Fr. *échancrures*; Ger. *Bugel*; It. *fascie*). A curve or bend of a rib or ribs. The curves of the waist are called 'middle bouts' (or 'C-bouts'); the upper curves, near the neck, are called 'upper bouts', and the lower curves 'lower bouts' (see fig.5).

Bowstick. The wooden stick to which the bowhair is attached. Generally made of pernambuco wood, it is round or octagonal in shape and tapers slightly from frog to head.

Brand. The name or other distinguishing mark of a bow maker. It is usually stamped into the bowstick above the frog.

Bratsche (Ger.). The German term for the viola; it derives from the Italian 'braccio' (*see* VIOLA DA BRACCIO).

Bridge (Fr. *chevalet*; Ger. *Steg*; It. *ponticello*). A thin wedge, usually of maple, inserted between the belly and the strings; it raises the strings to a required distance above the belly and fingerboard, as well as transmitting vibrations to the belly. The thin edge is at the top and is in contact with the strings, which are kept apart by notches. The top is arched to enable the player to bow each string separately. The bridge is open in design and is cut away at the bottom leaving 'feet' that are fitted to the arched belly; it is kept in position by the tension of the strings. (See figs.2 and 6.)

Chamber bass. A small-sized double bass.

Chanterelle (Fr.: 'the singing one'). The highest-pitched string of any instrument. In the violin family it is usually applied only to the violin E string. The term may have originated with the hurdy-gurdy, which has one or two melody strings and others that supply only drones.

Chin rest (Fr. *mentonnière*; Ger. *Kinnhalter*; It. *mentoniera*). A device clamped to the lower part of string instruments played on the arm, generally at the left side of the tailpiece. It serves to separate the chin from the instrument, thus ensuring that the transmission of vibrations is not obstructed, and at the same time gives the player a firm grip with the chin. In his *Violin-Schule* (1832) Spohr claimed to have invented the chin rest and illustrated it placed directly over the tailpiece (see fig.16).

Cinquième [quinte] (Fr.: 'fifth'). A term generally given to the first viola part in the five-part string ensemble of 17th-century France; in the 24 Violons du Roi (established 1626) it referred to the third viola.

Contrabass (Fr. *contrebasse*; Ger. *Kontrabass*; It. *contrabasso, contrabbasso*; Sp. *contrabajo*). A term for the double bass.

Contralto viola. *See* ALTO.

Corner-block. *See* BLOCK.

Crémaillère (Fr.). DENTATED BOW.

Dämpfer (Ger.). MUTE.

Dentated bow (Fr. *Crémaillère*). A type of bow with a movable frog in use before *c*1750. In order to set the frog in one of several positions, an iron catch or loop attached to it was engaged by one of several teeth on top of the bowstick (see fig.51*b*).

Dragonetti bow. A type of double bass bow. It was named after the bass player Domenico Dragonetti (1736–1846) and in use in England until the early 20th century. The bow was characterized by a large gap between the hair and the bowstick; it was held endways in the manner of the modern Simandl bow (see fig.43).

End-button [endpin, tailpin]. A term for the knob that is let into the bottom-block of instruments of the violin family. The tailgut is looped over it to secure the tailpiece (see figs.2 and 5).

Endpin [spike, tailpin] (Fr. *pique*; Ger. *Stachel*; It. *puntale*). A retractable

APPENDIX ONE

steel spike or piece of wood fixed to the lower part of the cello or double bass to support the instrument and to regulate its distance from the floor (see fig.36). The adjustable endpin, now almost universally used, was apparently first adopted by A. F. Servais c1846, although a fixed endpin was known much earlier (see fig.30). A detachable cello endpin that permits the instrument to be held in a more horizontal position has also been invented (fig.37). The term is further applied to the END-BUTTON.

English violet. A type of VIOLA D'AMORE, with seven principal and 14 sympathetic strings. It may be identical with the violetta marina.

E-viola. The name given to an experimental instrument constructed in 1961 by Otto Sand, who aimed to expand the sonority and range of an ordinary viola by fitting it with a fifth string.

Eye. A term for the circular inlay found on both sides of the frog of the bow (see fig.49c).

Ferrule. A band of metal, usually silver, positioned where the bow hair leaves the frog; it spreads the hair into a uniform ribbon (see figs.51c and 54c). Although claimed to be the invention of François Tourte (1747–1835), it was probably introduced earlier.

f-hole. See SOUNDHOLES.

Fiddle. A colloquial term for a member of the violin family or for the KIT. During the Middle Ages and early Renaissance the term also referred to a particular type of instrument known today as the medieval fiddle.

Fine-tuner. See TUNER.

Fingerboard (Fr. *touche*; Ger. *Griffbrett*; It. *tastiera, tasto*). The part of the instrument over which the strings are stretched and against which the fingers of the player's hand press down the strings; it extends from the end of the pegbox to well beyond the neck, over and above the belly, towards the bridge; it is generally made of ebony. It is glued to the upper surface of the neck and is usually rounded throughout its surface to allow the bow to touch each string separately. It is generally narrower at the pegbox end than at the bridge end (see figs.2 and 5).

French bow [Bottesini bow]. A type of double bass bow that is played overhand. It resembles the modern cello bow in appearance, although the stick is shorter, thicker, heavier and more sharply curved inwards (see fig.42a). Introduced relatively late in the 19th century, it is used almost exclusively in France, England and the USA.

Fret. A strip of gut, bone, ivory, wood or metal, placed across the fingerboard of certain string instruments, usually at intervals of a semitone. The violone, a double-bass viol and the ancestor of the double bass, had gut frets (see p.186 and fig.40a). Frets have occasionally been used on the violin to help the beginner play in tune.

239

Frog [heel, nut] (Fr. *hausse, talon*; Ger. *Frosch*; It. *tallone*). The device which secures the hair to the bow and holds it away from the stick at the lower end (where the player grasps the bow); it also serves to regulate the tension of the bow hair by means of a screw mechanism. At an early stage in its evolution the frog was horn-shaped and fixed, but by the late 17th century various methods of adjusting the hair were being developed (*see* DENTATED BOW and figs.49 and 51).

Geige (Ger.). A term meaning violin or 'fiddle'. In the Middle Ages it was used to refer to any bowed string instrument. By the 16th century a distinction was made between *grosse Geigen* (viols) and *kleine Geigen* (violins). Praetorius (*Syntagma musicum*, ii, 2/1619) used the term *Geigen* for members of the violin family and *Violen* for viols; he also distinguished between the *rechte Discant-Geig* ('treble violin proper') and the *klein discant Geig* (VIOLINO PICCOLO).

German bow. *See* SIMANDL BOW.

Guitar violoncello. *See* ARPEGGIONE.

Hair. A term for the ribbon of horsehair, about 1cm wide, that is fixed to the bowstick (see figs.51 and 53); it comprises 150–200 hairs and is adjusted to the required tension by a screw mechanism in the frog. White horsehair is used for violin bows and (usually) for viola and cello bows; double bass bows generally have black hair, which is stronger.

Handbassel (Ger.). *See* VIOLA DA SPALLA.

Harmonicello. A bass string instrument built by J. C. Bischoff in 1794. A variant of the cello, it had five gut playing strings and ten sympathetic metal ones.

Haute-contre [haute-contre taille] (Fr.). A term generally given to the second viola part in the five-part string ensemble of 17th-century France; in the 24 Violons du Roi (established 1626) it referred to the first viola.

Head [point]. A term for the part of the bowstick that holds the hair in position at the end opposite to the frog. Modern bows have a hatchet-shaped head which is faced with a protective plate, generally made of ivory (see fig.53). Earlier types were known as the 'pike's' head, the 'swan-bill' and the 'battle-axe' (see figs.49 and 52).

Heel. *See* FROG.

Inlay. Material set into the wood. The PURFLING helps to protect the edges of the instrument and is also ornamental. Decorative inlays, which may be of mother-of-pearl or ivory, are sometimes found in the back, ribs, scroll, tailpiece, fingerboard or pegs (see figs.15, 28a and 29). Bows usually have a circular inlay ('eye') in the frog (see. fig.49c).

Kit [kytte] (Fr. *poche, pochette, sourdine*; Ger. *Posch, Tanzmeistergeige, Taschengeige*; It. *canino, pochetto, sordina, sordino*; Lat. *linterculus*). A small, unfretted fiddle, generally with four strings, made in a variety of shapes. It was played from the 16th century to the 19th and often used by dancing masters. The earliest kits were members of the rebec family and were either pear-shaped or shaped like a narrow boat and had vaulted backs. In the late 17th century kits resembling the viol, violin or guitar were made, with a slightly arched back and a long neck. The tuning is generally in 5ths, sometimes at the pitch of the violin, but more often a 4th or a 5th higher and occasionally (in three-string instruments) an octave. A violin-shaped instrument by Stradivari (dated 1717) is in the Paris Conservatoire museum.

Label. The means by which a maker marks an instrument as his work. It is glued to the inside of the back and is visible through the soundholes. Labels were originally handwritten, but later were printed; forgeries are common.

Lapping. A term for the protective band of leather, whalebone or silver wire that covers the bowstick above the frog. It provides grip for all fingers, and prevents wear of the stick (see fig.49c).

Linings [side-linings]. The thin strips of softwood fitted inside the body of the instrument to provide greater support for the ribs where they meet the belly and the back (see fig.2). They are glued along the edges of the ribs and form joints with the corner-blocks.

Luthier (Fr.; It. *liutaio*). Originally the word for a lute maker, it has become the general term for a maker of violins or other string instruments and is often used similarly in English and German.

Machine head. A mechanical tuning device used in place of a wooden peg on double basses and occasionally cellos. It has a worm-gear mechanism to enable a metal string to be held at great tension with no slippage. Worm-gear heads were used on double basses in the 18th century.

Mute (Fr. *sourdine*; Ger. *Dämpfer*; It. *sordino*). A device, often in the form of a three-pronged clamp (sometimes two- or five-pronged), which is placed in contact with the bridge in order to absorb some of the vibrations and thus change the volume and quality of the sound (see Chapter 9, §3). It may be made of metal (particularly steel and aluminium), ivory, bakelite or wood (especially ebony and boxwood) (see fig.12a). The degree of muting and the difference of tone-colour depend on the materials used as well as the mute's mass and the firmness with which it is attached.

Neck (Fr. *manche*; Ger. *Hals*; It. *mancio*). The projecting handle of the instrument, to which part of the fingerboard is fastened; it is usually made of maple and is joined to the body by nailing or gluing (or both) (see fig.2).

New Violin Family [Violin Octet]. A consort of eight acoustically balanced instruments in graduated sizes and tunings, designed by Carleen Hutchins and her associates (1963–5) after research by

VIOLIN FAMILY

Frederick Saunders. The instruments range from the treble violin (body length 28.6 cm; tuned an octave above the normal violin) to the contrabass violin (body length 130 cm; tuned like the double bass). The mezzo, alto and baritone violins are re-scaled versions of the violin, viola and cello respectively: the body length of the alto (50.8 cm) makes it preferable to play the instrument like a cello, but with a longer endpin. The soprano is tuned an octave above the normal viola and is comparable in size to a three-quarter violin; the tenor, tuned G-d-a-e', is similar in size to the three-quarter cello; and the small bass violin, tuned a 4th above the double bass, is the size of a three-quarter bass.

Nut (Fr. *sillet*; Ger. *Sattel*, *Obersattel*; It. *capo tasto*). The thin ridge, generally of ebony or other hardwood, inserted between the pegbox and fingerboard (see fig.5). It raises the strings above the fingerboard to allow the open strings to sound freely from nut to bridge; it also holds the strings at fixed distances apart and adds a frictional resistance that helps the pegs in holding the strings. The term can also refer to the FROG.

Octobass. A large three-string double bass, tuned C'-G'-C, built by J.-B. Vuillaume in 1851. Berlioz thought highly of the instrument, which is in the Paris Conservatoire museum.

Peg (Ger. *Wirbel*). A wooden pin with a protruding flattened knob, usually made of ebony or rosewood; it is inserted into a hole in the pegbox (see figs.2 and 5). It serves to secure the string in position and to regulate its tension. The string is threaded through a hole in the shaft.

Pegbox (Fr. *cheviller*; Ger. *Wirbelkasten*; It. *cassa dei bischeri*). The wooden box-like structure, open on top, into which are fitted the pegs that hold the strings in place and regulate their tension (see fig.5). The tapered pegs are inserted into holes in the sides of the pegbox and run from one side to the other, the shank of each peg being at right angles to the string.

Piccolo bass. A term for a small double bass used in jazz. It has thin strings and is tuned an octave higher than the standard instrument.

Point [tip]. A common term for the HEAD of the bow; it can also refer specifically to the sharpened end of the head.

Ponticello (It.). BRIDGE.

Purfling (Fr. *filet*; Ger. *Einlage*; It. *filetto*). A narrow inlay of wood inset in a trough cut just inside the border edge of the belly and back (see figs.2 and 5). It consists of three narrow strips, the middle one being of white or yellow wood and the outer ones of black wood. It helps to protect the edges of the instrument and serves also as ornamentation.

Quartgeige (Ger.). A small violin, or VIOLINO PICCOLO, tuned a 4th higher than the violin.

APPENDIX ONE

Quinte (Fr.: 'fifth'). An 18th-century term for the viola and for the viola player. It was also generally used to designate the first viola part in the five-part string ensemble of 17th-century France (see also CINQUIÈME).

Quinton. A five-string instrument in use during the 18th century. It combined characteristics of the violin and the viol; it had frets and sloping shoulders, but its body otherwise resembled that of a violin.

Resin. *See* ROSIN.

Ribs (Fr. *éclisses*; Ger. *Zargen*; It. *fascie*). The sides that connect the belly and the back of a string instrument. They are generally made of hardwood, particularly maple; they should be the same texture, and preferably from the same piece of wood, as the back. In the violin they consist of six curved strips, one for each bout (see fig.2). Their height varies according to the model (as a rule, instruments with low arching of the belly and back have higher ribs), and in instruments of the same family generally increases in relation to the size of the instrument.

Rosin [resin, colophony, colophonium, colophane] (Fr. *colophane*; Ger. *Kolophonium*, *Geigenharz*; It. *colofonia*). A solid substance obtained from the distillation of oil of turpentine which is rubbed on the hair of the bow to give the hair the necessary 'bite' on the strings. It is hard and brittle, its colours varying from amber to dark brown, and is cast into rounded or rectangular shapes. Pure rosin is best for violin, viola and cello bows, but the double bass bow requires a stiffer preparation made of pure rosin and white pitch in equal proportions.

Saddle. A small piece of hardwood, often ebony, inserted into the centre of the base edge of the belly, by removing some (or all) of the purfling. It carries the tailgut over the edge of the belly and prevents the tailpiece from touching the belly (see figs.2 and 5).

Screw button [screw cap]. A term for the metal knob that forms part of the screw mechanism of the FROG (see fig.51*c*).

Scroll. The end of the neck, carved in the shape of a scroll; it is usually made of maple. In the 17th and 18th centuries it was sometimes carved as an animal or human head. Its function is decorative, although in earlier times the instrument was often hung up by it.

Shoulder rest [shoulder pad]. A pad or other device that is attached to a violin or viola at the base of its back to help support the instrument under the chin. Several modern types of rest have metal legs with rubber-covered feet that fit onto the edges of the back, so that the rest is not in direct contact with the back and does not absorb vibrations.

Simandl bow [German bow]. A type of double bass bow, named after the Viennese teacher Franz Simandl (1840–1912); it is used almost exclusively in Germany, Austria and central Europe. It combines the modern head and incurve of the French bow with a greater space

243

VIOLIN FAMILY

between hair and stick at the frog, which is itself shaped differently. It is held endways (see figs.42*b* and 43).

Slide (Fr. *recouvrement*). A term for the rectangular plate made of mother-of-pearl that covers the bowhair on the lower face of the frog, between the ferrule and the back-plate (see figs.51*c* and 54*c*). It is said to have been invented by François Tourte (1747–1835), but was probably introduced earlier.

Sordino (It.). MUTE.

Soundbox. The body of the instrument. It acts as a resonator (see Chapter One, §1(ii) and Chapter Nine).

Soundholes [f-holes] (Fr. *ouïes*; Ger. *Schallöcher*; It. *occhi*). The two openings cut in the belly on either side of the bridge to enhance the instrument's tone quality and increase the volume of sound; they are also essential for the insertion and adjustment of the soundpost. In instruments of the violin family they are f-shaped (viols have C-shaped holes). (See also Chapter Nine, §1.)

Soundpost (Fr. *âme*; Ger. *Stimme*, *Stimmstock*; It. *anima*). A small wooden pillar (about 6 mm in diameter in the violin), generally of pine or spruce, inserted vertically between the belly and back, under the side of the bridge carrying the highest-sounding string: its position is not directly under the foot of the bridge but on a line with it slightly towards the tailpiece (see fig.2). It serves to relieve the downward pressure of the strings and bridge on the belly, and to transmit the vibrations of the belly and ribs to the back. It also immobilizes the foot of the bridge near to it, so that the other foot vibrates with comparative freedom and helps to transmit the vibrations to the wide areas of the belly (see Chapter Nine, §1).

Soundtable. *See* BELLY.

Sourdine (Fr.). MUTE.

Spike. *See* ENDPIN.

String (Fr. *corde*; Ger. *Saite*, *Streich-*; It. *corda*). In a musical instrument a length of any material that can produce a musical sound when held stretched and then plucked, bowed, struck, or otherwise excited. Gut, silk and wire, and more recently plastic, are the most common materials, but many others have been used. Violin strings were traditionally made from the twisted gut of lambs. By the early 18th century the lowest string (G) and occasionally the D string were overspun with silver or copper wire. Early in the 20th century the use of steel E strings became common; some are covered with a ribbon of aluminium. Aluminium-covered A and D strings with a gut core are common, as are silver-covered G strings; G strings may also be gold-covered. A plastic core is sometimes used instead of gut. (See also Chapter One, §3(i) and Chapter Nine.)

APPENDIX ONE

String bass. A colloquial term for the double bass.

Stroh violin. A type of violin developed by Augustus Stroh (1828–1914) in London *c*1900 for use in gramophone recording studios; at the time it was impossible to make satisfactory recordings of a group of ordinary string instruments because all sounds needed to be directed at a single large horn. The instrument incorporated elements of the gramophone and had a body consisting of a long, narrow piece of wood, of which the upper surface served as a fingerboard; a flexible membrane was mounted at one side of the bridge with a straight metal horn attached to it. A concert model had a second, smaller horn that could be directed towards the player. The Stroh violin was later used as a folk instrument in Romania (see Chapter Four, §1).

Table. *See* BELLY.

Tailgut. A loop of gut, wire or nylon attached to the tailpiece, which it secures by passing around the end-button (see fig.2).

Taille (Fr.: 'tenor'). A term generally given to the third viola part in the five-part string ensemble of 17th-century France; in the 24 Violons du Roi (established 1626) it referred to the second viola.

Tailpiece (Fr. *cordier, tirecordes*; Ger. *Saitenhalter*; It. *cordiera*). A string holder to which the strings are attached at the lower end of the instrument. It consists of a piece of wood (generally ebony), or, for high-tension metal strings, metal, secured by the TAILGUT, which is looped over the end-button (see figs.2 and 5).

Tailpin. A term for the ENDPIN of the cello and double bass. It is also occasionally applied to all instruments of the violin family for the END-BUTTON.

Tenor violin. A term for a string instrument, most often a type of viola or small cello. Its earliest usage referred to a three-string viola, but from the 16th century it was commonly applied to a large viola (see fig.29) that was tuned like a modern viola and normally used for the lower part of the viola range (the smaller 'alto' or 'contralto' viola favoured a higher tessitura). The term also referred to a small type of cello with a tuning between that of a modern viola and cello; it was used only occasionally and was virtually obsolete after the mid-17th century.

Terzgeige (Ger.). A small violin, or VIOLINO PICCOLO, tuned a 3rd higher than the violin.

Tip. *See* POINT.

Top [top plate]. *See* BELLY.

Top-block. *See* BLOCK.

Tuner [adjuster, fine-tuner]. A metal, screw-like device used to fine-tune steel strings; it is located where the string is secured to the tailpiece (see fig.2).

VIOLIN FAMILY

Underslide (Fr. *coulisse*). A thin metal plate attached to the upper surface of the frog. It prevents contact between the frog and the bowstick and consequently minimizes wear from friction. It is said to have been invented by François Lupot (1774–1837). (See fig.51*c*.)

Varnish. The clear, protective lacquer that coats the wood of string instruments; it acts as a preservative. Although it cannot improve the tone of an instrument, if incorrectly applied it could prevent the best tone-qualities being realized.

Viola alta. A large viola introduced in 1876 by Herman Ritter. An exact enlargement of a violin, but tuned like a viola, it was built in Würzburg by K. A. Hörlein (1829–1902) to reproduce the violin's acoustical properties. It had a large body (*c*48 cm) for improved resonance; in 1898 a fifth string (*e″*) was added. Although used at Bayreuth and by the Ritter Quartet, it became redundant, probably because of its unwieldy size.

Viola da braccio [viola da braz, viola da brazzo] (It.). A generic term for bowed string instruments played on the arm (It. *braccio*) as opposed to one played on or between the knees, i.e. viola da gamba (*gamba*: 'leg'; *viola* was a general word for a bowed string instrument). It was also the 16th- and 17th-century term for a member of the violin family (including the cello).

Viola d'amore (Fr. *viole d'amour*; Ger. *Liebesgeige*). A type of viola popular during the late 17th and 18th centuries. It is normally about the size of a viola and is played under the chin, but it has the flat back, wide ribs and sloping shoulders characteristic of the viol; it is unfretted. Usually there are seven playing strings, which cross the top of the bridge, and seven sympathetic strings, which run through the bridge and under the fingerboard into separate pegs in the pegbox.

Viola da spalla (It.). An 18th-century name for a small bowed string instrument with four to six strings; it was held across the player's chest by a strap over the shoulder (It. *spalla*). The *Handbassel* was probably identical with the viola da spalla; J. Adlung (*Anleitung zu der musik-alischen Gelahrtheit*, 1758) considered the term a synonym for violoncello.

Viola di fagotto (It.; Ger. *Fagottgeige*). A bowed string instrument played on the arm like a viola, but with the tuning and range of a cello. As some of its strings were overspun with copper wire, it produced a buzzing sound like a bassoon (It. *fagotto*). It is described in various 17th- and 18th-century books, including Daniel Speer, *Grundrichtiger . . . Unterricht der musicalischen Kunst* (1687). It was sometimes confused with the *Handbassel* (see VIOLA DA SPALLA).

Violalin. A five-string viola made by Friedrich Hillmer of Leipzig before 1800; it was still being played in public by his son Joseph in 1840. Like the *viola pomposa*, Woldemar's *violon-alto* and Ritter's *viola alta*, the instrument was an attempt at the combination of violin and viola.

Viola pomposa (It.). A bowed string instrument played on the arm. Its five strings were tuned either *c-g-d'-a'-e"*, or possibly *d-g-d'-g'-c"*, and it was in use from *c*1725 to *c*1770. It was called *violino pomposa* by some writers and others confused it with the VIOLONCELLO PICCOLO.

Violetta (It.). A term used at various times to mean viol, violin or viola. In the 16th century it was used to refer to violins as a class and could also mean 'viol'; in the 17th and 18th centuries it usually meant 'viola'.

Violetta marina (It.). A bowed string instrument with sympathetic strings, developed by Pietro Castrucci (1679–1752). It probably resembled the viola d'amore, and may have been identical with the English violet.

Violetta piccola (It.). A term normally denoting a descant viol, but also used by Praetorius (*Syntagma musicum*, ii, 2/1619) to mean violin.

Violina. A mechanical instrument constructed in Vienna in 1911. It consisted of three violins grouped around a common axis and a rotating bow (see fig.7).

Violine (Ger.). Violin.

Violinista. A mechanical instrument constructed in 1920. It consisted of an ordinary violin placed in a mobile cradle, which, when rotated, caused the individual strings to be played. The bow could move at any desired speed and various bowstrokes such as *martelé*, *spiccato* and *staccato* could be used.

Violino (It.). Violin.

Violin Octet. *See* NEW VIOLIN FAMILY.

Violino grande (It.: 'large violin'). A type of violin with an expanded range and sonority constructed by H. O. Hansson (1963–6) for the violinist Bronisław Eichenholz. It is similar in size to a viola and has five strings, tuned in fifths from *c*.

Violino piccolo (It.). A small violin in existence from the 16th century until *c*1750. In the 17th and 18th centuries it was usually tuned a 4th higher than the normal violin and sometimes called *Quartgeige* in German. Sometimes the tuning was a 3rd higher than usual (Ger.: *Terzgeige*). Praetorius described it as 'Klein discant Geig'.

Violino pomposa. *See* VIOLA POMPOSA.

Violon (Fr.). Violin.

Violon-alto. A viola with five strings tuned *c-g-d'-a'-e"*. It was designed by M. Woldemar of Orleans, *c*1788.

Violoncello d'amore. A small cello with sympathetic strings as on the VIOLA D'AMORE.

247

Violoncello piccolo (It.: 'little violoncello'). A small cello in use in the first half of the 18th century. J. S. Bach composed solo parts for it in nine of his Leipzig cantatas; some contemporary writers confused the instrument with the viola pomposa.

Violoncello portatile. A collapsible cello made by John Wilde (d 1770). When assembled it had a box-like shape that resembled the 'porta cello' sometimes used by beginners today.

Violoncino (It.). A term for a cello first found in a volume of sonatas by G. B. Fontana (Venice, 1641). It was in use until the early 18th century.

Violone (It.: 'large viol'). In modern terminology, the double-bass viol, the ancestor of the double bass. In 16th-century Italy it was a generic term for the viol family but by c1600, in Italy and elsewhere, it had come to mean a large five-string or six-string bass viol, tuned either in 4ths or a combination of 3rds and 4ths. In Italian sources from 1700 to 1750 'violone' may also refer to the cello.

Virtuosa. The first mechanical violin, constructed in the USA in 1908. It consisted of an ordinary violin placed inside an instrument containing levers and mechanical 'fingers'; a disc replaced the bow.

Wedge. (1) The small block of wood that serves to secure the hair in the frog and the head of the bow (see figs.51 and 53).

(2) The piece of wood inserted between the neck and fingerboard when the neck projected straight from the body (before c1800). Later, when the bridge was heightened and the tensions of the strings increased, the neck was tilted back to compensate for the increased angle of the strings and the wedge became redundant (see fig.13).

Worm-gear head. *See* MACHINE HEAD.

APPENDIX TWO

Index of Violin and Bow Makers

Cross-references within this appendix are distinguished by the use of small capitals, with a large capital for the initial letter of the entry referred to, for example: *See* SMITH, JOHN; or, in running prose, JOHN SMITH.

Adam. French family of bow makers. Jean (*fl* c1790–1820) made rather inelegant, utilitarian bows; those of his son Jean Dominique (1795–1865) were more carefully finished. Some of the bows by Jean Dominique's son, Grand-Adam (1823–69), are equal to the best Parisian work of the time.

Albani, Mathias (1621–1712). Tyrolean violin maker. Active in Bolzano, he made instruments modelled on A. and H. Amati lines. Although false Albani labels appeared from c1640 on many 18th-century German violins and from c1690 much of the work bearing the authentic label was probably done by his sons Michael and Joseph, the Albani influence was strong among 18th-century Tyrolean makers.

Alberti, Ferdinando (*fl* Milan, c1737–63). Italian violin maker. He took over the shop of Giovanni Grancino. His violins are reminscent of Grancino's, and have good tonal qualities, but the craftsmanship lacks refinement and symmetry.

Aldric, Jean-François (1765–1843). French violin maker. One of the third generation of a Mirecourt family of makers, he settled in Paris in 1785. His instruments, patterned on the Stradivari model, are among the best produced by the French. His cellos are outstanding and much in demand.

Allen, Samuel (1848–c1905). English bow maker. He worked for W. E. Hill & Sons c1880–1891 as a maker and repairer of bows, then independently. He is best known for his cello bows, patterned in most respects after Tourte.

Alvey, Brian (*b* 1949). English bow maker. He was apprenticed to W. E. Hill & Sons and remained with the firm until 1978. His gold and tortoise-shell mounted bows retain much of the Hill style.

Amati. Italian family of violin makers, active in Cremona. Andrea (c1511–c1580) probably originated the present form of the violin, viola and cello. He used contemporary knowledge of measurement and proportion in his design, and this classical construction gives instruments of the Cremonese school much of their visual superiority and may also influence their tone. Most of Andrea's surviving instruments date from 1564–74. His sons Antonio (*b* *c*1540) and Girolamo (Hieronymus) (i) (1561–1630), 'the brothers Amati', inherited the business in 1580. They continued to develop the craft, producing instruments of improved strength, and were possibly the first to make alto violas. Their work was copied and counterfeited in Italy and abroad, and their influence was particularly strong in England in the late 18th century. Girolamo's son Nicolo (1596–1684), the most highly regarded of the Amatis, favoured a wider model (the 'Grand Amati') and made mostly violins, which are noted for their tone and ease of response. He was the only important maker to survive famine and plague in Italy in the 1630s and later trained Andrea Guarneri, Francesco Rugeri and Antonio Stradivari. His son Girolamo (Hieronymus) (ii) (1649–1740) was a fine maker but not equal to the other members of the family; he seems to have made few instruments after 1700.

Antoniazzi. Italian family of violin makers. They may be related to Gregorio Antoniazzi (*fl* *c*1732–50), whose instruments have some affinity with those of Montagnana. Gaetano (1823–97) studied in Cremona before establishing himself in Milan. His work also appears under the label of Monzino e Figlio, where he may have been employed. His son Ricardo (1860–1913) worked in the Bisiach and Monzino workshops in Milan. Ricardo's instruments, based on the Stradivari model, are superior to his father's and are among the best Italian work around 1900. Gaetano's younger son, Romeo (1862–1922), worked briefly in Milan, then in Cremona. He attracted many pupils who became good makers. His instruments, also based on classical models, differ slightly from his brother's.

Bailly, Paul Joseph (1844–1907). French violin maker. He was a pupil of Jules Gaillard and Nicolas Vuillaume in Mirecourt and joined J.-B. Vuillaume's workshop in Paris in 1864. After 1868 he worked in Lille, then in Douai (where he made violins for the Academy of Music), Mirecourt, Brussels and London, and for Harry Dykes in Leeds, before settling in Paris. He made *c*3000 instruments, mostly violins on Stradivari or Guarneri models, and won awards at the Paris Exposition of 1878. His daughter Jenny succeeded him *c*1897.

Bairhoff, Giorgio (1712–86). German violin maker. He apparently moved to Naples early in life and appears to have been a pupil of the Gagliano family, whose pattern he followed. He worked in Naples from 1740, chiefly on violins.

Baldantoni, Giuseppe (1784–1873). Italian violin maker, active in Ancona. His instruments are of an original design based on the theories of Antonio Bagatella (1755–1829). They have a distinctive orange varnish and a rich tone.

APPENDIX TWO

Balestrieri, Tomaso (*fl c*1750–80). Italian violin maker, active in Mantua. His instruments follow the style of Cremona, where he may have been trained. His best violins are patterned on a flat Stradivari model and produce a powerful sound.

Banks, Benjamin (1727–95). English violin maker. He worked in Salisbury and did much to raise the standard of English violin making. He is best known for his cellos, which are patterned after Amati or Stradivari models and resemble Forster's in appearance and tone. Some of his later instruments were made for and branded by Longman & Broderip; bows carrying his brand were probably made for him. His son James made instruments in Salisbury until the business moved to Liverpool in 1811; he then concentrated on repairs.

Bausch, Ludwig Christian August (1805–71). German bow maker. He studied in Dresden. After working in Russia, Dresden, Dessau and Wiesbaden he established Ludwig Bausch & Son in Leipzig in 1865. His bows are flexible and sturdy and combine the best of French and German styles. Under his sons Otto and Ludwig the firm produced bows until 1908.

Beare. English family of violin dealers and restorers. John (1842–1928) became a dealer in 1865. In 1892 he divided his business: Beare & Son, established with his son Walter, are wholesalers of new instruments and accessories; John & Arthur Beare (originally Beare, Goodwin and Co.) specialize in early instruments. John's son Arthur (1875–1945) studied the violin in Leipzig before joining the firm. He had an excellent reputation as both craftsman and dealer. His son William Arthur (*b* 1910) studied in Mirecourt and worked in the firm from 1929, succeeding as chairman in 1954. He made more than 30 violins and was an authority on early instruments. His stepson, Charles (*b* 1937), trained in Mittenwald and New York and joined the firm in 1961; he specializes in restoration.

Becker. American family of violin makers. Carl G. Becker (1887–1975), grandson of the violin maker Herman Maklett, worked in Chicago for Lyon & Healy and John Hornsteiner, then joined William Lewis & Son as repair shops supervisor. He also made instruments under his own name and (from 1936) with his son Carl F. Becker (*b* 1919). They introduced improvements in restoration, particularly of varnish, and in 1968 set up their own workshop. Geraldine (*b* 1955) works with her father.

Bellarosa, Vittorio (*b* 1907). Italian violin maker. He studied at Mittenwald, with Vito in Rotello and with Fredi in Rome before settling in Naples (*c*1930). His violins are Neapolitan in style and resemble the Gagliano school. They are often mistaken for early 19th-century instruments.

Bellini, Luiz (*b* 1935). American violin maker. Born in Brazil of Italian parents, he studied wood carving at the Escola Technica Getulio Vargas and was then apprenticed to Guido Pascoli. He moved to the USA in 1960 and worked for Rembert Wurlitzer (1960–68) and Jacques Français (1968–75) as a restorer before making violins independently in Jackson Heights, NJ. He has three main models: Guarneri del Gesù's 'Lord Wilton' (1742) and 'Kreisler' (1733), and Stradivari's 'Baron Knoop' (1715). He is considered the best contemporary Guarneri copyist and has developed a varnish similar to the original Cremonese in appearance. His violins are branded as well as bearing a label.

Bellosio, Anselmo (1743–93). Italian violin maker, active in Venice. He probably trained under Giorgio Seraphin, whom he succeeded in business in 1777. Owing to their fine quality, his instruments have been attributed to earlier and better-known makers. His pupils and successors Pietro Novello and Marco Antonio Cerin were unable to sustain the business, effectively ending the 18th-century Venetian school of violin making.

Benti, Matteo (?1579–after 1660). Italian instrument maker. His instruments were prized by his contemporaries, but no extant instrument can be definitely attributed to him.

Beretta, Felice (*fl* 1758–89). Italian violin maker, active in Como. His better instruments are similar to those of Giuseppe Guadagnini, with whom he probably studied, but are inferior in craftsmanship.

Bergonzi. Italian family of violin makers, active in Cremona in the 18th century. Carlo (1683–1747) probably studied with the Guarneris and for many years may not have had his own workshop. His best violins, influenced by Stradivari and Guarneri models, were made in 1730–40. The slightly inferior work of his son Michel Angelo (*c*1722–after 1758) is evident in his later violins. Michel Angelo continued the Cremonese tradition apart from the varnish, which he either did not inherit or abandoned, and the secret was lost. His son Nicola (after 1746–after 1796) made violins of varying quality. The work of Nicola's brothers, Carlo and Zosima, is almost unknown.

Bernardel. French family of violin makers. Auguste Sébastien Philippe (1798–1870) was apprenticed in Mirecourt before working for Lupot and C. F. Gand in Paris. From 1826 he worked independently in Paris, producing violins and cellos mostly patterned on Stradivari. His sons Ernest Auguste (1826–99) and Gustave Adolphe (1832–1904) succeeded him in 1866 and joined Gand Frères to form Gand & Bernardel Frères; the business passed to Albert Caressa in 1901. Other members of the family include Auguste Sébastien's brother Louis (1806–47), and Léon (1953–1931), son of Ernest Auguste, who had a shop in Paris from 1898.

Bertolotti, Gasparo. *See* GASPARO DA SALÒ.

Betts, John (1755–1823). English violin maker and dealer. He worked in London from 1780. His early violins resemble those of his teacher Richard Duke, but by 1790 he was making instruments that show the influence of Stradivari. He employed the best craftsmen, who continued to produce instruments and bows of all qualities after his son took over the business. One of the first to import Italian instruments, he bought the 'Betts' Stradivari (1704) for £1. The firm, Arthur & John Betts, closed *c*1850.

Burgess, David (*b* 1953). American violin maker. He trained as a violinist until he was 18, but had begun to repair violins by 1967 and worked for David Saunders in Seattle (1968–71), then for Hans Weisshaar in Los Angeles (1971–6) as a repairman. His personal model is based on the Stradivari pattern and he has won many awards, the first in 1974. His instruments are signed on the inside of the soundboard as well as bearing a label.

Cahusac. English family of makers, dealers and music publishers. They made woodwind instruments and violins. Thomas (i) (*d* 1798) worked at the sign of the Two Flutes and Violin (later 196 Strand) and was known as the oldest maker in London. His son Thomas (ii) (*fl* 1781–1814) worked independently in London until 1794, when he joined his father and his brother William (*fl* 1794–1816); the firm became Cahusac & Sons (later T. & Wm. Cahusac). Thomas (ii) moved to different premises in 1800; William continued the family business until 1816.

Calcagni, Bernardo (*fl* *c*1710–50). Italian violin maker, active in Genoa. Most of his violins are average instruments, patterned after Stradivari and Guarneri models. Late in life he formed a partnership with Antonio Pazarini (*c*1720–44).

Camilli, Camillo (*c*1704–1754). Italian violin maker. He worked in Mantua, where he may have been a pupil of Antonio Zanotti. His violins resemble those of Pietro Guarneri, who also worked in Mantua, but have Amati-like scrolls.

Calvarola, Bartolommeo (*fl* Bergamo and Bologna, *c*1750–75). Italian violin maker. His violins are based on the model of Francesco Rugeri, but are more slender and are unique in the narrow cutting of their scrolls. His violas and cellos are more full-bodied.

Candi, Cesare (1869–1947). Italian violin maker. He studied with Raffaele Fiorini in Bologna, then joined his brother Oreste (1865–1938) in Genoa. He won distinction at exhibitions throughout Italy for his violins, which combine elements of Stradivari and Amati. He also made bows and other instruments, some elaborately inlaid, including guitars, lutes and mandolins.

Capela, Antonio (*b* 1932). Portuguese violin maker. He was taught by his father, Domingos (1904–79), then studied in Paris, Mirecourt and Cremona. His instruments are patterned after Stradivari, Guarneri 'del

VIOLIN FAMILY

Gesù' and Montagnana, and have won many honours at international competitions.

Carcassi. Italian family of violin makers. Lorenzo and Tomaso (both *fl* c1750–80) worked in Florence. Their many instruments resemble those of G. B. Gabbrielli, with whom they may have studied, but appear strongly influenced by Stainer. The quality is variable.

Casini, Antonio (c1630–after 1705). Italian violin maker; he worked for the Duke of Modena, supplying violins and other instruments. The best of his few surviving instruments are the violas and double basses, and the violins patterned after the large Amati model.

Castagneri, Andrea (*fl* c1730–60). Italian violin maker; he studied with his father, Gian Paolo, a Cremonese maker who worked in Paris. He is regarded as the best maker in Paris in the mid-18th century. His instruments combine elements of both French and Italian schools; similar violins are sometimes misattributed to him.

Castello, Paulo (*fl* c1750–80). Italian violin maker, active in Genoa. His violins, loosely patterned after the Stradivari model, rarely show good craftsmanship apart from the soundholes, but the varnish is good and they have a warm tone.

Catenari [Catenar, Gatenar], **Enrico** (*fl* 1671–1720). Italian violin maker. Active in Turin, he was associated with Goffredo Cappa, as either pupil or teacher; both were strongly influenced by Amati. The workmanship and tone of Catenari's instruments are good.

Catlin, George (1777 or 1778–1852). American instrument maker. He worked in Hartford, Conn., and in Philadelphia after 1815, making woodwind, string and keyboard instruments. His violins are rare.

Celoniato, Giovanni Francesco (*fl* c1720–54). Italian violin maker. He was a pupil of Goffredo Cappa in Saluzzo before settling in Turin. His instruments show influences of Amati, Stradivari and Bergonzi, but have individual characteristics. Their good craftsmanship is not reflected in their tone, which is consistent only in the cellos.

Cerin, Marco Antonio (1774–after 1808). Italian violin maker. One of the last significant makers of the 18th-century Venetian school, he studied with Anselmo Bellosio, assisting in the making of Bellosio's last instruments.

Ceruti. Italian family of violin makers. Giovanni Battista (c1755–after 1817) worked in Cremona. He was the pupil and successor of Lorenzo Storioni, whom he surpassed in craftsmanship and individuality. He was succeeded by his son Giuseppe (c1787–1860), whose instruments are similar to his father's. Giuseppe's son Enrico (1808–83) retained both the Cremonese influence and his family's individuality in his violins; he was a prolific maker.

Chanot. French family of violin makers. Joseph Chanot worked in

254

Mirecourt in 1780. His son François (1787–1823) invented a guitar-shaped instrument on his own concept of acoustical principles, with a flat table and no soundpost (examples are in the Paris Conservatoire). François' brother Georges (i) (1801–73) studied with Simon Lété. He worked in Paris and was second only to J.-B. Vuillaume as a copyist of Stradivari and Guarneri; he was also a dealer and restorer. His son-in-law Joseph Chardon succeeded to the business. Georges (ii) (1831–93), son of Georges (i), worked in London from 1851. His sons Georges-Adolphe (1855–1911) and Joseph-Anthony (1865–1936) worked in Manchester and London respectively.

Chardon, André (1887–1963). French bow maker. He was the grandson of Joseph Marie Chardon (1843–1930), who had succeeded Georges Chanot; he studied in Paris with his father, Georges (1870–1949). His bows, made after the Dominique Peccatte model, are among the best by 20th-century makers. He was also an eminent violin maker.

Chiocchi, Gaetano (1814–81). Italian violin maker. He studied philosophy, medicine and music, and became music director of Padua's ballet theatre. Apparently self-taught, he made violins that are a highly original version of the Brescian concept and have outstanding tonal qualities. They are often inlaid with a five-layer purfling. His output was small.

Chrétien, Hippolyte. French violin maker. *See* SILVESTRE.

Clagget, Charles (1740–95). Irish violinist and inventor. In 1776 he settled in London to devote himself to the mechanical improvement of instruments, including the tuning and temperament of violins and keyboard instruments. None of his devices survived.

Clutterbuck, John (*b* 1949). English bow maker. He was apprenticed to W. E. Hill & Sons and worked briefly for the firm before establishing a partnership with Stephen Bristow; they worked jointly under the name J. S. Rameau. Clutterbuck set up independently in Bicester in 1977.

Collin-Mezin, Charles Jean Baptiste (1841–1923). French violin maker. After studying in Mirecourt, he worked for C. F. Vuillaume in Brussels before establishing himself in Paris in 1867. He had an excellent reputation in his own time, but his instruments, though precisely made on the Mirecourt Stradivari model, are not outstanding; tonally, the cellos have matured better than the violins and violas. He was among the first to advocate the use of metal A and E strings for violins.

Contreras, José (*fl* c1740–75). Spanish violin maker. He worked in Madrid but may have studied in Italy. One of the first repairmen, he worked on several Stradivari instruments which became the model for his own violins. His work compares favourably with that of his Italian contemporaries. He was succeeded by his son José (*d* 1827).

Cordano, Jacopo [Giacomo] **Fillippo** (*fl* Genoa, mid- to late 18th century). The labelling and dating of his instruments are uncertain, partly due to the existence of two different models, both of the Amati type, bearing his name. His cellos and larger violins show his best work.

Corte, Alfonso dalla (*fl* Naples, *c*1860–85). Italian violin maker. His instruments are patterned mainly after the Gagliano school, though his work is heavier. Despite his individual style, anonymous instruments have been misattributed to him.

Costa, Felix Mori (*fl* Parma, *c*1800–25). Italian violin maker. His violins are reminiscent of Landolfi's small model; most are made of plain wood but with varnish of good texture.

Costa, Pietro Antonio dalla [della] (*c*1740–68). Italian violin maker. He worked principally in Treviso, and possibly in Mantua and Venice. His violins are expertly made after the model of the Amati brothers. Mozart owned one of his instruments; otherwise he was little known and few of his violins survive. The theory that there were two makers, Pietro and Antonio dalla Costa, is unsupported.

Craske, George (1795–1888). English violin maker of German descent. He is reputed to have been a pupil of William Forster and to have made his earliest instruments for Thomas Dodd and Clementi & Co. He worked in Leeds, Sheffield, Manchester and Salford, then settled in Stockport. Most of his violins follow the Guarneri 'del Gesù' model; the rest, as well as the violas and cellos, are patterned after Stradivari. His instruments are strongly made and powerful, but lack Italian timbre. After his death W. E. Hill & Sons sold his remaining stock under a joint label.

Cross, Nathaniel (*fl* London, *c*1720–51). English violin maker. His instruments are patterned after Stainer and are distinctive for their purfling, which is set in a groove. His best work was done after he became a partner of Barak Norman around 1715.

Cunha, José da (*b* 1955). American bow maker. He was apprenticed to William Salchow in New York and joined his workshop. His bows are modelled after the Tourte–Peccatte school.

Cuypers [Kuypers, Kuppers], **Johannes Theodorus** (1724–1808). Dutch violin maker, active in The Hague. He was one of the first makers in northern Europe to work on the Stradivari pattern, though with distinctive personal details. His sons, Johannes Franciscus (1766–1828) and Johannes Bernardus (1781–1840), were less distinguished makers.

Dall'aglio [Dalaglio], **Giuseppe Joseph** (*fl* Mantua, 1795–1840). Italian violin maker. His instruments reflect the influences of Pietro Guarneri and Camillo Camilli. They are of robust build and individual character, with the curve of the centre bouts cut to swing deeper than usual.

D'Attili, Dario (*b* 1922). American violin maker and restorer, of Italian birth. He studied at the Emil Herrmann workshop, New York, with Fernando Sacconi and worked with him until Sacconi died (1973). They joined REMBERT WURLITZER in 1950; D'Attili was manager in 1964–74 and then became associated with William Moennig & Son, Philadelphia. His instruments are patterned after the old Italians, especially Pietro Guarneri, and show a keen understanding of their sound and workmanship. He is an authority on old instruments.

De Comble, Ambroise (*fl* Tournay, *c*1740–85). Netherlands violin maker. The theory that he was a pupil of Stradivari is not supported by the style of his work, which combines Italian and Flemish elements. His violins, of consistently good quality, have unusual features, such as low-cut soundholes.

Deconet, Michele (*c*1712–after 1780). Italian violin maker of Alsatian birth, active in Venice. Initially a soldier and violinist, he probably studied violin making with Pietro Guarneri, though his work is equally influenced by Montagnana. He was the most prolific Venetian maker after about 1750; his earlier violins are his best.

Degani. Italian family of violin makers. Its most important member, Eugenio (1840–1915), studied with his father, Domenico (1820–87). He worked in Montagnana and Trieste and settled in Venice after 1888. His instruments have strong individual details and are scrupulously made, after his own model or those of the great 18th-century makers. His son and pupil Giulio Ettore (1875–1953) joined the business in 1898, when it became Degani e Figlio, and moved to Cincinnati in 1935; he returned to Venice in 1943. His violins, equal to Eugenio's, are based on the Stradivari model. (Some inferior, spurious instruments bearing his label have appeared in America.) Eugenio's nephew and pupil Giovanni Schwarz (*d* 1952) may have collaborated on instruments bearing Eugenio's label after 1900.

Derazy, (Jean Joseph) Honoré (1794–1883). French violin maker. He worked in several workshops in Mirecourt and Paris including that of J.-B. Vuillaume, where he made many of the violins with inlaid work and carved scrolls in the style of Tieffenbrucker (known as the 'Duiffoprugcar' violins). His best work is mostly based on the Stradivari model. Good instruments carrying his label were made by assistants, though not to his standard. His son and pupil Justin Amadée (1839–90), a prolific though not outstanding maker, succeeded him after 1879.

D'Espine, Alessandro [Alexandre] (*b* 1775; *fl* Turin, 1823–46). Italian violin maker, probably of French origin. He was reputedly a pupil of G. B. Ceruti in Cremona and was associated with Pressenda in Turin, but his instruments retain a French character. His craftsmanship was invariably good, but the violins patterned after the Guarneri 'del Gesù' model are better tonally than those after Stradivari.

Dodd. English family of bow makers and instrument sellers, active in London. Most 18th-century English bows are unmarked, but have been attributed to Edward Dodd (i) (1705–1810). His son John (1752–1839) was the greatest English bow maker before Tubbs. He probably began to make bows between 1780 and 1790, before the improvements that had occurred in France had reached England. His later bows incorporate all the innovations and are of high quality, though modern players find the violin and viola bows too short. John's brother Thomas (d 1834) was a music seller and dealer as well as a maker. Violins from his shop were of good quality, modelled after Stradivari, and most were probably made by assistants, including Bernard Fendt and Lott senior. Bows sold under his brand include some by Thomas Tubbs. James (i) (d after 1824) worked with his father, Edward (i), c1802–7. His sons, James (ii) (1792–1865) and Edward (ii) (1797–1851), worked together as bow makers until 1832; Edward then made only violin strings. James made many bows for the trade, including Betts; his early cello bows show much of his best work.

Duke, Richard (*fl* c1750–85). English violin maker. He may have been a pupil of Wamsley or Thomas Smith. Regarded by his contemporaries as the best maker in London, he greatly improved the London school of instrument making. He taught Joseph Hill, John and Edward Betts, and his son Richard. His Stradivari copies rank among the best English violins, though most of his instruments were on the Stainer model. He also made violas and cellos. Many worthless 19th-century imitations bear his name.

Eberle, Johann Ulrich (1699–1768). Austro-Bohemian string instrument maker. He was apprenticed in Vils before studying in Prague with Thomas Edlinger. His best violins are modelled on Italian lines, resembling but surpassing Edlinger's. His violas d'amore are much in demand.

Eberle, Tomaso (*fl* Naples, c1753–92). Italian violin maker, probably of Austrian (Tyrolean) ancestry. Probably a pupil of Nicola Gagliano and one of the best followers of the Gagliano school, Eberle made instruments that vary from their model in the purfling, scrolls and soundholes. Tonally they are warmer but less powerful.

Edlinger, Thomas (1662–1729). Bohemian violin maker of German birth. He trained in Augsburg before settling in Prague. A fine teacher, he is considered the founder of the old Prague school. His work loosely follows the Stainer model. He was succeeded by his son, Joseph Joachim (1693–1748), who continued to follow his model despite visits to Italy.

Emiliani, Francesco (*fl* Rome, c1700–c1740). Italian violin maker. Like many of his contemporaries, he followed either the Stainer or Amati patterns. His instruments are slender and well made, with similarities to those of his teacher David Tecchler.

APPENDIX TWO

Eulry, Clément (*fl* late 18th–early 19th century). French bow maker. Now believed to have been the teacher rather than the pupil of Nicolas Maire or Pajeot *fils*, he made bows similar to theirs but less carefully finished. He is thought to be the first maker to use a metal thumb facing on the frog.

Eury, Nicolas (*fl* Paris, 1810–30). French bow maker. He was a member of a Mirecourt family of violin makers. His work is comparable to that of Tourte. His bows are rare and details of his work are confused, because many bows were probably unstamped and other makers' bows have been stamped with his name.

Fabris, Luigi (*fl* Venice, *c*1850–80). Italian violin maker. His instruments are based on a flat model, mostly after the Guarneri 'del Gesù' pattern, with some after Stradivari. Lack of care in the craftsmanship is balanced by a good, robust tone. Many flat-modelled violins have been misattributed to Fabris.

Fagnola, Annibale (*c*1865–1939). Italian violin maker. He worked in Turin from 1890, making reproductions, chiefly of Pressenda's instruments, which were often sold as originals. By 1905 he was working under his own label, exporting most of his instruments to England. His personal model has been widely copied.

Fendt. English family of violin makers of Austrian origin, active in London. Bernard (1756–1832), who may have been related to the Paris maker François Fent, went to England via Paris and worked for Thomas Dodd from 1800, then for Betts. The eldest of his four sons, Bernard Simon (1800–51), was an outstanding workman; he was employed by Betts before forming a partnership with George Purdy. Martin (1812–?*c*1850) and Francis did little work; Jacob (1815–49) is believed to have made imitations of Guarneri instruments.

Fétique. French family of bow makers. Victor (1872–1933) was apprenticed in Mirecourt and worked there for C. N. Bazin before joining Caressa & Français in Paris in 1901; he worked independently from 1913. His bows are patterned after the Voirin model, but lack distinction. Victor's brother Jules (1875–1951) also worked for Bazin, then became assistant to Eugène Sartory; he joined Caressa & Français in 1917. His best work resembles and is comparable to Sartory's.

Finkel. Swiss bow makers. They continued the line of bow makers started by Ewald WEIDHAAS in Markneukirchen. Siegfried Finkel (*b* 1927) was apprenticed to Ewald's son Paul and joined his workshop. (He also became Paul's son-in-law.) He worked independently in Brienz from 1952. His bows are well-made Germanic interpretations of the Peccatte model. Siegfried's son and pupil Johannes (*b* 1947) worked for Beare in London, Weisshaar in Los Angeles and Moennig & Son in Philadelphia, and returned to his father's workshop in 1974. His early work was also based on the Peccatte model. Reproductions of earlier makers followed, but since his return to Brienz his bows have shown French as well as German characteristics.

Fiorini, Giuseppe (1861–1934). Italian violin maker. He was trained by his father, Raffaele Fiorini, in Bologna, where he worked until 1888. In 1889 he moved to Munich, where he established the firm Rieger & Fiorini, and in 1915 moved to Zurich. He returned to Italy in 1923 and established himself in Rome in 1927. He made an extensive study of Stradivari's tools and methods and maintained an Italian style despite his long association with German violin making. His work is elegant and he is regarded as one of the finest 20th-century Italian makers. His instruments are branded under the tailpiece as well as bearing a label.

Fonclause, Joseph (1800–64). French bow maker. He studied in Mirecourt and worked for Tourte, Lupot and J.-B. Vuillaume in Paris before setting up independently c1840. His bows have an odd sweep along the front ridge but are otherwise typical of his time. Few bows bear his own brand, but he produced many for Vuillaume.

Forster. English family of violin makers and music publishers. William (i) (1739–1808) was taught by his father in Cumberland before settling in London in 1759. At first he made copies of Stainer instruments, then (from c1770) worked after Cremonese models, particularly the Amatis. His output included cellos and double basses (three were made for the king). The earliest known violins by his son, William (ii) (1764–1824), were made in 1779. The two worked together, identifying their instruments by adding 'Senr' or 'Junr' to the printed label. Their cellos were owned by all leading English cellists of the time. Though mostly patterned after Amati, some are in the style of Stainer and later instruments show the influence of Stradivari. William (ii) took over the publishing side in 1786. His son Simon Andrew (1801–70), also a maker, succeeded to the business and wrote, with W. Sandys, *The History of the Violin* (1864).

Français, Jacques Pierre (*b* 1923). American violin dealer and restorer, of French birth. He came of a family that first worked with Nicolas Lupot. He studied with Victor Aubry in Le Havre and Georges Apparut in Mirecourt, then worked for Wurlitzer in New York and later established his own business there. He is America's leading dealer, restorer and repairman.

Gabbrielli, Giovanni Battista (*fl* c1740–70). Italian violin maker. The most significant of the 18th-century Florentine makers, he may also have taught his colleagues. His work was influenced by Stainer but his violins are usually closer to a Cremonese model. He also made violas and cellos.

Gaggini, Pierre (*b* 1903). French violin maker. He studied with his uncle Albert Louis Blanchi (1871–1942) before establishing himself in Nice. He attracted a strong following, especially in France, and won several awards. His violins and cellos are based on the Stradivari model; the violas are similar to the 'Tertis' model. Bows carrying his stamp were usually made by others and finished by Gaggini.

Gagliano. Italian family of violin makers, active in Naples. Their large output includes fine 18th-century instruments, but the quality declined with the increased demand of the 19th century. Alessandro (*fl* c1700–c1735) was the first known Neapolitan maker. His instruments, made on his own model, have great character and the cellos are especially good. Violins made by his sons Nicola (i) (*fl* c1740–c1780) and Gennaro [Januarius] (*fl* c1740–c1780) are considered the best of the Gaglianos. Nicola was influenced by Stradivari; Gennaro, the better craftsman, made copies of Amati and Stradivari. Both made cellos on the Stradivari model and introduced the narrow design later followed by most Neapolitan makers. Nicola's son Ferdinando (*fl* c1770–c1795) was probably taught by Gennaro, whose style he followed. Ferdinando's three brothers collaborated to some extent: Giuseppe [Joseph] (*fl* c1770–c1800) was taught by his father and his early work was excellent, but instruments made later with Antonio (i) (*fl* c1780–c1800) are inferior to his own; Giovanni [Johannes] (*fl* c1785–after 1815), whose instruments are similar to those of Gennaro and Ferdinando, worked independently from c1800. Giovanni's sons, Nicola (ii) (*fl* c1800–c1825), Raffaele (*d* 1857) and Antonio (ii) (*d* 1860), were competent but undistinguished makers.

Gagliano, Carlo (*fl* late 18th century). Italian violin maker. He worked in Belluno and was not connected with the Gagliano family of Naples.

Gand. French family of violin makers. Charles Michel worked first in Mirecourt, then (c1780) moved to Versailles. His son François, 'Gand *père*' (1787–1845), studied with Nicolas Lupot, worked briefly with his father and then for the dealer and restorer Köliker in Paris. In 1820 he purchased Köliker's business and in 1824 succeeded Lupot, whose daughter he had married. His few surviving instruments are excellent. His brother Guillaume Charles Louis (1792–1858) worked for Lupot before succeeding his father in Versailles; his instruments resemble Lupot's. Gand *père*'s sons Charles Adolpe (1812–66) and Charles Nicolas Eugène (1825–92) made few instruments. They inherited the business, which became Gand Frères in 1855. On Charles Adolphe's death the firm merged with BERNARDEL, becoming Gand & Bernardel Frères.

Garimberti, Ferdinando (*b* 1894; *d*). Italian violin maker. Initially a cellist, he began making violins on the advice of the Antoniazzi brothers and worked independently in Milan. His instruments were made on a personal model inspired by Stradivari. He won several awards and was associated with the international school of violin making in Cremona.

VIOLIN FAMILY

Gasparo da Salò [Bertolotti] (1540–1609). Italian maker of string instruments. He came of a family of makers and in 1562 settled in Brescia, working first with Girolama Virchi and then independently. Most in demand are his tenor violas (see fig. 28*a*), many of which have been reduced in size, and his double basses, which were championed by Dragonetti. He also made violins, viols and a cittern. His son Francesco (*b* 1565) continued the family trade, but Gasparo's position as leading maker in Brescia was taken over by his pupil Maggini.

Gatenar, Enrico. *See* CATENARI, ENRICO.

Geissenhof, Franz (1754–1821). Austrian violin maker. He was apprenticed to Johann Georg Thir in Vienna and succeeded him. His style evolved gradually from old Viennese to direct copying of Stradivari. In this respect his career parallels that of his contemporary Lupot in Paris: they both surpassed ordinary origins to become skilled interpreters of the work of Stradivari.

Gennaro, Giacomo [Januarius, Jacobus] (*fl* Cremona, *c*1640–55). Italian violin maker. He studied with Nicolo Amati, whose pattern he followed so closely that many of his instruments have been attributed to that maker. Instruments are rarely found under his original label, on which he used the latinized form of his name.

Gigli, Giulio Cesare (*fl* Rome, *c*1720–62). Italian violin maker. Working in the style of Tecchler, he made instruments differing in the waists, edges and scrolls, but matching Tecchler's in elegance.

Gilkes, Samuel (1787–1827). English violin maker. He was a pupil of Charles Harris and worked for William Forster and possibly for Betts. His small output favoured the Amati model, though some violins were patterned after Stradivari; his late instruments are particularly fine. His son and successor, William (1811–75), did not match him, but his double basses are in demand.

Gillet, Louis (1891–1970). French bow maker. He was apprenticed in Mirecourt and had workshops there, in Nancy and in Chalon-sur-Saône. He made bows for Eugène Sartory and Georges Dupuy and many, unstamped, for the trade, but kept the best for his own brand.

Gobetti, Francesco (1675–1723). Italian violin maker. Originally a shoemaker, he probably studied violin making with Matteo Goffriller. He worked only from *c*1710 to 1717, but ranks among the greatest Venetian makers for the tonal and visual qualities of his violins, which resemble those of Goffriller and Montagnana.

Goffriller [Gofriller], **Matteo** (*c*1659–1742). Italian string instrument maker. The first important Venetian maker, Goffriller is presumed to have studied with Martin Kaiser, to whose business he succeeded in 1690. There is wide variety in the patterns and quality of his work and many instruments have been attributed to more famous makers. He is best known for his cellos based on the large Amati pattern, most of which have since been cut down. His son Francesco (1692–*c*1740) worked in Venice and Udine but was less productive.

Gragnani, Antonio (*fl* Livorno, *c*1765–95). Italian violin maker. Though he probably studied in Florence, his instruments are similar to those of Stradivari in concept, with enlongated scrolls. His use of whalebone for the black purfling was almost unique in Italy. He was succeeded by his son Onorato.

Grancino, Giovanni (*fl* *c*1685–*c*1726). Italian violin maker. He was the most important maker in Milan before Guadagnini and Landolfi. His instruments, inspired by the Amati model, show competent workmanship but are made with less expensive wood than those of his Cremonese contemporaries. He made many cellos, most of them very large and since cut down. It is uncertain whether he had any connection with other makers named Grancino. Carlo Giuseppe Testore was his best pupil.

Grimm, Karl (1794–1855). German maker of string instruments. He was maker to the royal court in Berlin and had a reputation not only for his bowed string instruments patterned after Italian makers, but also for his harps. His business was taken over by C. Hellmig in 1851.

Guadagnini. Italian family of violin makers. Lorenzo (before 1690–1748) worked in Piacenza and possibly in Cremona with Giuseppe Guarneri (*b* 1666) or Carlo Bergonzi. His son Giovanni Battista [J. B.] (*c*1711–1786) was the most important Italian maker of the mid- to late 18th century. In 1740–49 Giovanni worked with his father in Piacenza and developed a personal model, then moved to Milan, where he made his finest instruments. His violins made after 1759 in Parma are unique for the position and style of their soundholes, and those made after 1771 in Turin were much influenced by the Stradivari instruments owned by his patron Count Cozio di Salabue. His own model was not copied for 100 years. His son Giuseppe, 'Il soldato' (*fl* *c*1770–1805), worked independently in Como, Pavia and Milan. Giuseppe's brother Gaetano (*d* 1831) worked with his father in Turin and remained there. Descendants continued working into the 20th century; they included Felice, Carlo, another Gaetano, Antonio and Francesco.

Guarneri. Italian family of violin makers. Andrea (*c*1626–1698) studied and worked with Nicolo Amati in Cremona, but his instruments show a distinctive personal concept. His output included small (alto) violas and he was among the first to make small cellos. His son Pietro Giovanni, 'da Mantova' (1655–1720), worked with him from *c*1670, but by 1683 had settled in Mantua, where he was also a court musician. His instruments are similar to his father's, but more carefully made. Pietro's brother Giuseppe Giovanni Battista (1666–1739 or 1740), one of the greatest makers, stayed in Cremona and inherited his father's business in 1698, though his influence is evident from 1680. He developed an original style that is closer to his brother's than to Andrea's. There are no violins with his label later than 1720. His sons Pietro and Giuseppe worked with him from c1715. Pietro, 'da Venezia' (1695–1762), later settled in Venice, where he worked under his own label from 1730. His style became a blend of the Cremonese and Venetian schools and his cellos were particularly successful. (Bartolomeo) Giuseppe, 'del Gesù' (1698–1744), shares Stradivari's reputation as the greatest of all makers. He developed a unique style that combined his father's model with other influences, including Stradivari and the Brescians, and produced instruments outstanding for their craftsmanship and the power and beauty of their tone. His nickname derives from his cipher IHS.

Guersan, Louis (c1713–after 1781). French violin maker. He was a pupil of Claude Pierray and succeeded to his business, producing violins, violas, quintons and pardessus viols based on his own model but similar to Pierray's. His best work is excellent.

Guillami, Juan (fl c1720–65). Spanish violin maker. He worked in Barcelona, but had probably studied in Italy because his instruments, largely after Stradivari, are reminiscent of the 18th-century Gagliano school. His son, Juan (d c1818–20), failed to gain recognition.

Hardie, Matthew (1755–1826). Scottish violin maker. He may have been taught by John Blair, who later became his assistant, or by Panormo. While based on early Stradivari and Amati models, his violins are not copies, unlike those of his English contemporaries. His pupils included his son Thomas (1802–58), his cousin Peter Hardie and David Stirrat.

Hart. English family of violin makers and dealers. John Thomas (1805–74) was a pupil of Samuel Gilkes and opened his own business in London c1825. Primarily a dealer, he formed collections of early instruments. His son George (i) (1839–91), who continued the business as Hart & Son, is known chiefly for his writings on violins. He was succeeded by his sons, George (ii) (1860–c1931) and Herbert (1883–1953), who expanded the trade to include new instruments made in France and by the VOLLER brothers. The firm closed in 1939.

Hel, (Pierre) Joseph (1842–1902). French violin maker. He studied with Salzard in Mirecourt and worked for Sébastien Vuillaume in Paris and Nicolas Darche at Aix-la-Chapelle before establishing himself in Lille in 1865. His violins, patterned after the great Cremonese makers, rank among the best of the French school. His son Pierre Jean Henri (1884–1937) succeeded him in 1902, after studying at the Bazin workshop in Mirecourt. He won international awards for his instruments and was an expert restorer.

Henry, Joseph (1823–70). French bow maker. He studied in Paris with Peccatte, with whose work his is often confused. He made bows

for dealers such as Chanot and Gand Frères, and worked briefly with
SIMON. He established his own business in Paris in 1851.

Hill. English firm of violin and bow makers, restorers and valuers.
Joseph (1715–84) was a pupil of Peter Wamsley before establishing his
own business in London. His work was of variable quality, but was
refined and elegant at its best and his cellos are made on a good pattern.
His son William (1745–90) probably assisted him before setting up
independently, working after his father's patterns. William's brother
Lockey (1756–1810), a prolific but inferior maker, was surpassed by
his son Henry Lockey, 'the second Lockey Hill' (1774–1835). Henry
Lockey worked for John Betts before opening his own business in
Southwark *c*1810. He was influenced by instruments he saw while
working for Betts, especially those by Stradivari and Vincenzo
Panormo; his violins and cellos are among the best English instruments.
He was assisted by his son Joseph (*c*1805–1837), a talented craftsman.
Joseph's brother William Ebsworth (1817–95) pioneered techniques of
restoration that saved many fine instruments. Under his sons William
Henry (1857–1927), Arthur Frederick (1860–1939), Alfred Ebsworth
(1862–1940) and Walter Edgar (1871–1905) the business contributed to
the history of the violin through restoration, research and publications
(Alfred Ebsworth was the world expert on old violins). The firm also
produced new instruments, partly in the French tradition, and a bow
workshop was created in the 1890s. A team of makers, working after
the pattern of Samuel Allen, developed a bow of uniquely English style
and set an unequalled standard for quality. The business continued
under (Albert) Phillips Hill (1883–1981), his son Desmond (d'Artrey)
(*b* 1916) and Desmond's sons Andrew Phillip (*b* 1942) and David
Roderick (*b* 1952). The firm moved to Great Missenden, Buckinghamshire, in 1974.

Hoffmann, Johann Christian (1683–1750). German maker of string
instruments, the most famous of a family active in Leipzig between
1650 and 1750. He made instruments for the Dresden court and for J. S.
Bach. His instruments include all the standard members of the violin
family and the violoncello piccolo, as well as lutes, theorbos and viols.
His brother Christian Gottlieb (1691–1735) made violins and viols.

Hofmans, Mathijs (*fl* Antwerp, *c*1670–*c*1700). Belgian violin maker.
He was probably a pupil of Hendrik Willems of Ghent. Considered the
greatest of Belgian makers, he was influenced by the Amatis and made
violins noted for their elegance and tonal excellence.

Homolka, Ferdinand (August Vincenč) (1828–90). Bohemian
violin maker. The leading member of a family of makers, he studied
with his father, Emanuel Adam (1796–1849). He worked for various
makers in Prague, Vienna and Linz, and independently in Prague from
1857. His instruments are well made and he was the family's most
successful copyist of the Stradivari model. Other makers included his

uncle Ferdinand Joseph (1810–62), his brother Vincenč Emanuel (1826–61), his son Eduard Emanuel Karel (1860–1933) and his grandson Eduard Ferdinand (1896–1915).

Horil, Jakob (*fl* c1720–60). Violin maker of Bohemian descent. He worked in Vienna and in Rome. His earlier instruments, after the Stainer model, indicate Tyrolean training, but his later violins show Italian influence. His work is superior to similar models by his German and Austrian contemporaries.

Husson. The name of several French bow makers. Claude-Charles (1811–93) was a founder member of Jérome Thibouville-Lamy & Cie. Charles Claude (i) (*fl* mid-19th century) taught Alfred Lamy and J. A. Vigneron. His bows resemble those of early Parisian makers. His son and pupil Charles Claude (ii) (1847–1915) was apprenticed to J.-B. Vuillaume and A. J. Lamy and worked for Gand & Bernardel Frères before working independently in Paris. His bows are similar to his father's, but heavier in build. August (1870–1930) was no relation of the above. He worked for Vuillaume, Bazin and Thomassin, and for Vigneron, whose style he followed; he later worked independently in Paris.

Jacobsz [Jacobs], **Hendrik** (1629 or 1630–99). Netherlands violin maker, active in Amsterdam. He was the most celebrated of Netherlands makers, but few instruments made entirely by him survive. His copies of the Amati 'grand pattern' are elegant, with distinctive jet-black whalebone for the dark purfling and varnish of Italian quality. His stepson, PIETER ROMBOUTS, assisted and later succeeded him.

Januarius, Jacobus. *See* GENNARO, GIACOMO.

Johnson, John (*fl* London, c1745–62). English violin maker. His violins, based on the Stainer model, show uneven craftsmanship. His fairly consistent use of maple is unusual for his time.

Kennedy, Thomas (1784–1870). English violin maker. The son and pupil of John Kennedy (c1730–1816), he came of a family that included several violin makers. Before establishing himself in London, he worked for Thomas Powell and William Forster. His cellos and double basses show his best work.

Klotz [Kloz]. German family of violin makers, active in Mittenwald. The most famous Klotz instruments date from the 18th century. Mathias (1653–1743), the first violin maker in Mittenwald, was apprenticed to the Paduan lute maker Giovanni Railich and seems not to have made violins until long after his return to Mittenwald in 1678. His instruments show both Italian and German influences. Of his sons, Georg (1687–1737), Sebastian (1696–c1760) and Johann Carl (1709–c1770), Sebastian was the best and most prolific maker. Sebastian's sons Aegidius (1733–1805) and Joseph (1743–late 18th century) each had an individual style.

APPENDIX TWO

Kulik, Jan (1800–72). Bohemian violin maker. He trained under K. Sembera in Prague and Martin Stoss in Vienna and became one of the best Bohemian makers of his time. His earlier violins are patterned after various Italian models, his later ones mainly after Andrea Guarneri. His cellos have a better tone and are patterned after either Stradivari or a design by the engineer Leopold Savoi.

Kuypers [Kuppers], Johannes Theodorus. See CUYPERS, JOHANNES THEODORUS.

Lafleur, Jacques (1757–1832). French violin and bow maker. He was apprenticed in Mirecourt and went to Paris in 1783. His bows, which resemble those of the early Adam school, are rare. His brand was occasionally used by Maire and Pajeot *fils*.

Lafleur, Joseph René (1812–74). French bow maker. The son of Jacques Lafleur, whose work he surpassed, and initially a violinist, he seems to have learnt his craft through observation of existing bows. His association with Nicolas Maire, who had succeeded to Jacques' workshop, probably helped to develop his style.

Lamy, Alfred Joseph (1850–1919). French bow maker. He studied in Mirecourt with Charles Claude Husson (i) and worked for Gautrot in Château-Thierry, then for F. N. Voirin in Paris. He copied Voirin's model, which he continued to use when he later worked independently. The work of his son Alfred (after 1875–1944), who succeeded him, is similar.

Landolfi, Carlo Ferdinando (*fl* c1750–c1775). Italian violin maker. He worked in Milan, where he may have been associated with G. B. Guadagnini, whose influence is apparent. His instruments, which include violas and cellos, show individual characteristics and neat workmanship. His main pupils were Pietro Giovanni Mantegazza and his own son Pietro Antonio (*fl* c1760–c1785).

Lavazza, Antonio Maria (*fl* c1703–32). Italian violin maker. He worked in Milan and may have been taught by the Grancinos, but his few surviving instruments are based on a modified Stradivari pattern. The work of his son Santino shows greater influence of the Grancino and Stradivari styles.

Lee, John Norwood (*b* 1953). American bow maker. He trained as an oboist, but from 1977 worked for Bein & Fushi on violin repairs; he soon became interested in bows and learnt bow making with the firm. His own robust style is recognizable in his copies of 19th-century models. His personal work is usually gold-mounted; stars added to his brand usually denote bows, of lesser quality, made by assistants.

Lemböck, Gabriel (1814–92). Austrian violin maker of Hungarian birth. He was apprenticed in Budapest and worked for other makers in Vienna before opening his own workshop there in 1840. His instruments are boldly modelled and well made, and usually pattered after Maggini, Stradivari, or the 'Canon' of Guarneri 'del Gesù'.

Lewis, Edward (*fl* London, *c*1687–*c*1745). English violin maker. One of the best craftsmen of his time, he may have worked for the Jaye family. His model was a personal one, with some Brescian influence. Few of his instruments survive.

Lídl. Czech instrument makers. The firm was founded in Brno in 1909 by Joseph Lídl (1864–1946); it produced brass and string instruments and accordions. When Joseph's son Václav (*b* 1894) took over the business in 1918, he opened factories elsewhere in Czechoslovakia; he later worked in Vienna.

Lorenzini, Gasparo (*fl* Piacenza, 1743–1804). Italian violin maker. He claimed to be a pupil of Guadagnini, whose influence is evident in his work. His violins are good tonally; unfortunately few survive.

Lott, John [Jack] **Frederick** (early 1800s–1871). English violin maker. The son of John Frederick Lott (1775–1853), who made cellos and basses for Thomas Dodd, he trained as a violin maker but worked in other fields until *c*1843. He was the finest maker, and the best imitator of the work of Guarneri 'del Gesù' and Stradivari, in London in the 19th century; his violins are tonally comparable to the Italians. Like Fendt, with whom he probably worked, he made instruments that looked old and used, but his aim was to capture the mood rather than to make exact copies.

Luff, William (*b* 1904). English violin maker. One of the finest 20th-century English makers, he trained at Dykes & Son. He worked independently from 1932 and in 1945–55 was a repairman for J. & A. Beare before again setting up his own workshop. Most of his violins are copies of the Guarneri 'del Gesù' model. He also made violas and a cello.

Lupot, Nicolas (1758–1824). French violin maker of German birth. He is considered the greatest French maker. He studied and worked with his father, François (i), in Orleans and in 1794 went to Paris to work with François-Louis Pique. After perfecting his model based on Stradivari, he opened his own workshop in Paris in 1798. He produced mainly violins, and by 1810 had reached his highest level of achievement, which he maintained. His most important pupils were Gand, who succeeded him, and Bernardel. His brother, François (ii) (1774–1837), was principally a bow maker, rivalling François Tourte.

Maggini, Gio(vanni) Paolo (*c*1581–*c*1632). Italian violin maker. He was a pupil of Gasparo da Salò and became the best-known maker of the Brescian school. He produced mostly violins, in response to the instrument's growing popularity, though he also made alto violas and small-sized cellos; he may have been the first to make these smaller violas and cellos. His greatest achievement was in the broad tone of his violins and their compact form, emulated and adapted by both Guarneri and Stradivari. He also made double basses, viols and citterns. Many copies of his instruments were made in the 19th century.

Maire, Nicolas (1800–78). French bow maker. A member of a Mirecourt family which included violin makers, he was trained in the Lafleur workshop in Paris, where he may have worked with Pajeot, and in 1833 succeeded Jacques Lafleur. His work varies in style, but not in its fine craftsmanship.

Maline, Guillaume (*b* 1793; *d* *c*1850–60). French bow maker. He worked for J.-B. Vuillaume in Paris and made unbranded sticks for other Parisian makers. The heads of his bows are patterned after Peccatte but most of the frogs and screw buttons are of the Vuillaume type.

Mantegazza. Italian family of violin makers and restorers. The best-known, Pietro Giovanni (*fl* *c*1757–*c*1800), was a pupil of Landolfi. He worked in Milan with his brother Domenico. Towards 1790 they began making alto violas, possibly with other members of the family. Francesco and Carlo, probably of the second generation, were well known as restorers.

Marchi, Giovanni Antonio (1727 or 1728–1810). Italian violin maker. He worked in Bologna and possibly in Milan. His violins, which are rare, are patterned after Gagliano.

Marconcini, Luigi (*fl* Ferrara and Bologna, *c*1760–91). Italian violin maker. His instruments are built on a Stradivari outline and his best work is in his cellos, which are large. The work of his son Giuseppe (1772–1841), who studied with Storioni, is generally considered superior.

Mariani, Antonio (*fl* Pesaro, *c*1635–85). Italian violin maker. He was reputedly a pupil of Maggini, but his model is original and reminiscent of Gasparo da Salò; many similar instruments have been attributed to him. He made large and small violas and cellos as well as violins. Instruments made by his son and pupil Luigi ('Ludovico'; *fl* Pesaro, *c*1690–1702) are similar in style, but less elongated.

Maucotel. French family of violin and bow makers and dealers. Charles (1807–after 1860) was apprenticed in Mirecourt. He worked for Gand in Paris and William Davis in London and from 1850 had his own workshop in London. His brother Charles Adolphe (1820–58) also studied in Mirecourt and had his own business in Paris. Both worked after the Stradivari and Guarneri patterns. Charles Adolphe's grand-nephew Ernest (1867–?) was taught by Paul Bailly and then by an uncle in Moscow. He worked for Silvestre in Paris and became his partner. As Silvestre & Maucotel they produced good violins and bows; the firm later became Maucotel & Deschamp.

Maussiel, Leonard (1685–after 1765). German violin maker. He was probably apprenticed to his grandfather, Matthias, in Augsburg. His instruments follow the Stainer and Tecchler models but are more individual than copies. His scrolls are often carved as a lion's or woman's head.

Melegari, Enrico Clodoveo (*fl* Turin, *c*1860–88). Italian violin maker. His instruments are made on an original pattern which follows classical proportions. Violins dated after 1888 were probably completed by his brothers Michele and Pietro, who were his assistants.

Mezzadri, Alessandro (*fl* Ferrara, *c*1690–1732). Italian violin maker. His two careers of maker and performer resulted in a meagre output of instruments, the best of which have probably been relabelled with more famous names. His violins are based loosely on the Amati pattern, while his violas derive from larger Brescian models.

Millant. French family of violin and bow makers. The brothers Roger (*b* 1901) and Max (*b* 1903) were apprenticed with their grandfather Sébastien Auguste Deroux, then worked for Dykes & Son in London and in 1923 opened their own business in Paris. They made violins and cellos on an original pattern based on Stradivari and Guarneri models, and violas similar to the 'Tertis'; they also published books on violin making. Roger's son Jean-Jacques (*b* 1928) was apprenticed in Mirecourt; he worked independently in Paris from 1951 and was named 'Meilleur Ouvrier de France' in 1971. His bows follow the Peccatte school. Max's son Bernard (*b* 1929) served apprenticeships in violin and in bow making and achieved distinction in both, working independently in Paris. His bows are similar in style to his cousin's.

Miremont, Claude-Augustin (1827–87). French violin maker. He studied in Mirecourt with his father, Sébastien. He worked in Paris for Lafleur and Bernardel and from 1852 in New York. In 1861 he set up his own shop in Paris, where he produced his best work. Pierre Fournier used one of his cellos.

Montagnana, Domenico (*c*1687–1750). Italian string instrument maker. He was probably a pupil and assistant of Matteo Goffriller before opening his own workshop in Venice; he may also have been associated with Gobetti. From 1720 his output was large; it includes violins on several patterns and large, powerful cellos with a sound quality equal to the great Cremonese instruments. His surviving viola, used by Lionel Tertis, was the inspiration for the 'Tertis' model adopted by many modern makers.

Mount, William Sidney (1807–68). American painter and violinist. He patented an 'improved' violin model which in its final form (1857) had a guitar-shaped body, a concave back and reversed soundholes. Called 'The Cradle of Harmony', it was supported by musicians, but was never mass-produced.

Nemessányi, Samuel Felix (1837–81). Hungarian violin maker. The

APPENDIX TWO

best Hungarian maker of his time, he trained in Pest and Prague before establishing himself in Pest in 1863. His violins, though usually after the Guarneri 'del Gesù' model and occasionally after Stradivari and Maggini, are not Italianate in appearance or tone. His cellos are much sought after.

Nicolas, Didier (1757–1833). French violin maker. Nicknamed 'le Sourd', he was apprenticed and worked in Mirecourt. His violins are fuller and heavier than their Stradivari model, with an unusually large distance between the soundholes. Instruments from his later years were made by assistants and vary in quality; his brand was later used by Derazy, Mougenot and Laberte & Magnie.

Niggell, Sympert (1710–85). German violin maker. He was the foremost 18th-century maker at Füssen. His work, of graceful proportions, is reminiscent of the Albani and Stainer models.

Nürnberger, (Franz) Albert (1854–1931). German bow maker. He worked with his father, also Franz Albert, in Markneukirchen. His brand was also used by his son Karl Albert (b 1906), so that it is difficult to distinguish their work. Bows from the early 20th century are superior to later models.

Oddone, Carlo Giuseppe (1866–c1936). Italian violin maker. He studied in Turin and worked for F. W. Chanot in London before returning to Turin, where he established a fine reputation. His work is mostly patterned after Guarneri and Stradivari.

Odoardi, Giuseppe (1746–after 1786). Italian violin maker. Nicknamed 'Il Vilano D'Ascoli', he was self-taught and produced around 200 instruments. His style was mainly patterned on Stradivari, but was also influenced by Montagnana and Mariani. Antonio Odoardi was probably his nephew.

Ouchard. French family of bow makers. Emile François (1872–1951) studied with Eugène Cuniot-Hury in Mirecourt and succeeded to his business. His son and pupil Emile A. (1900–69) was the most important member of the family. He worked in Paris, New York and Chicago, and returned to France in the mid-1950s. His bows are similar to those of the Voirin–Lamy school. Emile's son and pupil Bernard (b 1925) worked with him and then with Pierre Vidoudez in Geneva until he was appointed professor of bow making at the Mirecourt school in 1971.

Pacherele [Pacherel], **Pierre** (1803–71). French violin maker. He was apprenticed in Mirecourt, then worked in Nice and Genoa and for G. F. Pressenda in Turin before establishing himself in Nice. He was influenced by Pressenda, but his style remained more French than Italian. His few cellos are excellent.

Pajeot [Pageot] [first name unknown] (1791–1849). French bow maker. His father, Louis Simon (c1750–92), was also a bow maker.

VIOLIN FAMILY

Pajeot was associated with Nicolas Maire as student and business partner, and they were both associated with Jacques Lafleur in Paris as pupils or makers. Pajeot's bows are excellent but rare.

Pallotta, Pietro (*fl* Perugia, *c*1788–1821). Italian violin maker. His instruments, mostly patterned after a slender model, are tonally good and are well made, apart from the scrolls. He was not prolific.

Pamphilon, Edward (*fl* London, *c*1670–95). English violin maker. His violins and violas, though small, have characteristics of the larger, Brescian model. The craftsmanship is uneven but the varnish is excellent.

Panormo, Vincenzo (1734–*c*1813). Sicilian violin maker. A self-taught maker, active in London, France and possibly Ireland, he settled in London (1789), where he assisted John Betts and became the leading maker. His work was mostly patterned after Stradivari, though the violins made in France appear more French than Italian; most of his instruments are unlabelled. His son Joseph (*c*1775–*c*1840) worked with him and made good quality instruments. His son George Lewis (*d c*1850) made guitars and fine bows.

Parker, Daniel (*fl* London, *c*1700–30). English violin maker. He was probably a pupil of Barak Norman (*c*1670–*c*1740). He followed the vogue of copying the Stradivari model, with details conforming to contemporary practices of English workmanship, and is considered the best early English maker. He was equally successful with violas of various sizes. Fritz Kreisler often used one of his violins.

Peccatte, Dominique (1810–74). French bow maker. He was apprenticed to a violin maker in Mirecourt. In 1826 he went to work for J.-B. Vuillaume in Paris, where he learnt bow making from Persois and met Tourte. He became an outstanding bow maker, second only to Tourte, and by 1837 had taken over Lupot's workshop, where he continued to make bows for Vuillaume. He returned to Mirecourt in 1847. His brother François (1820–55), also a good bow maker, worked in Mirecourt and Paris. François' son Charles (1850–1920) was taught by Voirin; he worked for Lenoble, then independently in Paris.

Pedrazzini, Giuseppe (1879–1958). Italian violin maker. Active in Milan, he apparently studied with the Antoniazzi brothers. Their influence shows in his violins, which are based on the Stradivari pattern with distinctively rounded curves. His instruments are tonally equal to those of the best of his Italian contemporaries.

Peresson, Sergio (*b* 1913). American violin maker of Italian birth. The leading North American maker, he learnt violin making as a hobby in Italy before working professionally in Venezuela. In 1963 he worked with Moennig & Son and soon set up his own shop in New Jersey. His work is based on a combination of the Stradivari and Guarneri 'del Gesù' models; his violas are especially successful.

Perry, Thomas (1744 or *c*1757–1818). Irish violin maker, active in Dublin. He may have been related to the French violin making family Pierray. He made high-quality violins after the Amati model and used a joint label with his son-in-law William Wilkinson. The latter, an inferior craftsman, seems to have contributed little to instruments made before 1818 and his later work, under the label Perry and Wilkinson, degraded Perry's reputation.

Persois [Persoit] [first name unknown] (*fl* first half of 19th century). French bow maker. Possibly the first bow maker to work for J.-B. Vuillaume, he was employed by him for *c*15 years. His branded bows, which are rare and in demand, resemble those of Tourte.

Pierray, Claude (*fl* Paris, *c*1710–*c*1725). French violin maker. He was the finest early French maker. His violins, more elegant than those of his contemporary Jacques Bocquay, often pass as Italian. His cellos, though small, are also of good quality.

Pique, François-Louis (1758–1822). French violin maker. He was apprenticed in Mirecourt. He had his own shop in Paris from *c*1778 and was Luthier du Conservatoire. He was closely associated with Lupot and almost his equal in craftsmanship. The pattern of his instruments is similar to Lupot's, but larger, and their work has sometimes been misattributed.

Plani, Agostino de (*fl* *c*1750–80). Italian violin maker. He was the least characteristic maker of the 18th-century Genoan school. A Bavarian influence is evident in his work, which is negligible in both style and tone.

Platner, Michael (*fl* Rome, *c*1720–50). Violin maker, probably of Austrian (Tyrolean) origin. He may have been a pupil of Tecchler in Rome, but followed the Stainer pattern. His craftsmanship was excellent.

Poggi, Ansaldo (1893–1984). Italian violin maker. Originally a violinist, he studied violin making in Zurich with Giuseppe Fiorini and around 1920 established his own workshop in Bologna. He won several awards for his violins, which are based on the Stradivari model and noted for their exceptional tone.

Pollastri, Augusto (1877–1927). Italian violin maker. He studied with Raffaele Fiorini in Bologna, where he worked independently from around 1900. His pattern, dubbed 'il modello Pollastri', is based on the Stradivari model. His brother and pupil Gaetano (1886–1960) worked independently after 1927. Gaetano's style is similar and he used the same logo, but his work does not match Augusto's.

Postacchini, Andrea (1786–1862). Italian violin maker. The disparity in the quality of workmanship and in the labelling between his early and late instruments and the length of his working life led to the belief that there were two makers, father and son. His instruments, including violas and cellos, are based mostly on a personal model and are tonally of high quality.

Postiglione, Vincenzo (1831–1916). Italian violin maker. He was apprenticed in Naples and set up his workshop there. His craftsmanship is consistently good and most of his work is typically Neapolitan, following the Gagliano school; he sometimes copied other masters, including Guarneri 'del Gesù'. His large output includes viols and violas d'amore as well as the standard members of the violin family.

Prescott, Abraham (1789–1858). American maker of bowed string instruments and keyboard instruments. He trained as a cabinet maker in Deerfield, NH, and began to make large cellos (described as 'bass viols' or 'church basses') in 1809. He later moved to Concord and from 1836 concentrated on the manufacture of organs and similar instruments. His former apprentices, the brothers David and Andrew Dearborn, took over the manufacture of string instruments in 1848. Prescott's double basses are played by leading orchestral and jazz musicians.

Pressenda, Giovanni Francesco (?1777–1854). Italian violin maker, active in Turin. He and his pupil Giuseppe Rocca are considered the finest Italian makers of the 19th century. Always strongly influenced by Stradivari, Pressenda's style changed from the broad, flat, early model to a fully arched pattern and gradually returned to a flatter model that was particularly successful. He also made cellos and small violas. His violins were copied by ANNIBALE FAGNOLA.

Pyne, George (1852–1921). English violin maker. Although he worked for Edward Withers for about 20 years, he was apparently self-taught. His violins are competently made and tonally have matured well. They are based on the models of the old Cremonese masters.

Rameau, J. S. Name used by the 20th-century bow makers JOHN CLUTTERBUCK and Stephen Bristow during their partnership.

Retford, William Charles (1875–1970). English bow maker. He worked in London for W. E. Hill & Sons from 1892 to 1956, collaborating with the HILL brothers on the development of the Hill bow. After his retirement he worked at home in Hanwell and wrote *Bows and Bow Makers* (1964).

Richardson, Arthur (1882–1965). English violin maker. He was trained as a foundry worker and was an amateur violin maker before working professionally. He ranks among the best 20th-century English makers for his violins, which are based on Stradivari and Guarneri models. He collaborated with Lionel Tertis in producing a number of 'Tertis' model violas.

Richaume, André (1905–66). French bow maker. He was apprenticed with Emile François Ouchard in Mirecourt before joining his uncle Victor Fétique in Paris. He worked independently from 1923 and in 1957 was named 'Meilleur Ouvrier de France'. He was a leading

APPENDIX TWO

maker under his own brand and supplied fine bows to other Parisian makers.

Rivolta, Giacomo (*fl* Milan, *c*1800–1850). Italian violin maker. His work shows the influence of both the Gagliano and the Grancino schools. Of his output of bowed string instruments, his cellos, based on a Stradivari model, are most important.

Rocca, Giuseppe (1807–65). Italian violin maker. He studied with Pressenda in Turin and worked independently there from *c*1839. His work was increasingly influenced by Stradivari, and his best violins, made in 1845–50 and tonally outstanding, are based on either a Stradivari or a Guarneri pattern. He moved to Genoa *c*1860. His son and pupil Enrico (1847–1915) made violins from 1878.

Rogeri, Giovanni Battista (*fl c*1670–*c*1705). Italian violin maker. He was a pupil of Nicolo Amati. Active in Brescia, he introduced features of his predecessor Maggini into some of his violins. By 1690 he had surpassed most of his contemporaries and his best violins are tonally equal to the best of the Amatis. He also made fine cellos. He was assisted by his son Pietro Giacomo (*fl c*1690–1720), also a fine craftsman. Their work is not similar to that of Francesco Rugeri, who was once thought to be related.

Rombouts, Pieter (1667–?1740). Netherlands violin maker. He studied with his stepfather Hendrik Jacobsz in Amsterdam. His bold approach to instrument making is evident in all his work, particularly in his designs, decorative details and varnish, and his style is recognizable in Jacobsz's later instruments. He did not use his own label until *c*1708 and was less prolific from that time.

Rubio, David (Joseph) (*b* 1934). English instrument maker. He trained as a doctor, but became a guitarist and then a guitar maker and opened a workshop in New York in 1964. He returned to England in 1967 and expanded his range to include harpsichords, viols and lutes, and violins, violas and cellos of pre-19th-century design. His workshop is in Cambridge.

Rugeri [Ruggeri, Rugieri], **Francesco** ['Il Per'] (1620–*c*1695). Italian violin maker. He worked in Cremona and may have been the first pupil of Nicolo Amati, whose style he copied closely; he sometimes used Amati's label. He established his own workshop *c*1641 and was later assisted by his sons Vincenzo and Giacinto, who were both active until about 1730. Francesco was probably the first Cremonese maker to produce a smaller-sized cello.

Sacconi, (Simone) Fernando (1895–1973). Italian maker and restorer of violins. He learnt violin making with Giuseppe Rossi and also studied drawing and sculpture. He had extraordinary ability as a copyist of old instruments and as a restorer, and developed techniques for making invisible repairs. He went to New York in 1931 to work on

VIOLIN FAMILY

repairs and restorations for Emil Herrmann. In 1950 he and his pupil Dario D'Attili joined Rembert Wurlitzer and established a workshop where many of the best American repairers were trained. He spent his last years in Cremona teaching violin making and writing his book *I 'segreti' di Stradivari* (1972).

Salchow, William (*b* 1926). American bow maker. He studied as a cellist and was a cello salesman for Wurlitzer before learning bow making in Mirecourt. From 1960 he worked independently in New York, making bows that follow French lines but with characteristics of the early work of the Dodd family.

Salomon, Jean Baptiste Deshayes (*fl c*1740–72). French violin maker. He was possibly the brother of the maker Saloman di Rheims but worked in Paris. The quality of his work varied and most of his best violins, which resemble those of Gabbrielli, were made before 1750. He also made small violas, cellos and harps. After his death his business was continued by his widow, under the direction of Jean Theodore Namy.

Sannino, Vincenzo (1879–after 1966). Italian violin maker. He learned violin making at an early age; he worked in Naples until 1914 and in Rome from 1925. His style has an affinity with the classic Neapolitan school, whose methods he studied. He also copied other masters; much of his best work has false labels.

Santagiuliana, Giacinto (*fl* Vicenza and Venice, *c*1770–1830). Italian violin maker. His violins are inspired by the Amati family but have the fullness of the larger Guarneri models. Gaetano, probably a younger brother, worked in Vicenza and had a similar style.

Sartory, Eugène (1871–1946). French bow maker. He was taught by his father in Mirecourt, then worked in Paris for Charles Peccatte and Alfred Lamy before setting up his own workshop in 1893. His bows were influenced by Voirin and Lamy but are stronger in the hand and to the eye. Ysaÿe was among his patrons, and his bows are popular today.

Scarampella, Giuseppe (1838–1902). Italian violin maker. He studied with Nicolo Bianchi in Paris in 1865 and worked in Florence from 1866 for Luigi Castellani, whom he later succeeded as curator of the Cherubini Conservatory collection. He made few instruments, mostly violins patterned after Stradivari and Guarneri, but his craftsmanship was consistently good. His brother Stefano was his pupil.

Scarampella, Stefano (1843–1927). Italian violin maker, brother and pupil of GIUSEPPE SCARAMPELLA. Active in Mantua, he was a prolific maker, but most of his work is not equal to his brother's. His violins are based loosely on the Stradivari, Guarneri and Balestrieri models and, despite poor craftsmanship, usually have good tone. Owing to increased demand for their instruments, many violins bearing the Scarampellas' labels are fakes.

276

APPENDIX TWO

Schwarz, Giovanni (*d* 1952). Italian violin maker, nephew of Eugenio DEGANI.

Seraphin [Serafin, Serafino], **Sanctus** [Santo] (1699–after 1758). Italian violin maker, active in Venice from *c*1720. By 1730 he had developed a style that combined the influence of Amati with his own Venetian design, and his best instruments, which are outstanding in tone and appearance, were made before 1740. He retired in 1744. His nephew (and presumably his pupil) Giorgio (*c*1726–1775), also a fine craftsman, worked independently from 1742 and later succeeded to the business of his father-in-law, Domenico Montagnana.

Sijde [Syde], **Willem van der** (*fl* Amsterdam, 1664–*c*1700). Netherlands violin maker. His violins, made on a personal model, are distinctive for their rolled edges, bold purfling, flat tables and sound-holes carved close to the purfling. In spite of his individuality, he is considered an important member of the late 17th-century Amsterdam school.

Silvestre. French family of violin makers. Pierre (1801–59) studied with Blaise at Mirecourt before working in Paris with Lupot and Gand *père*. From 1829 he worked independently at Lyons and in 1831 was joined by his brother Hippolyte (1808–79), who had worked for Blaise and in Paris for J.-B. Vuillaume. Their work, which is equal to the best of their contemporaries, was made and labelled jointly, though Pierre is regarded as the finer maker. Their nephew Hippolyte Chrétien (1845–1913) studied at Mirecourt and with his uncle Hippolyte and in 1865 succeeded to the business. He moved to Paris in 1884 and the firm became Silvestre & Maucotel in 1900, later Maucotel & Deschamp.

Simon, P(aul) (1808–82). French bow maker. One of the most important 19th-century bow makers, he was apprenticed in Mirecourt. He worked in Paris successively for Peccatte, J.-B. Vuillaume and Gand Frères, and in 1847 purchased Peccatte's business. His bows have two styles of head, a modified Peccatte model and a larger, personal model.

Soliani, Angelo (1752–after 1810). Italian violin maker. He worked in Modena, producing instruments reminiscent of the Guadagnini model. His violins show good craftsmanship and have a clear and flexible, though small, tone.

Sorsana, Spiritus (*fl c*1715–40). Italian violin maker. He was the only maker of note to work in Cuneo. Though probably a pupil of Gioffredo Cappa, he made violins of an individual, square-shouldered pattern that shows little of Cappa's influence.

Sprenger, Eugen (1882–1953). German string instrument maker and restorer. He studied with his father, Anton, then worked briefly for his brother Adolf in Stuttgart, and in Munich, Switzerland, France and England, before opening his own shop in Frankfurt in 1907. His instruments are well built, with a powerful tone. He patented his own

VIOLIN FAMILY

viola model and wrote *Die Streichinstrumente und ihre Behandlung* (1951). His son and pupil Eugen (*b* 1920), who took over the business in 1950, specializes in restoration and reconstruction of historical instruments.

Staghmeulen, Johannes Baptista van der (*fl* Antwerp, late 17th century). Netherlands violin maker. His background is obscure but his style is a blend of Flemish and Italian; the violas in particular show Brescian influence.

Stainer [Steiner], Jacob [Jakob] (?1617–1683). Austrian violin maker. He was apprenticed to a German maker in Italy, then travelled in Italy, Germany and Austria, selling instruments and doing repairs, before settling in Absam in 1655. He supplied instruments to the Tyrolean court and fulfilled many other commissions. He made some of his finest instruments after 1675, although he had begun to suffer from bouts of insanity. His craftsmanship is comparable to Stradivari's and the silvery tone of his violins was regarded as ideal for more than 150 years. He also made alto and tenor violas, cellos, double basses and viols.

Stainer, Markus [Marcus] (*c*1633–1693). Austrian violin maker. He made fine instruments and was formerly thought to be a brother of JACOB STAINER.

Storioni, Lorenzo (1751–*c*1800). Italian violin maker. He worked in Cremona, absorbing and furthering the traditions of his predecessors, but his merit has been obscured by the use of his label in violins by lesser Italian makers of the time. His violins, though rough by Cremonese standards, are well proportioned and show the influence of Guarneri 'del Gesù'. In his later instruments the more delicate work of his pupil J. B. Ceruti is evident. He also made cellos and small violas.

Stradivari, Antonio (1644–1737). Italian maker of violins and other string instruments. A pupil of Nicolo Amati, he may have been apprenticed first as a woodcarver. His few early violins, termed 'Amatisé', are Cremonese in character but not outstanding instruments. From 1680 the Amati influence faded and his instruments became more robust and more powerful. After 1690 his individuality was more marked by wider purfling, bolder soundholes, stronger arching and a deeper-coloured varnish, and he introduced the 'long Strad', a model probably designed to bring to his instruments the more powerful tonal qualities of the older Brescian makers. By 1699 his sons Francesco (1671–1743) and Omobono (1679–1742) were probably his assistants. His finest instruments were made in 1700–20 and include the 'Betts' (1704), the 'Alard' (1715) and the 'Messiah' (1716) violins, and the smaller-sized cellos, which have exceptional sound-carrying qualities; the cellos served as a model for most makers from the early 19th century. After 1720 he used wood of slightly inferior quality, but his superb craftsmanship was maintained almost to the end of his life. Since the end of the 18th century he has been regarded as the greatest of all makers.

APPENDIX TWO

Syde, Willem van der. *See* SIJDE, WILLEM VAN DER.

Tarisio, Luigi (*c*1790–1854). Italian dealer and collector. He bought and sold violins which he found in small towns in northern Italy and rescued many fine instruments by taking them to Paris for restoration. In 1827 he had acquired the 'Messiah' Stradivari and at his death he owned 30 Stradivaris and 120 other Italian masterpieces; all of which were purchased by Vuillaume.

Tassini, Bartolomeo (*fl c*1740–60). Italian violin maker. Although he was active in Venice, his work shows an unusual mixture of Milanese and German influences. His best work resembles that of the Testores, with whom he may have studied.

Taylor, Malcolm (Morris) (*b* 1933). English bow maker. He was apprenticed with W. E. Hill & Sons and worked there until 1973, when he set up independently; his workshop is in Barnstaple, Devon. He follows the Hill pattern, but his bows are slightly heavier and those for viola and cello are his best. John Clutterbuck, Stephen Bristow and Brian Alvey were his pupils at Hill's.

Taylor, Michael (John) (*b* 1949). English bow maker. He was trained at Ealing Strings, London. His bows, based mostly on the Tourte model, combine French patterns with English solidity and are of the finest craftsmanship.

Tecchler, David (*c*1666–after 1747). Italian violin maker of German birth. The leading maker of the Roman school, he probably studied in Augsburg before settling in Rome at a time when there was great demand for violins and cellos. He based his work mainly on Cremonese patterns and is known chiefly for his cellos, most of which were large but have since been cut down. Francesco Emiliani was one of his pupils.

Testore. Italian family of violin makers active in Milan. Though once derided as 'cheapjacks', they answered the need for inexpensive instruments and their work is now more highly valued. Carlo Giuseppe (*fl* 1690–*c*1720), the most skilled, made instruments that resemble those of his teacher Grancino, except in the design of the scroll, which became a family trademark. His son Carlo Antonio (*fl c*1720–after 1760) copied his style but was a less careful craftsman. He was assisted late in life by his son Giovanni. Carlo Antonio's brother Paolo Antonio (*fl c*1725–60) incorporated personal details that were not always successful, but produced some instruments of good quality. Paolo Antonio's son Pietro (*fl c*1750–60) was possibly the clumsiest of all violin makers, but his violas are equal in tone to those of his relatives.

Thibout, Jacques Pierre (1779–1856). French violin maker. He worked in Caen for Jean Gabriel Köliker before setting up in Paris in 1807. He became violin maker to the Opéra and won medals at the Paris exhibitions. His violins, patterned after the Stradivari model, combine French timbre with Italian flexibility of tone.

Thomassin, Louis (1855–between 1900 and 1910). French bow maker. After working with Bazin in Mirecourt, he went to Paris in 1872 to work for F. N. Voirin; he and Alfred Lamy continued the business after Voirin's death. From 1891 he had his own workshop, where he made bows modelled after Voirin and some Tourte copies. His son and pupil Claude (1870–1942) also worked in Paris and made elegant bows patterned after Voirin.

Tielke, Joachim (1641–1719). German string instrument maker. He may have studied with Gottfried Tielke (possibly his older brother) in Italy before settling in Hamburg in 1667. His instruments were often lavishly decorated and were much in demand. Many survive, mostly viols, though he also made violins, lutes, guitars and citterns.

Tobin, Richard (*c*1777–*c*1841). Irish violin maker. He studied and worked with Thomas Perry before joining John Betts in London around 1813. There is little record of him after Betts's death in 1823, although he probably continued to supply dealers, and there are no instruments bearing his own label. His violins, patterned after the Stradivari model, are among the best English work of the time.

Tononi. Italian family of violin makers. Giovanni (*d* 1713) worked in Bologna. He was a careful craftsman and based his work on Amati models. His son Carlo (*d* after 8 March 1730), a more important maker, produced instruments on improved versions of his father's models and often had several assistants involved in the making of one violin. He moved to Venice *c*1715; the violins made there in the 1720s have a different character, and his role in their construction is uncertain. He also made cellos and small violas.

Tourte. French family of bow makers. The working life of (?Louis) Tourte *père* [*le vieux*] (*fl* Paris, *c*1740–80) coincided with the evolution of the transitional bow. His bows varied in length and design until the late models, which were close to the modern bow. His son Tourte *l'aîné* (*fl c*1765–*c*1800) was probably the Xavier Tourte active in Paris at the time, though there has been doubt even about *l'aîné*'s existence, owing to the disparity in design and quality of bows attributed to him. Tourte *père*'s son François (Xavier), *le jeune* or *le frère puîné* (1745–1835), produced bows of superb craftsmanship and playing qualities, and is regarded as the 'Stradivari of the bow'. He was apprenticed as a clock maker but joined the family workshop in the early 1770s and by 1790 had established the model that became the standard modern bow. Though some experts claim that there were three stages in the development of his style, no chronology of the changes can be made, because he did not stamp his bows.

Trapani, Raffaele (*fl* Naples, *c*1800–1830). Italian violin maker. His work shows a curious mixture of influences: the outline follows the

Neapolitan, Gagliano pattern but the details are Brescian, giving his violins a clumsy appearance.

Tubbs. English family of bow makers, active in London. Thomas (*fl* c1790–c1830), a contemporary of Dodd and Tourte, witnessed the modernization of the bow. The quality of his work was variable. Bows made by his son William (*fl* c1825; *d* ?1878) are rare, though he may also have supplied dealers. William's son and pupil James (1835–1919) worked at first for W. E. Hill & Sons. After setting up independently (c1870) he developed his own style, distinctive both visually and to the player. His output, with the help of his son Alfred (*d* 1912), amounted to c5000 bows for violin, viola and cello. Edward Tubbs, who may have been James's brother, worked in New York at the turn of the century.

Urquhart, Thomas (*fl* London, c1650–80). English violin maker. He was probably a pupil of Jacob Rayman, a Tyrolean maker who worked in London from about 1620. His violins are well made and have a good tone; they have often been sold as more important Italian instruments.

Valenzano, Giovanni Maria (c1770–c1830). Italian violin maker. He is recorded as having worked in Asti, Naples, Padua, Trieste, Valenza, Marseilles, Montpellier, Nice and Barcelona as well as in Rome, where he settled (1825) and made his best instruments. His violins are based on an Amati model.

Vangelisti, Pier Lorenzo (*fl* Florence, c1700–c1745). Italian violin maker. His instruments foreshadow those of G. B. Gabbrielli, though they lack their elegance, and are sometimes misattributed to Gabbrielli. His name appears as 'Evangelisti' on some of his labels.

Vatelot, Etienne (*b* 1925). French violin maker and restorer. He studied in Paris with his father, Marcel, a leading maker, then in Mirecourt with Dieudonné. He returned to Paris to study repairs, then rejoined his father, whose business he took over in 1959. He is an expert on early instruments and noted for his skill in tonal adjustments. His book *Les archets français* (1976) is the definitive work on French bows.

Ventapane, Lorenzo (*fl* c1800–c1840). Italian violin maker. Active in Naples, he appears to have been a pupil of either Giovanni Gagliano or Nicola Gagliano (ii), whose work his own resembles. The quality of his work was variable but all his violins have the characteristic Neapolitan tone.

Vigneron, Joseph Arthur (1851–1905). French bow maker. He was apprenticed in Mirecourt with Charles Claude Husson (i) and worked for Gand & Bernardel Frères in Paris before opening his own shop there (c1888). He developed an individual style and his best bows are equal to the finest of his day, but much of his output, though solidly made, lacks grace. He was succeeded by his son and pupil André (1881–1924), a

VIOLIN FAMILY

prolific maker, whose style was derived from his father's. André supplied unstamped bows to other makers.

Vinnacia. Italian family of violin and mandolin makers, active in Naples from the mid-18th to the late 19th centuries. Gennaro (*fl* *c*1750–80) and his sons Antonio, Giovanni and Vincenzo, as well as other makers of the first two generations, made violins and mandolins. Most of the violins are patterned after the Gagliano school; Vincenzo also used the Guarneri model. Later generations produced few instruments of the violin family.

Voirin, François Nicolas (1833–85). French bow maker. He was apprenticed in Mirecourt and worked for J.-B. Vuillaume in Paris before setting up his own business there. His bows are more delicate than those of previous generations and are sometimes considered too light. After his death his wife continued the business, using his brand on his pupils' work.

Voller. Family of violin makers, probably of English origin. Three brothers, Arthur, Charles and William, were active in London from the early 1890s to around 1935. Until the turn of the century they were associated with Hart & Son, producing copies of Stradivari and Guarneri 'del Gesù' violins that were of exceptional quality. They then worked independently, producing instruments in the style of Italian makers, and sometimes offering their violins as Italian originals. Even today their instruments are not always recognized as fakes.

Vuillaume, Jean-Baptiste (1798–1875). French violin maker and dealer. He trained with his father in Mirecourt, then worked for Chanot and Simon Lété in Paris and in 1828 set up his own workshop there. His first instruments were in the French tradition but he was renowned both in Paris and abroad for his later work, which resembled that of the Cremonese school. As a dealer he handled many fine instruments and he made copies of Stradivari, Guarneri 'del Gesù', Amati and Maggini violins. Most of the best French bow makers were his workmen and pupils, including Eulry, Persois, Peccatte, Lenoble and Voirin, and his influence was apparent all over France, particularly in Mirecourt. His brother and pupil Nicolas-François (1802–76) worked in Brussels and was also a copier. A nephew, Sébastien (1835–75), was a maker of note.

Wamsley [Walmsley, Warmsley], **Peter** (*fl* London, *c*1725–45). English maker of violins, violas and cellos. He was a pupil of Nathaniel Cross and, like him, followed the Stainer pattern. The foremost English maker of his time, he was later criticized for having worked the wood too thin. His cellos are the forerunners of the English school, often regarded as second only to the best of the Italians. He also made violas of good size.

Watson, William D(avid) (*b* 1930). English bow maker. He was a pupil of Retford at W. E. Hill & Sons in London and worked for the firm before setting up independently in 1962; he moved to Denham, Buckinghamshire in 1963. His bows are strong and precisely made. He is also well known as a restorer of old bows.

Weidhaas. German bow makers. Ewald (1868–1939) was apprenticed to Hermann Pfretzschner. His son and pupil Paul (1894–1962) worked for Fétique in Paris and then established a workshop in Markneukirchen. Paul's son-in-law Siegfried FINKEL has continued the Weidhaas tradition of bow making.

Weisshaar, Hans (*b* 1913). American violin maker of German birth. He studied in Mittenwald and in Switzerland, the Netherlands and Germany. In 1937 he emigrated to the USA, where he worked for Lewis & Son in Chicago and Emil Herrmann in New York, and in 1947 established his own business in Hollywood, California. His excellent restorations have brought him an international reputation.

Widhalm, Leopold (1722–76). German violin maker. He worked in Nuremberg and was the most important 18th-century German maker outside Mittenwald. His violins follow the Stainer model. Instruments with the same label dated after 1800 were probably made by his sons.

Withers. English family of violin makers, repairers and dealers, active in London. Edward (i) (1808–75) founded the firm by purchasing that of R. and W. Davis. A pupil of John Lott, he made instruments of fine quality. His son and apprentice Edward (ii) (1844–1915) also worked with John Lott. He made *c*200 instruments and, like his father, copied the work of Stradivari and Guarneri. After his death his sons Edward Sidney Munns (1870–1955), Bernard Sidney (1873–1942) and Douglas Sidney (1879–1962) continued the business, but the emphasis shifted to repairing and dealing. Bernard's son Edward Stanley (*b* 1904) was succeeded by Dietrich M. Kessler in 1969. George (*c*1850–*c*1920), brother of Edward (ii), had his own dealing and restoration business and was joined by his sons Guarnerius and Walter George; his firm closed in 1932.

Wornum [Wornham]. English family of music publishers and instrument makers, active in London. Robert (1742–1815) was a publisher and he also made violins and cellos. Succeeding generations concentrated on the manufacture of pianos.

Wurlitzer. American firm of instrument makers and dealers. Franz Rudolph (1831–1914) came of a family of instrument makers who had worked in Saxony since the 17th century. He emigrated to the USA in 1853 and settled in Cincinnati, where he began dealing in instruments. His business expanded and later included the manufacture and sale of all types of instruments in various branches. His son Rudolph Henry (1873–1948) went to Berlin, where he studied violin playing, the history of instruments, acoustics and violin making. On his return he

VIOLIN FAMILY

supervised the firm's collection and made the violin department a world centre for rare string instruments. Rudolph's son Rembert (1904–63) studied in Mirecourt under Amédée Dieudonné and with Alfred Hill in London. In 1949 he established the violin department as a separate company in New York and in 1950 was joined by FERNANDO SACCONI. It was continued after his death by his widow, with Sacconi and DARIO D'ATTILI, until 1974.

Zanoli, Giacomo (*fl c*1725–65). Italian violin maker. He probably studied with his father, Giovanni Battista, in Verona and then worked in Venice and Padua before taking over his father's business. His instruments, mostly after the small Amati pattern, are competently made but not outstanding.

Bibliography

VIOLIN

M. Agricola: *Musica instrumentalis deudsch* (Wittenberg, 1529/R1969, enlarged 5/1545)

S. di Ganassi: *Regola rubertina* (Venice, 1542–3/R1970)

P. Jambe de Fer: *Epitome musical* (Lyons, 1556); repr. in Lesure (1958–63)

R. Rognoni: *Passaggi per potersi essercitare* (Venice, 1592)

L. Zacconi: *Prattica di musica* (Venice, 1592/R1967)

M. Praetorius: *Syntagma musicum*, i (Wittenberg and Wolfenbüttel, 1614–15/R1968); ii (Wolfenbüttel, 1618; 2/1619/R1958 and 1980, Eng. trans., ed. D. Z. Crookes, 1986); iii (Wolfenbüttel, 1618, 2/1619/R1958 and 1976)

F. Rognoni: *Selva de varii passaggi* (Milan, 1620/R1970)

M. Mersenne: *Harmonie universelle* (Paris, 1636–7/R1963; Eng. trans., 1957)

G. Zannetti: *Il scolaro* (Milan, 1645)

J. A. Herbst: *Musica moderna prattica* (Frankfurt, 2/1653)

B. Bismantova: *Compendio musicale* (Ferrara, 1677/R1978)

Anon.: *Nolens volens* (London, 1695)

D. Merck: *Compendium musicae instrumentalis Chelicae, das ist: kurtzer Begriff, welcher Gestalten die Instrumental-Music auf der Violin, Pratschen, Viola da Gamba, und Bass gründlich und leicht zu erlernen seye* (Augsburg, 1695)

G. Muffat: *Florilegium secundum* (Passau, 1698); ed. H. Rietsch, DTÖ, iv, Jg.ii/2 (1895/R)

M. Corrette: *L'école d'Orphée, méthode pour apprendre facilement à jouer du violon dans le goût françois et italien avec des principes de musique et beaucoup de leçons* (Paris, 1738/R1972, enlarged 2/1779, ?3/1790)

J.-J. C. de Mondonville: Introduction to *Les sons harmoniques*, op.4 (Paris and Lille, c1738)

F. Geminiani: *Le prime sonate a violino e basso . . . nuovamente ristampate, e con diligenza corrette, aggiuntovi – ancora per maggior facilità le grazie agli adagi, ed i numeri per la trasposizione della mano* (London, 1739) [op.1 (1716), rev. with added ornaments and fingerings]

———: *Sonate a violino e basso*, op.4 (London, 1739)

VIOLIN FAMILY

R. Crome: *The Fiddle New Model'd, or a useful Introduction for the Violin* (London, *c*1750)

F. Geminiani: *The Art of Playing on the Violin* (London, 1751; facs. ed. D. D. Boyden, 1952)

J. J. Quantz: *Versuch einer Anweisung die Flöte traversiere zu spielen* (Berlin, 1752, 3/1789/*R*1952; Eng. trans., 1966)

L. Mozart: *Versuch einer gründlichen Violinschule* (Augsburg, 1756/*R*1976, enlarged 3/1787/*R*1956; Eng. trans., 1948, rev. 2/1951/*R*1985)

L'abbé *le fils* [Saint-Sévin]: *Principes du violon* (Paris, 1761/*R*1961, 2/1772)

G. Tartini: *L'arte del arco* (Paris, 1758); repr. in J. B. Cartier: *L'art du violon* (1798)

————: *Lettera* [dated 1760] *del defonto Sig. Giuseppe Tartini alla Signora Maddalena Lombardini*, L'Europa letteraria, v/2 (Venice, 1770; Eng. trans., 1771/*R*1967)

————: *Traité des agréments de la musique* (Paris, 1771); ed. E. Jacobi (1961) [incl. Eng. and Ger. trans. and facs. of orig. It. MS, in the Conservatorio di Musica Benedetto Marcello, Venice]

G. Löhlein: *Anweisung zum Violinspielen . . . mit 24 kleinen Duetten erläutert* (Leipzig, 1774)

M. Corrette: *L'art de se perfectionner dans le violon où l'on donne à étudier des leçons sur toutes les positions . . . suite de l'école d'Orphée* (1782/*R*1973)

A. Lolli: *L'école du violon en quatuor* (Berlin and Amsterdam, *c*1784)

A. B. Bruni: *Caprices et airs variés en forme d'étude pour un violon seul*, op.1 (Paris, 1787)

F. Galeazzi: *Elementi teorico-pratici di musica con un saggio sopra l'arte di suonare il violino analizzata, ed a dimostrabili principi ridotta . . .*, i (Rome, 1791, rev. 2/1817); ii (Rome, 1796)

J. A. Hiller: *Anweisung zum Violinspielen für Schulen und zum Selbstunterrichte* (Leipzig, 1792)

R. Kreutzer: *40 études ou caprices pour le violon* (Paris, ?1796)

J. B. Cartier: *L'art du violon* (Paris, 1798, enlarged 3/*c*1803/*R*1973) [incl. G. Tartini: *L'arte del arco*]

M. Woldemar: *Méthode pour le violon* (Paris, 1798, rev. 2/*c*1800 as *Grande Méthode ou étude élémentaire pour le violon*)

P. Gaviniès: *Les vingt-quatre matinées* (Paris, *c*1800)

P. Baillot, P. Rode and R. Kreutzer: *Méthode de violon* (Paris, 1803)

P. Rode: *24 caprices en forme d'études* (Berlin, *c*1815)

F. Fiorillo: *Etudes de violon formant 36 caprices* (Vienna, n.d.)

N. Paganini: *24 capricci* (Milan, 1820)

B. Campagnoli: *Nouvelle méthode de la mécanique progressive du jeu de violon*, op.21 (Leipzig, 1824; It. trans., n.d.; Eng. trans., 1856)

K. Guhr: *Über Paganinis Kunst, die Violine zu spielen* (Mainz, 1829)

L. Spohr: *Violin-Schule* (Vienna, 1832; Eng. trans., 1843)

BIBLIOGRAPHY

P. Baillot: *L'art du violon: nouvelle méthode* (Paris, 1834)

F.-J. Fétis: *Biographie universelle des musiciens et bibliographie générale de la musique* (Brussels, 1835–44, 2/1860–65/R1963)

G. Dubourg: *The Violin* (London, 1836, 5/1878)

J.-D. Alard: *École de violon* (Paris, 1844)

N. Paganini: *Etudes en 60 variations sur l'air Barucabà pour violon solo,* op.14 (Paris and Mainz, 1851)

H. Wieniawski: *L'école moderne,* op.10 (Leipzig, [1854])

F.-J. Fétis: *Antoine Stradivari, luthier célèbre* (Paris, 1856; Eng. trans., 1864/R1964)

C.-A. de Bériot: *Méthode de violon,* op.102 (Paris, 1858)

F. Regli: *Storia del violino in Piemonte* (Turin, 1863)

F. David: *Violinschule* (Leipzig, 1864)

W. Sandys and S. A. Forster: *The History of the Violin* (London, 1864)

H. W. Ernst: *6 mehrstimmige Studien* (Hamburg, 1865)

F. David: *Die hohe Schule des Violinspiels* (Leipzig, 1867–72, 2/1903)

J. W. von Wasielewski: *Die Violine und ihre Meister* (Leipzig, 1869, 8/1927)

A. K. Tottmann: *Führer durch den Violinunterricht* (Leipzig, 1873, rev. 4/1935 as *Führer durch die Violinliteratur: ein kritisches, systematisches und nach den Schwierigkeitsgraden geordnetes Verzeichnis*)

L. A. Vidal: *Les instruments à archet, les faiseurs, les joueurs d'instruments, leur histoire* (Paris, 1876–8/R1961)

J.-F. Mazas: *75 Etudes mélodiques et progressives pour violon,* op.36 (Brunswick, 1880)

G. Hart: *The Violin and its Music* (London, 1881)

O. Ševčík: *Schule der Violintechnik,* op.1 (Prague, 1881)

J. Rühlmann: *Die Geschichte der Bogeninstrumente* (Brunswick, 1882)

W. Huggins: 'On the Function of the Soundpost', *Proceedings of the Royal Society of London,* xxxv (1883), 241

E. Heron-Allen: *Violin-making, as it Was and Is: Being a Historical, Theoretical, and Practical Treatise on the Art and Science of Violin-making* (London, 1884, 2/1885/R1984)

A. Pougin: *Viotti et l'école moderne de violon* (Paris, 1888)

The Strad (1890–)

E. Heron-Allen: *De Fidiculis Bibliographia: being an Attempt towards a Bibliography of the Violin and all Other Instruments played with a Bow* (London, 1890–94/R1961)

O. Ševčík: *Schule der Bogentechnik,* op.2 (Leipzig, 1895)

L. Torchi: *La musica strumentale in Italia nei secoli XVI, XVII e XVIII* (Turin, 1901)

W. H., A. F. and A. E. Hill: *Antonio Stradivari: his Life and Work* (London, 1902, 2/1909/R1963)

J. Joachim and A. Moser: *Violinschule* (Berlin, 1902–5; 2/1959, ed. M. Jacobsen)

G. Fry: *The Varnishes of the Italian Violin-makers* (London, 1904)

VIOLIN FAMILY

W. M. Morris: *British Violin Makers* (London, 1904, rev. 2/1920)

O. Ševčík: *Violinschule für Anfänger*, opp.6, 7, 8 and 9 (Leipzig, 1904–8)

A. Schering: *Die Geschichte des Instrumental-Konzerts* (Leipzig, 1905, 2/1927/R1965)

M. Schneider: 'Zu Bibers Violinensonaten', *ZIMG*, viii (1906–7), 471; ix (1907–8), 29

L. Hupfeld: *DEA-Violina* (Leipzig, 1909)

C. Flesch: *Urstudien* (Berlin, 1911)

M. Pincherle: 'La technique du violon chez les premiers sonatistes français (1695–1723)', *BSIM*, vii/8–9 (1911/R1973), 1-32; vii/10 (1911), 20

B. Studeny: *Beiträge zur Geschichte der Violinsonate im 18. Jahrhundert* (Munich, 1911)

A. A. Bachmann: *Les grands violonistes du passé* (Paris, 1913)

A. Dolmetsch: *The Interpretation of the Music of the XVIIth and XVIIIth Centuries* (London, 1915, 2/1946/R1969)

L. Capet: *La technique supérieure de l'archet* (Paris, 1916)

D. Fryklund: *Studien über die Pochette* (Sundsvall, 1917)

G. Beckmann: *Das Violinspiel in Deutschland vor 1700* (Leipzig, 1918)

A. Moser: 'Die Violin-Skordatur', *AMw*, i (1918–19), 573

J. Wolf: *Handbuch der Notationskunde*, ii (Leipzig, 1919/R1963), 63, 237 [on scordatura]

L. Auer: *Violin Playing as I Teach it* (New York, 1921)

D. C. Dounis: *The Artist's Technique of Violin Playing*, op.12 (New York, 1921)

A. Jarosy: *Die Grundlagen des violinistischen Fingersatzes* (Berlin, 1921; Eng. trans., 1933, as *A New Theory of Fingering*)

W. L. von Lütgendorff: *Die Geigen- und Lautenmacher vom Mittelalter bis zur Gegenwart* (Frankfurt am Main, 6/1922/R1968)

M. Pincherle: *Les violonistes, compositeurs et virtuoses* (Paris, 1922)

L. de La Laurencie: *L'école française de violon de Lully à Viotti* (Paris, 1922–4/R1971)

C. Flesch: *Die Kunst des Violin-Spiels*, i (Berlin, 1923, 2/1929; Eng. trans., 1924); ii (Berlin, 1928; Eng. trans., 1930)

W. J. Giltay: *Bow Instruments: their Form and Construction* (London, 1923)

A. Moser: *Geschichte des Violinspiels* (Berlin, 1923, rev., enlarged 2/1966–7)

A. Pougin: *Le violon, les violonistes et la musique du violon du XVIe au XVIIIe siècle* (Paris, 1924)

L. Auer: *Violin Masterworks and their Interpretation* (New York, 1925)

A. A. Bachmann: *An Encyclopedia of the Violin* (New York, 1925/R1966)

A. Bonaventura: *Storia del violino, dei violinisti e della musica per violino* (Milan, 1925)

L. Auer: *Graded Course of Violin Playing* (New York, 1926)

F. von Reuter: *Führer durch die Solo-Violinmusik* (Berlin, 1926)

BIBLIOGRAPHY

A. Lefort and M. Pincherle: 'Le violon', *EMDC*, II/iii (1927), 1800

M. Pincherle: *Feuillets d'histoire du violon* (Paris, 1927) [incl. G. B. Viotti: *Méthode*]

G. R. Hayes: *Musical Instruments and their Music: 1500–1750* (London, 1928–30)

G. Kinsky, R. Haas and H. Schnoor: *Geschichte der Musik in Bildern* (Leipzig, 1929; Eng. trans., 1930, 2/1951)

E. and E. Doflein: *Geigenschulwerk* (Mainz, 1931, 2/1951; Eng. trans., 1957)

R. Haas: *Aufführungspraxis der Musik* (Wildpark-Potsdam, 1931)

F. Hamma: *Meisterwerke italienischer Geigenbaukunst* (Stuttgart, 1931, rev. 2/1964 as *Meister italienischer Geigenbaukunst*, with Eng. trans., rev. 4/1976)

W. H., A. F. and A. E. Hill: *The Violin Makers of the Guarneri Family* (London, 1931)

E. Lesser: 'Zur Scordatura der Streichinstrumente', *AcM*, iv (1932), 123, 148

R. Vannes: *Essai d'un dictionnaire universel des luthiers* (Paris, 1932, 2/1951/R1972 as *Dictionnaire universel des luthiers* and R1981 incl. suppl. 1959)

E. van der Straeten: *The History of the Violin* (London, 1933/R1968)

I. M. Yampol'sky: *Osnovï skripichnoy applikaturï* [The principles of violin fingering] (Moscow, 1933, enlarged 3/1955; Eng. trans., 1967)

T. Russell: 'The Violin "Scordatura" ', *MQ*, xxiv (1938), 84

E. Reeser: *De klaviersonate met vioolbegeleiding in het Parijsche muziekleven ten tijde van Mozart* (Rotterdam, 1939)

F. Farga: *Geigen und Geiger* (Zurich, 1940; Eng. trans., 1950, rev., enlarged 2/1969, 7/1983)

N. Bessaraboff: *Ancient European Musical Instruments* (Cambridge, Mass., 1941)

D. C. Dounis: *New Aids to Technical Development*, op.27 (London, 1941)

P. G. Gelrud: *A Critical Study of the French Violin School (1782–1882)* (diss., Cornell U., 1941)

B. F. Swalin: *The Violin Concerto: a Study in German Romanticism* (Chapel Hill, 1941)

J. H. Fairfield: *Known Violin Makers* (New York, 1942, 4/1983)

A. Veinus: *The Concerto* (New York, 1944)

E. N. Doring: *How Many Strads?* (Chicago, 1945)

E. H. Meyer: *English Chamber Music* (London, 1946, rev. 2/1982 as *Early English Chamber Music: From the Middle Ages to Purcell*)

J. Michelman: *Violin Varnish . . . 1550–1750* (Cincinnati, 1946)

S. Babitz: *Principles of Extensions in Violin Fingering* (Los Angeles, 1947; rev., enlarged 2/1974)

F. Hamma: *Meister deutscher Geigenbaukunst* (Stuttgart, 1948; Eng. trans., 1961)

VIOLIN FAMILY

E. N. Doring: *The Guadagnini Family of Violin Makers* (Chicago, 1949)

R. H. Rowen: *Early Chamber Music* (New York, 1949/*R*1974)

W. C. Gates: *The Musical Literature for Unaccompanied Solo Violin* (diss., U. of North Carolina, 1950)

B. Schwarz: *French Instrumental Music between the Revolutions (1789–1830)* (diss., Columbia U., 1950; New York, 1987)

I. M. Yampol'sky: *Russkoye skripichnoye iskusstvo: ocherki i materialï* [Russian violin playing: essays and materials], i (Moscow, 1951)

K. Jalovec: *Italští houslaři* [Italian violin makers] (Prague, 1952; Eng. trans., 1952 and 1957)

R. and M. Millant: *Manuel pratique de lutherie* (Paris, 1952, 2/1979)

M. Riley: *The Teaching of Bowed Instruments from 1511 to 1756* (diss., U. of Michigan, 1954; Ann Arbor, 1986)

W. Kolneder: *Aufführungspraxis bei Vivaldi* (Leipzig, 1955, 2/1973)

A. Wirsta: *Ecoles de violon au XVIIIme siècle* (diss., U. of Paris, 1955)

A. Buchner: *Hudební nástroje od pravěku k dnešku* [Musical instruments through the ages] (Prague, 1956; Eng. trans., 1956, 4/1962)

S. Babitz: 'Differences between 18th-century and Modern Violin Bowing', *Score*, no.19 (1957), 34; rev. as *Bulletin no.2, Early Music Laboratory* (Los Angeles, 1970)

C. Flesch: *Memoirs* (London, 1957, 2/1958; Ger. orig., Freiburg, 1960, 2/1961)

F. Lesure: 'L'*Epitome musical* de Philibert Jambe de Fer (1556)', *AnnM*, vi (1958–63), 341–86

S. Babitz: *The Violin: Views and Reviews* (Urbana, Ill., 2/1959)

K. Jalovec: *Čeští houslaři* [Czech violin makers] (Prague, 1959; Eng. trans., 1959)

W. S. Newman: *The Sonata in the Baroque Era* (Chapel Hill, 1959, rev. 4/1983)

B. Seagrave: *The French Style of Violin Bowing and Phrasing* (Stanford, Calif., 1959)

J. Wilson, ed.: *Roger North on Music* (London, 1959)

W. Henley: *Universal Dictionary of Violin and Bow Makers* i–v (Brighton, 1959–60); vi, ed. C. Woodcock as *Dictionary of Contemporary Violin and Bow Makers* (Brighton, 1965)

A. H. Benade: *Horns, Strings, and Harmony* (Garden City, NY, 1960)

C. Flesch: *Alta scuola di diteggiatura violinistica* (Milan, 1960; ed. and trans. B. Schwarz, 1966, as *Violin Fingering: its Theory and Practice*)

W. Primrose: *Technique is Memory: a Method for Violin and Viola Players Based on Finger Patterns* (Oxford, 1960)

A. Baines, ed.: *Musical Instruments through the Ages* (Harmondsworth, 1961, 2/1966/*R*1976)

A. Hutchings: *The Baroque Concerto* (London, 1961, rev. 3/1973)

R. Aschmann: *Das deutsche polyphone Violinspiel im 17. Jahrhundert* (Zurich, 1962)

BIBLIOGRAPHY

I. Galamian: *Principles of Violin Playing and Teaching* (Englewood Cliffs, NJ, 1962, 2/1985 with postscript by E. A. H. Green)

C. M. Hutchins: 'The Physics of Violins', *Scientific American*, ccvii (1962), Nov, 78

R. Donington: *The Interpretation of Early Music* (London, 1963, rev., enlarged 3/1974)

W. S. Newman: *The Sonata in the Classic Era* (Chapel Hill, 1963, rev. 3/1983)

J. Szigeti: *A Violinist's Notebook* (London, 1964)

C. R. Boxer: *The Portuguese Seaborne Empire: 1415–1825* (London, 1965)

D. D. Boyden: *The History of Violin Playing from Its Origins to 1761* (London, 1965/R1975)

M. K. Farisch: *String Music in Print* (New York, 1965, suppl. 1968, 2/1973)

E. Leipp: *Le violon, historique, esthétique, facture et acoustique* (Paris, 1965; Eng. trans., 1969)

W. Senn: 'Streichinstrumentenbau', *MGG*

W. Senn, F. Winckel and E. Winternitz: 'Violine', *MGG*

J. Szigeti: *Beethovens Violinwerke: Hinweise für Interpreten und Hörer* (Zurich, 1965) [enlarged Ger. trans. of J. Szigeti: *The Ten Beethoven Sonatas for Piano and Violin* (Urbana, Ill., 1965)]

I. Galamian and F. Neumann: *Contemporary Violin Technique:* i, *Scale and Arpeggio Exercises* (New York, 1963); ii, *Double and Multiple Stops* (New York, 1966)

J. W. Hartnack: *Grosse Geiger unserer Zeit* (Munich, 1967)

C. M. Hutchins: 'Founding a Family of Fiddles', *Physics Today*, xx (1967), 23 [on the New Violin Family]

W. P. Malm: *Music Cultures of the Pacific, the Near East and Asia* (Englewood Cliffs, NJ, 1967, 2/1977)

O. Möckel: *Die Kunst des Geigenbaues* (Hamburg, 3/1967, rev. 4/1977, 6/1984)

L. N. Raaben: *Sovetskiy instrumental'niy kontsert* [The Soviet instrumental concerto] (Leningrad, 1967)

B. G. Seagrave and J. Berman: *The A.S.T.A. Dictionary of Bowing Terms* (Urbana, Ill., 1968, 2/1976)

K. M. Stolba: *A History of the Violin Etude to about 1800* (Fort Hayes, 1968–9/R1979)

J. Backus: *The Acoustical Foundations of Music* (New York, 1969)

D. D. Boyden: *Catalogue of the Hill Collection of Musical Instruments in the Ashmolean Museum, Oxford* (London, 1969)

F. Neumann: *Violin Left Hand Technique: a Survey of the Related Literature* (Urbana, Ill., 1969)

W. S. Newman: *The Sonata since Beethoven* (Chapel Hill, 1969, rev. 3/1983)

J. Szigeti: *Szigeti on the Violin* (London, 1969, 2/1979)

VIOLIN FAMILY

A. Gingrich: *A Thousand Mornings of Music: the Journal of an Obsession with the Violin* (New York, 1970)

S. Milliot: *Documents inédits sur les luthiers parisiens du XVIIIe siècle* (Paris, 1970)

Y. Menuhin: *Six Lessons with Yehudi Menuhin* (London, 1971/R1974 as *Violin: Six Lessons with Yehudi Menuhin*)

A. Wirsta: *L'enseignement du violon au XIXème siècle* (Paris, 1971–4)

S. and S. Applebaum: *The Way they Play* (Neptune City, NJ, 1972)

W. Kolneder: *Das Buch der Violine* (Zurich, 1972, 3/1984)

R. Millant: *J. B. Vuillaume: sa vie et son oeuvre* (London, 1972)

S. M. Nelson: *The Violin and Viola* (London, 1972)

H. K. Goodkind: *Violin Iconography of Antonio Stradivari, 1644–1737* (Larchmont, NY, 1973)

C. M. Hutchins and M. Bram: 'The Bowed Strings – Yesterday, Today, and Tomorrow', *Music Educators Journal* (1973), Nov, 20

A. Loft: *Violin and Keyboard: the Duo Repertoire* (New York, 1973)

E. Melkus: *Die Violine* (Berne, 1973)

J. Wechsberg: *The Glory of the Violin* (New York, 1973)

B. Geiser: *Studien zur Frühgeschichte der Violine* (Berne and Stuttgart, 1974)

A. Woollen: 'New Instruments Unveiled in Britain', *The Strad*, lxxxv (1974–5), 265

Violinspiel und Violinmusik in Geschichte und Gegenwart: Internationaler Kongress am Institut für Aufführungspraxis der Hochscule für Musik und darstellende Kunst: Graz 1972 (Vienna, 1975)

L. C. Witten jr: 'Apollo, Orpheus and David: a Study of the Crucial Century in the Development of Bowed Strings in North Italy 1480–1580 as seen in Graphic Evidence and some Surviving Instruments', *JAMIS*, i (1975), 5–55

Journal of the Violin Society of America (1975–)

J. H. Chestnut: 'Mozart's Teaching of Intonation', *JAMS*, xxx (1977), 254

R. Donington: *String Playing in Baroque Music* (London, 1977)

A. Gaugé: ' "La lutherie" at Mirecourt', *Journal of the Violin Society of America*, iii/3 (1977), 68

E. Dann: 'The Second Revolution in the History of the Violin: a Twentieth-century Phenomenon', *Journal of the Violin Society of America*, iv/1 (1977–8), 46; repr. in *College Music Symposium*, xvii/2 (1977), 64

M. Brinser: *Dictionary of Twentieth Century Violin Makers* (Irvington, NJ, 1978)

R. Stowell: *The Development of Violin Technique from L'abbé le fils to Paganini* (diss., U. of Cambridge, 1978)

C. Taylor: 'The New Violin Family and its Scientific Background', *Soundings*, vii (1978), 101

BIBLIOGRAPHY

L. Vorreiter: 'Zur Entstehungsgeschichte der Violine', *Musikinstrument*, xxvii/1 (1978), 30

F. Prochart: *Der Wiener Geigenbau im 19. und 20. Jahrhundert* (Tutzing, 1979)

B. C. Wade: *Music in India: the Classical Traditions* (Englewood Cliffs, NJ, 1979)

W. Apel: 'Studien über die frühe Violinmusik, VIII: die italienischen Hauptquellen von 1680 bis 1689', *AMw*, xxxvii (1980), 206–35

M. Campbell: *The Great Violinists* (London, 1980)

S. W. McVeigh: *The Violinist in London's Concert Life, 1750–1784: Felice Giardini and his Contemporaries* (diss., U. of Oxford, 1980)

C. Vettori: *Linee classiche della liuteria italiana* (Pisa, 1980)

G. Tumminello: *Arte, artigianato, società: dall' albero al violino, lavoro e creatività* (Cremona, 1981)

B. Barilli: *Il sorcio nel violino* (Turin, 1982)

J. S. and W. R. Robinson: *The Guarneri Mold and Modern Violin Making* (Oklahoma City, 1982)

H. Roth: *Master Violinists in Performance* (Neptune City, 1982)

W. Thomas: *Traditional Music in Wales: a Bibliography* (Cardiff, 1982)

I. Vigdorchik: *The Acoustical Systems of Violins of Stradivarius and other Cremona Makers* (Westbury, NJ, 1982)

W. Apel: *Die italienische Violinmusik im 17. Jahrhundert* (Wiesbaden, 1983)

A. Cohen: 'A Cache of 18th-century Strings', *GSJ*, xxxvi (1983), 37 [on the making of silk strings]

R. Gerle: *The Art of Practising the Violin* (London, 1983)

P. Marcan: *Music for Solo Violin Unaccompanied: a Performer's Guide to the Published Literature of the 17th, 18th, 19th and 20th Centuries* (High Wycombe, 1983)

M. Robinson: *Focus on Music: the Violin and Viola* (London, 1983)

B. Schwarz: *Great Masters of the Violin: from Corelli and Vivaldi to Stern, Zukerman, and Perlman* (New York, 1983)

B. R. Toskey: *Concertos for Violin and Viola: a Comprehensive Encyclopedia* (Seattle, 1983)

D. Gill, ed.: *The Book of the Violin* (New York, 1984)

D. Johnson: *Scottish Fiddle Music in the 18th Century: a Musical Collection and Historical Study* (Edinburgh, 1984)

W. Kolneder: *Harmonielehre für Geiger und Spieler anderer Melodieinstrumente* (Wilhelmshaven, 1984)

A. Lolov: 'Bent Plates in Violin Construction', *GSJ*, xxxvii (1984), 10

R. Stowell: 'Violin Bowing in Transition', *Early Music*, xii (1984), 316

P. Walls: 'Violin Fingering in the 18th Century', *Early Music*, xii (1984), 300

E. J. Ward: *The Strad Facsimile: an Illustrated Guide to Violin Making* (Honolulu, 1984)

VIOLIN FAMILY

I. Watchorn: 'Baroque Renaissance', *The Strad*, xcv (1984–5), 822 [on violins]

P. Barbieri: 'Giordano Riccati on the Diameters of Strings and Pipes', *GSJ*, xxxviii (1985), 20

K. Coates: *Geometry, Proportion, and the Art of Lutherie: a Study of the Use and Aesthetic Significance of Geometry and Numerical Proportion in the Design of European Bowed and Plucked String Instruments in the Sixteenth, Seventeenth, and Eighteenth Centuries* (New York, 1985)

R. Doerr: *Violin Maker's Handbook* (Battle Creek, MI, 1985)

B. Haynes: 'J. S. Bach's Pitch Standards: the Woodwind Perspective', *American Musical Instrument Society*, xi (1985), 55–113

S. Monosoff: 'Violin fingering', *Early Music*, xiii (1985), 76

K. Osse: *Violine: Klangwerkzeug und Kunstgegenstand: ein Leitfaden für Spieler und Liebhaber von Streichinstrumenten* (Wiesbaden, 1985)

R. Stowell: *Violin Technique and Performance Practice in the Late Eighteenth and Early Nineteenth Centuries* (Cambridge, 1985)

D. Cox: 'The Baroque Violin', *Journal of the Violin Society of America*, viii/1 (1986), 57

W. S. Gorrill and N. Pickering: 'Strings: Facts and Fallacies', *Journal of the Violin Society of America*, viii/1 (1986), 27

W. Hamma: *Violin-makers of the German School* (Tutzing, 1986)

R. Hargrave: 'Safety Pins', 'Tried and Tested', 'Keeping Fit', *The Strad*, xcvii (1986–7), 116, 194, 257 [Cremonese construction methods]

Y. Menuhin: *The Compleat Violinist: Thoughts, Exercises, Reflections of an Itinerant Violinist* (New York, 1986)

W. L. Monical: 'Violin', *New Harvard Dictionary of Music*, ed. D. Randel (Cambridge, Mass., 1986)

R. Regazzi: *Il manoscritto liutaria di G. A. Marchi, Bologna 1786* (Bologna, 1986) [with Eng. trans.]

A. Dipper and D. Woodrow: *Count Ignazio Alessandro Cozio di Salabue: Observations on the Construction of Stringed Instruments and their Adjustment, 1804, 1805, 1809, 1810, 1816*, Technical Studies in the Arts of Musical Instrument Making (Taynton, Oxfordshire, 1987)

C. Beare: *The Venetian Violin Makers* (in preparation)

VIOLA

M. Mersenne: *Harmonie universelle* (Paris, 1636–7/R1963; Eng. trans., 1957)

J. J. Quantz: *Versuch einer Anweisung die Flöte traversiere zu spielen* (Berlin, 1752, 3/1789/R1952; Eng. trans., 1966)

M. Corrette: *Méthodes pour apprendre à jouer à la contre-basse à 3, à 4, et à 5 cordes, de la quinte ou alto et de la viole d'Orphée . . . avec des leçons et des sonates pour ces trois instrumens* (Paris, 1773/R1977)

BIBLIOGRAPHY

Complete Instructions for the Tenor Containing such Rules and Examples as are necessary for Learners with a selection of Favorite Song-tunes, Minuets, Marches, etc. Judiciously adapted for that Instrument by an Eminent Master (London, between 1782 and 1798)

M. Woldemar: *Méthode d'alto contenant les premiers élémens de la musique, les positions doigtées et les coups d'archets anciens et modernes, terminée par des variations d'alto et violon* (Paris, between 1795 and 1803)

F. Cupis: *Méthode d'alto précédé d'un abrégé des principes de musique de différents airs nouveaux dont plusieurs avec variations et terminée par un long caprice ou étude propre à perfectionner l'élève en peu de temp* (Paris, c1801)

M. J. Gebauer: *Méthode d'alto contenant les principes de musique avec les gammes accompagnées dans tous les tons suives de petites pièces en duo tirées des plus célèbres auteurs tels que Haydn, Mozart, Boccherini &c* (Paris, c1805)

A. B. Bruni: *Méthode pour l'alto-viola contenant les principes de cet instrument suivis de vingt cinq études* (Paris, c1816)

J.-J.-B. Martinn: *Nouvelle Méthode d'Alto Contenant des Gammes et Exercises dans tous les Tons, Douze Leçons en Duos et trois Sonates Faciles* (Paris, between 1826 and 1830)

H. Berlioz: *Grand traité d'instrumentation et d'orchestration modernes* (Paris, 1843, 2/1855; Eng. trans., 1855)

H. Ritter: *Die Geschichte der Viola alta und die Grundsätze ihres Baues* (Leipzig, 1876, 2/1877/R1969, 3/1885)

———: *Die fünfsaitige Alt-Geige* (Bamberg, 1898)

E. van der Straeten: 'The Viola', *The Strad*, xxiii–xxvi (1912–16) [series of articles]

R. Clarke: 'The History of the Viola in Quartet Writing', *ML*, iv (1923), 6

F. H. Martens: *String Mastery* (New York, 1923)

W. Altmann: 'Zur Geschichte der Bratsche und der Bratschten', *AMz*, lvi (1929), 971

———, ed.: *Die Bratsche: Mitteilungsblatt des Bratschisten-Bundes* (Leipzig, 1929–30)

W. W. Cobbett: *Cyclopedic Survey of Chamber Music*, iii (London, 1929–30, 2/1963)

W. Altmann and V. Borissovsky: *Literaturverzeichnis für Bratsche und Viola d'amore* (Wolfenbüttel, 1937)

L. Tertis: *Beauty of Tone in String Playing* (London, 1938)

R. Dolejši: *Modern Viola Technique* (Chicago, 1939) [based on Ševčík's teachings]

C. Sachs: *The History of Musical Instruments* (New York, 1940)

J. A. Watson: 'Mozart and the Viola', *ML*, xxii (1941), 41

E. N. Doring: *How Many Strads?* (Chicago, 1945)

H. Letz: *Music for the Violin and Viola* (New York, 194)

H. Besseler: *Zum Problem der Tenorgeige* (Heidelberg, 1949)

VIOLIN FAMILY

L. Tertis: *Cinderella no More* (London, 1953) [autobiography, with valuable appx and work-lists]

M. W. Riley: *The Teaching of Bowed Instruments from 1511 to 1756* (diss., U. of Michigan, 1954; Ann Arbor, 1986)

W. Piston: *Orchestration* (New York, 1955)

G. Pasqualini: 'Referendum internazionale sulla viola moderna', *Saint Cecilia*, viii (1959), 81; ix (1960), 73

H. Kunitz: *Violine/Bratsche* (Leipzig, 1960)

W. Primrose: *Technique is Memory: a Method for Violin and Viola Players Based on Finger Patterns* (Oxford, 1960)

C. M. Hutchins: 'The Physics of Violins', *Scientific American*, ccvii (1962), Nov, 78

D. D. Boyden: 'The Tenor Violin: Myth, Mystery, or Misnomer', *Festschrift Otto Erich Deutsch* (Kassel, 1963), 273

F. Zeyringer: *Literatur für Viola* (Hartberg, 1963, suppl. 1965, rev. 3/1985)

D. D. Boyden: *The History of Violin Playing from its Origins to 1761* (London, 1965/R1975)

W. Senn: 'Streichinstrumentenbau', *MGG*

A. Berner: 'Viola', *MGG*

H. Barrett: *The Viola: Complete Guide for Teachers and Students* (Birmingham, Alabama, 1972, rev. 2/1978)

S. Nelson: *The Violin and Viola* (New York, 1972)

A. Arcidiacono: *La viola: gli strumenti musicali* (Milan, 1973)

Newsletter of the American Viola Research Society (1973–8)

M. Rosenblum: 'The Viola Research Society', *American String Teacher*, xxiii, 2 (1973), 29

W. Lebermann: 'The Viola Concerti of the Stamitz Family', *Viola Research Society Newsletter* (1974), 3

L. Tertis: *My Viola and I: a Complete Autobiography* (London, 1974)

K. Ewald: *Musik für Bratsche* (Liestal, 1975)

Journal of the Violin Society of America (1975–) [vol.iii (1977) incl. articles by M. W. Riley]

T. Serly: 'A Belated Account of the Reconstruction of a 20th Century Masterpiece', *College Music Symposium*, xv (1975), 7 [on Bartók's Viola Concerto]

L. C. Witten jr: 'Apollo, Orpheus, and David: a Study of the Crucial Century in the Development of Bowed Strings in North Italy 1480–1580 as seen in Graphic Evidence and some Surviving Instruments', *JAMIS*, i (1975), 5–55

British Viola Research Society Newsletter (1976–83)

Y. Menuhin and W. Primrose: *Violin and Viola* (London, 1976)

T. J. Tatton: *English Viola Music, 1870–1937* (diss., U. of Illinois, Urbana, 1976)

Newsletter of the American Viola Society (1978–85)

BIBLIOGRAPHY

W. Primrose: *Walk on the North Side: Memoirs of a Violist* (Provo, Utah, 1978)

F. Zeyringer: *The Problem of Viola Size* (New York, 1979)

The Viola: Yearbook of the International Viola Research Society (Kassel, 1979–)

M. W. Riley: *The History of the Viola* (Ypsilanti, Mich., 1980) [incl. full bibliography]

U. Drünner: 'Das Viola-Konzert vor 1840', *FAM*, xxviii (1981), 153

D. Gill: 'Vihuelas, Violas and the Spanish Guitar', *Early Music*, ix (1981), 455

L. Inzaghi and L. A. Bianchi: *Alessandro Rolla Catalogo tematico delle opere* (Milan, n.d. [1981])

M. Awouters: 'X-raying Musical Instruments: a Method in Organological Study', *RBM*, xxxvi–xxxviii (1982–4), 213

British Viola Society Newsletter (1983–)

W. Lebermann: 'Das Viola-Konzert vor 1840, Addenda und Corrigenda', *FAM*, xxx (1983), 220

M. Robinson: *Focus on Music: the Violin and Viola* (London, 1983)

B. R. Toskey: *Concertos for Violin and Viola: a Comprehensive Encyclopedia* (Seattle, 1983)

Journal of the American Viola Society (1985–)

S. L. Kruse: *The Viola School of Technique: Etudes and Methods written between 1780 and 1860* (Ann Arbor, 1986)

D. Dalton: *Playing the Viola: Conversations with William Primrose* (Oxford, 1988)

VIOLONCELLO

M. Agricola: *Musica instrumentalis deudsch* (Wittenberg, 1529/R1969, enlarged 5/1545)

G. M. Lanfranco: *Scintille di musica* (Brescia, 1533)

P. Jambe de Fer: *Epitome musical* (Lyons, 1556); repr. in Lesure (1958–63)

L. Zacconi: *Prattica di musica* (Venice, 1592/R1967)

M. Praetorius: *Syntagma musicum*, i (Wittenberg and Wolfenbüttel, 1614–15/R1968); ii (Wolfenbüttel, 1618; 2/1619/R1958 and 1980, Eng. trans., ed. D. Z. Crookes, 1986); iii (Wolfenbüttel, 1618, 2/1619/R1958 and 1976)

M. Mersenne: *Harmonie universelle* (Paris, 1636–7/R1963; Eng. trans., 1957)

H. Le Blanc: *Défense de la basse de viole contre les enterprises du violon et les prétensions du violoncel* (Amsterdam, 1740/R1975); repr. in *ReM*, ix (1927–8)

VIOLIN FAMILY

M. Corrette: *Méthode théorique et pratique pour apprendre en peu de tems le violoncelle dans sa perfection. Ensemble de principes de musique avec des leçons*, op.24 (Paris, 1741/*R*1972, 2/1783)

J. B. Tillière: *Méthode pour le violoncelle contenant tous les principes nécessaires pour bien jouer de cet instrument* (Paris, 1764; Eng. trans., London, *c*1795 as *New and Compleat Instruction*, rev. 4/1901 by I. Danbe)

R. Crome: *The Compleat Tutor, for the Violoncello* (London, 2/*c*1765)

S. Lanzetti: *Principes ou l'application de violoncelle par tous les tons* (Amsterdam, before 1770)

F. Cupis: *Méthode nouvelle et raisonnée pour apprendre à jouer du violoncelle* (Paris, 1772)

J. B. Baumgartner: *Instructions de musique, théorique et pratique, à l'usage du violoncelle* (The Hague, *c*1774)

J. Gunn: *The Theory and Practice of Fingering the Violoncello* (London, 1789)

P. Baillot, J. H. Levasseur, C.-S. Catel and C.-N. Baudiot: *Méthode de violoncelle et de basse d'accompagnement* (Paris, 1804/*R*1974; Eng. trans., *c*1850)

J.-B. S. Bréval: *Traité du violoncelle*, op.42 (Paris, 1804)

J.-L. Duport: *Essai sur le doigté du violoncelle, et sur la conduite de l'archet* (Paris, *c*1813)

C. Baudiot: *Méthode de violoncelle*, op.25 (Paris, 1826–8)

F.-J. Fétis: *Antoine Stradivari, luthier célèbre* (Paris, 1856; Eng. trans., 1864/*R*1964)

P. Roth: *Führer durch die Violoncell-Literatur* (Leipzig, 1888, 2/1898)

J. W. von Wasielewski: *Das Violoncell und seine Geschichte* (Leipzig, 1889, enlarged, 3/1925/*R*1970; Eng. trans., 1894/*R*1968)

E. S. J. van der Straeten: *The Technics of Violoncello Playing* (London, 1898, 4/1923)

W. H., A. F. and A. E. Hill: *Antonio Stradivari: his Life and Work* (London, 1902, 2/1909/*R*1963)

L. Forino: *Il violoncello, il violoncellista ed i violoncellisti* (Milan, 1905, 2/1930)

B. Weigl: *Handbuch der Violoncell-Literatur* (Vienna, 1911, 3/1929)

C. Liégeois and E. Nogué: *Le violoncelle: son histoire, ses virtuoses* (Paris, 1913)

F. Vatielli: 'Primordi dell'arte del violoncello', *Harmonia* (Rome, 1913–14, 3/1927)

E. S. J. van der Straeten: *History of the Violoncello, the Viol da Gamba, their Precursors and Collateral Instruments* (London, 1915/*R*1971)

M. Vadding and M. Merseburger: *Das Violoncell und seine Literatur* (Leipzig, 1920)

A. Broadley: *The Violoncello: its History, Selection and Adjustment* (London, 1921)

D. Alexanian: *Traité théorique et pratique du violoncelle/The Technique of*

BIBLIOGRAPHY

Violoncello Playing (Paris, 1922) [Fr. and Eng. text; preface by Casals]

F. Kohlmorgen: *Die Brüder Duport und die Entwicklung der Violoncelltechnik von ihren Anfängen bis zur Zeit B. Rombergs* (Berlin, 1922)

E. Nogué: *La littérature du violoncelle* (Paris, 1925, 2/1931)

H. Becker and D. Rynar: *Mechanik und Aesthetik des Violoncellspiels* (Vienna, 1929/R1971)

H. Weber: *Das Violoncellkonzert des 18. und beginnenden 19. Jahrhunderts* (Tübingen, 1933)

E. Rapp: *Beiträge zur Frühgeschichte des Violoncellkonzerts* (Würzburg, 1934)

W. Vollmer: *Über die Erscheinung des Wolftons bei Streichinstrumenten, insbesondere beim Cello* (Karlsruhe, 1936)

E. Nogué: *Le violoncelle, jadis et aujourd'hui* (Paris, 1937)

W. Mirandolle: *De violoncel: haar bouw, geschiedenis en ontwikkelingsgang* (The Hague, 1943)

L. S. Ginzburg: *Istoriya violonchel'novo iskusstva* [The history of the art of cello playing], i–iv (Moscow, 1950–78); Eng. trans. 1983 as *History of the Violoncello*

E. Valentin: *Cello: Das Instrument und sein Meister Ludwig Hoelscher* (Pfullingen, 1955)

M. Eisenberg: *Cello Playing of Today* (London, 1957) [with M. B. Stanfield]

G. Waegner: *Die sechs Suiten für das Violoncello allein von J. S. Bach* (Berlin, 1957)

R. Eras: *Über das Verhältnis zwischen Stimmung und Spieltechnik bei Streichinstrumenten in Da-gamba-Haltung* (Leipzig, 1958)

F. Lesure: 'L'*Epitome musical* de Philibert Jambe de Fer (1556)', *AnnM*, vi (1958–63), 341–86

J. Bächi: *Von Boccherini bis Casals* (Zurich, 1961)

J. Starker: *An Organized Method of String Playing: Violoncello Exercises for the Left Hand* (New York, 1961)

A. C. Bacon: *The Evolution of the Violoncello as a Solo Instrument* (diss., Syracuse U., 1962)

E. Cowling: *The Italian Sonata Literature for the Violoncello in the Baroque Era* (diss., Northwestern U., 1962)

A. Dioli: *L'arte violoncellistica in Italia* (Palermo, 1962)

G. J. Kinney: *The Musical Literature for Unaccompanied Violoncello* (diss., Florida State U., 1962)

W. Pape: *Die Entwicklung des Violoncellspiels im 19. Jahrhundert* (Saarbrücken, 1962)

K. Marx: *Die Entwicklung des Violoncells und seiner Spieltechnik bis J. L. Duport (1520–1820)* (Regensburg, 1963)

G. J. Shaw: *The Violoncello Sonata Literature in France during the Eighteenth Century* (diss., Catholic U., Washington, DC, 1963)

S. Milliot: 'Réflexions et recherches sur la viole de gambe et le violoncelle en France', *RMFC*, iv (1964), 179–238

L. A. Potter: *The Art of Cello Playing* (Evanston, Ill., 1964)

M. K. Farish: *String Music in Print* (New York, 1965; suppl. 1968)

U. Zingler: *Studien zur Entwicklung der italienischen Violoncellsonate von den Anfängen bis zur Mitte des 18. Jahrhunderts* (diss., U. of Frankfurt, 1966)

J. Eckhardt: *Die Violoncellschulen von J. J. F. Dotzauer, F. A. Kummer, und B. Romberg*, Kölner Beiträge zur Musikforschung, li (Regensburg, 1968)

G. Mantel: *Cello Technik* (Cologne, 1972)

G. Blees: *Das Cello-Konzert um 1800* (Regensburg, 1973)

L. Malusi: *Il Violoncello* (Padua, 1973)

M. B. Stanfield: *The Intermediate Cellist* (London, 1973)

L. Lützen: *Die Violoncell-Transkriptionen Friedrich Grützmachers* (Regensburg, 1974)

E. Cowling: *The Cello* (London, 1975, 2/1983)

W. Schrammek: 'Viola pomposa und Violoncello piccolo bei Johann Sebastian Bach', *Wissenschaftliche Bach-Konferenz: Leipzig 1975*, 345

P. Tortelier: *How I Play, How I Teach* (London, 1975)

L. C. Witten jr: 'Apollo, Orpheus and David: a Study of the Crucial Century in the Development of Bowed Strings in North Italy 1480–1580 as seen in Graphic Evidence and some Surviving Instruments', *JAMIS*, i (1975), 5–55

J. Webster: 'Violoncello and Double Bass in the Chamber Music of Haydn and his Viennese Contemporaries, 1750–1780', *JAMS*, xxix (1976), 413

S. Bonta: 'From Violone to Violoncello: a Question of Strings', *JAMIS*, iii (1977), 64–99

———: 'Terminology for the Bass Violin in Seventeenth-century Italy', *JAMIS*, iv (1978), 5–42

P. Allsop: 'The Role of the Stringed Bass as a Continuo Instrument in Italian Seventeenth-century Instrumental Music', *Chelys*, viii (1978–9), 31

N. Pyron: *Everything you wanted to know about the Baroque Cello* (London, 1979)

S. Milliot: *Le violoncelle en France au XVIIIe siècle* (Lille, 1981)

C. Bunting: *Essay on the Craft of Cello-playing: i, Prelude, Bowing, Coordination; ii, the Left Hand* (Cambridge, 1982, rev. 2/1988, ed. D. C. Pratt)

R. Doppelbauer: *Der frühe Cellounterricht* (Wilhelmshaven, 1982)

W. Pleeth: *Cello* (London, 1982)

M.-G. Scott: 'Boccherini's B flat Cello Concerto: a Reappraisal of the Sources', *Early Music*, xii (1984), 355

M. Adeney: *Tomorrow's Cellist: Exploring the Basis of Artistry* (Oakville, Ont., 1984)

BIBLIOGRAPHY

E. Halfpenny: 'The Berkswell Cello', *GSJ*, xxxvii (1984), 2 [on an early 18th-century English cello]

D. Markevitch: *Cello Story* (Princeton, NJ, 1984)

A. Planyavsky: 'Violone und Violoncello im 17. Jahrhundert', *Musicologica austriaca*, no.4 (1984), 43

D. C. Pratt, ed.: *'Cello Technique 'from one note to the next'* (Cambridge, 1988) [rev. edn. of Bunting, 1982]

M. Campbell: *The Great Cellists* (London, 1988)

DOUBLE BASS

M. Agricola: *Musica instrumentalis deudsch* (Wittenberg, 1529/*R*1969, enlarged 5/1545)

M. Praetorius: *Syntagma musicum*, ii (Wolfenbüttel, 1618; 2/1619/*R*1958 and 1980; Eng. trans., ed. D. Z. Crookes, 1986)

J. J. Quantz: *Versuch einer Anweisung die Flöte traversiere zu spielen* (Berlin, 1752, 3/1789/*R*1952; Eng. trans., 1966)

M. Corrette: *Méthodes pour apprendre à jouer à la contre-basse à 3, à 4 et à 5 cordes, de la quinte ou alto et de la viole d'Orphée . . . avec des leçons et des sonates pour ces trois instrumens* (Paris, 1773/*R*1977)

J. G. Albrechtsberger: *Gründliche Anweisung zur Komposition* (Leipzig, 1790/*R*1968; Eng. trans., 1844)

C. von Dittersdorf: *Lebensbeschreibung* (Leipzig, 1801; Eng. trans., 1896/*R*1970)

J. Fröhlich: *Kontrabass-Schule* (Würzburg, 1829; Eng. trans., ?1840)

J. G. Albrechtsberger: *Sämtliche Schriften*, ed. I. X. Seyfried (Vienna, 1837)

J. Hindle: *Der Contrabass-Lehrer* (Vienna, ?1850)

G. Bottesini: *Metodo completo per contrabbasso* (Milan, n.d.; Fr. trans., 1869; Eng. trans., ?1870, 2/1876)

F. Simandl: *Neueste Methode des Contrabass-Spiels* (Vienna, 1874; Eng. trans., 1903/*R*1964)

A. C. White: *The Double Bass* (London. ?1893/*R*1934)

J. Reynolds: *A Scrap Book for the Use of Students of the Double Bass* (London, c1896)

E. Madenski: *Grundriss der Geschichte des Solospiels auf dem Kontrabass* (Vienna, 1903)

F. Warnecke: *'Ad infinitum': Der Kontrabass* (Hamburg, 1909)

E. Nanny: *Méthode complète de contrebass* (Paris, ?1924)

W. Altmann, ed.: *Der Kontrabass* [Mitteilungsblatt des Kontrabassisten-Bundes] (March 1929–Feb 1931)

K. Gullbrandsson: *Kontrabas skola* (Stockholm, 1941/*R*1953)

E. Halfpenny: 'A Note on the Genealogy of the Double Bass', *GSJ*, i (1948), 41

VIOLIN FAMILY

L. Montag: *Double-Bass Method* (Budapest, 1956)

M. Grodner: *A Comprehensive Catalog of Available Literature for the Double Bass* (Bloomington, 1958, 3/1974)

C. Bär: 'Zum Begriff des "Basso" in Mozarts Serenaden', *MJb 1960–61*, 133

E. Halfpenny: 'The Double Bass', *Musical Instruments through the Ages*, ed. A. Baines (Harmondsworth, 1961)

F. Zimmerman: 'The Double Bass in Ensemble', *American String Teacher*, xiv/4 (1964), 12

E. Cruft: *The Eugene Cruft School of Double Bass Playing* (London, 1966)

I. H. Cohen: *The Historical Development of the Double Bass* (diss., New York U., 1967)

R. Elgar: *Looking at the Double Bass* (St Leonards on Sea, 1967)

G. Karr, ed.: *Sound Post: the Double Bass* [journal of the International Institute for the String Bass] (1967–71)

L. Hurst: 'The Bass Extension Machine vs. the Five-string Bass', *The Instrumentalist*, xxii (1968), 77

P. Albright: *Original Solo Concertos for the Double Bass* (Rochester, NY, 1969)

A. Meier: *Konzertante Musik für Kontrabass in der Wiener Klassik: mit Beiträgen zur Geschichte des Kontrabassbaues in Österreich* (Griebing über Prien am Chiemsee, 1969)

B. Turetzky: 'The Bass as a Drum', *The Composer*, i (1969), 92

———: 'Vocal and Speech Sounds – a Technique of Contemporary Writing for the Contrabass', *The Composer*, i (1969), 118

A. Planyavsky: *Geschichte des Kontrabasses* (Tutzing, 1970, rev. 2/1984)

E. Cruft: '1903 – Then and Now: some Bass Reflections', *Recorded Sound*, xlii–xliii (1971), 758

G. Karr, ed.: *Probass* (1971–3) [successor to *Sound Post*]

A. Planyavsky: 'Mozarts Arie mit obligatem Kontrabass', *MJb 1971–2*, 313; Eng. trans. in *Bass World*, ii (1976), 187

J. Rives: *Famous Bass Players* (Sante Fe, 1972)

S. Carlin: *Il contrabbasso* (Ancona and Milan, 1974)

J. Webster: 'Violoncello and Double Bass in the Chamber Music of Haydn and his Viennese Contemporaries, 1750–1780', *JAMS*, xxix (1976), 413

F. Baines: 'What exactly is a Violone?', *Early Music*, v (1977), 173

P. Brun: *Histoire des contrebasses à cordes* (Paris, 1982)

M. Térey-Smith: 'Joseph Kämpfer: a Contrabass Virtuoso from Pozsony (Bratislava)', *SM*, xxv (1983), 183

A. Planyavsky: 'Violone und Violoncello im 17. Jahrhundert', *Musicologica austriaca*, no.4 (1984), 43

R. Slatford and S. Petitt: *The Bottom Line: New Prospects for Teaching and Learning the Double Bass* (London, 1985)

BIBLIOGRAPHY

BOW

M. Mersenne: *Harmonie universelle* (Paris, 1636–7/R1963; Eng. trans., 1957)

J. C. Weigel: *Musicalisches Theatrum* (Nuremberg, c1722/R1961)

M. Woldemar: *Méthode pour le violon* (Paris, 1798, rev. 2/c1800 as *Grande Méthode ou étude élémentaire pour le violon*)

F.-J. Fétis: *Antoine Stradivari, luthier célèbre* (Paris, 1856; Eng. trans., 1864/R1964)

J. Rühlmann: *Die Geschichte der Bogeninstrumente* (Brunswick, 1882)

H. Saint-George: *The Bow: its History, Manufacture and Use* (London, 1896, 2/1909)

A. Hammerich: 'Zur Frage nach dem Ursprung der Streichinstrumente', *IMusSCR, ii Basle 1906*, 225

F. W. Galpin: *Old English Instruments of Music: their History and Character* (London, 1910, rev. 4/1965 by T. Dart)

K. Schlesinger: *The Instruments of the Modern Orchestra and Early Records of the Precursors of the Violin Family*, ii (London, 1910)

C. Sachs: 'Die Streichbogenfrage', *AMw*, i (1918–19), 3

H. Panum: *Middelalderen strengeinstrumenter*, ii–iii (Copenhagen, 1928–31; Eng. trans., 1941)

G. Hayes: *Musical Instruments and their Music, 1500–1750*, ii (London, 1930)

R. Vannes: *Essai d'un dictionnaire universel des luthiers* (Paris, 1932, 2/1951/R1972 as *Dictionnaire universel des luthiers* and R1981 incl. suppl. 1959)

E. van der Straeten: *The History of the Violin* (London, 1933/R1968)

F. Wunderlich: *Der Geigenbogen: seine Geschichte, Herstellung und Behandlung* (Leipzig, 1936, 2/1952)

H.-H. Dräger: *Die Entwicklung des Streichbogens* (Kassel, 1937)

C. Sachs: *The History of Musical Instruments* (New York, 1940)

V. Denis: *De muziekinstrumenten in de Nederlanden en in Italië, naar hun afbeelding in de 15de-eeuwsche kunst* (Antwerp, 1944; part Eng. trans. in *GSJ*, ii, 1949)

F. Hamma: 'Der Bogen zum Streichinstrument', *IZ*, viii (1953), 25

A. Koenig: *Le violon et ses ancêtres* (Liège, 1954)

J. Roda: *Bows for Musical Instruments of the Violin Family* (Chicago, 1959)

B. A. Struve: *Protsess formirovaniya viol i skripok* [The process of making the viol and violin] (Moscow, 1959)

D. Droysen: *Die Saiteninstrumente des frühen und hohen Mittelalters (Halsinstrumente): Darstellung der Instrumententypen anhand ikonographischer und literarischer Quellen sowie romanischer und frühgotischer Plastik* (diss., U. of Hamburg, 1961)

R. Hammerstein: *Die Musik der Engel: Untersuchungen zur Musikanschauung des Mittelalters* (Munich, 1962)

K. Marx: *Die Entwicklung des Violoncells und seiner Spieltechnik bis J. L. Duport 1520–1820* (Regensburg, 1963)

W. Bachmann: *Die Anfänge des Streichinstrumentenspiels* (Leipzig, 1964, 2/1966; Eng. trans., 1969, as *The Origins of Bowing and the Development of Bowed Instruments up to the 13th Century*)

W. C. Retford: *Bows and Bow Makers* (London, 1964)

C. van Leeuwen Boomkamp and J. H. Van der Meer: *The Carel van Leeuwen Boomkamp Collection of Musical Instruments* (Amsterdam, 1971)

R. Millant: *J. B. Vuillaume: sa vie et son oeuvre* (London, 1972)

E. Vatelot: *Les archets français* (Nancy, 1976) [in Eng., Fr. and Ger.]

S. Monosoff, D. Boyden and others: 'The Baroque Bow Past and Present', *Journal of the Violin Society of America*, iii/4 (1977), 35–77 [symposium]

L. Malusi: *L'arco degli strumenti musicale: storia, tecnica, costruttori, valutazioni* (Padua, 1981)

D. Gill, ed.: *The Book of the Violin* (New York, 1984) [especially chap. by J. Liivoja-Lorius]

W. L. Monical: 'Bow', *The New Harvard Dictionary of Music*, ed. D. Randel (Cambridge, Mass., 1986)

ACOUSTICS

M. Praetorius: *Syntagma musicum*, ii (Wolfenbüttel, 1618, 2/1619/R1958 and 1980), 26

F. Savart: *L'institut*, viii/67–71 (1840)

M. G. J. Minnaert and C. C. Vlam: 'The Vibrations of the Violin Bridge', *Physica*, iv (1937), 361

W. Lottermoser and J. Meyer: 'Akustische Prüfung der Klangqualität von Geigen', *IZ*, xii (1957), 42

H. F. Meinel: 'Regarding the Sound Quality of Violins and a Scientific Basis for Violin Construction', *Journal of the Acoustical Society of America*, xxix (1957), 817

C. M. Hutchins, A. S. Hopping and F. A. Saunders: 'Subharmonics and Plate Tap Tones in Violin Acoustics', *Journal of the Acoustical Society of America*, xxxii (1960), 1443

C. M. Hutchins: 'The Physics of Violins', *Scientific American*, ccvii (1962), Nov, 78

J. C. Schelleng: 'The Violin as a Circuit', *Journal of the Acoustical Society of America*, xxxv (1963), 326

H. Fletcher and L. C. Sanders: 'Quality of Violin Vibrato Tones', *Journal of the Acoustical Society of America*, xli (1967), 1534

C. M. Hutchins: 'Founding a Family of Fiddles', *Physics Today*, xx (1967), 23 [on the New Violin Family]

BIBLIOGRAPHY

J. C. Schelleng: 'Acoustical Effects of Violin Varnish', *Journal of the Acoustical Society of America*, xliv (1968), 1175

L. Cremer: 'Die Geige aus Sicht des Physikers', *Nachrichten der Akademie der Wissenschaften in Göttingen*, ii, Mathematisch-Physikalische Klasse (1971), 12

C. M. Hutchins, K. A. Stetson and P. A. Taylor: 'Clarification of Free Plate Tap Tones by Hologram Interferometry', *Catgut Acoustical Society Newsletter*, no.16 (1971), 15

J. C. Schelleng: 'The Action of the Soundpost', *Catgut Acoustical Society Newsletter*, no.16 (1971), 11

L. Cremer: 'The Influence of "Bow Pressure" on the Movement of the Bowed String', *Catgut Acoustical Society Newsletter*, no.18 (1972), 13; no.19 (1973), 21

E. Jansson: 'On the Acoustics of the Violin', *IMSCR*, xi *Copenhagen 1972*, 462

I. M. Firth and J. M. Buchanan: 'The Wolf in the Cello', *Journal of the Acoustical Society of America*, liii (1973), 457

C. M. Hutchins: 'Instrumentation and Methods for Violin Testing', *Journal of the Audio Engineering Society*, xxi (1973), 563

C. M. Hutchins and M. Bram: 'The Bowed Strings – Yesterday, Today, and Tomorrow', *Music Educators Journal* (1973), Nov, 20

W. Reinicke: 'Übertragungseigenschaften des Streichinstrumentenstegs', *Catgut Acoustical Society Newsletter*, no.19 (1973), 26

J. C. Schelleng: 'The Bowed String and the Player', *Journal of the Acoustical Society of America*, liii (1973), 26

————: 'The Physics of the Bowed String', *Scientific American*, ccxxx (1974), Jan, 87

J. Meyer: 'An Acoustical Method of Violin Testing', *Catgut Acoustical Society Newsletter*, no.23 (1975), 2

C. M. Hutchins, ed.: *Musical Acoustics* (Stroudsburg, 1975–6) [incl. reprs. of almost all articles above]

D. F. Parsons: 'The Influence of String Partials on Violin Tone and an Electronic Method of Tuning String Instruments to Overtones', *Acustica*, xxxvii (1977), 222

M. E. McIntyre and J. Woodhouse: 'The Acoustics of Stringed Musical Instruments', *Interdisciplinary Science Reviews*, iii (1978), 157

E. B. Arnold and G. Weinrich: 'Method for Measuring Acoustic Radiation Fields', *Journal of the Acoustical Society of America*, lxviii (1980), 404

D. W. Haines: 'On Musical Instrument Wood', *Catgut Acoustical Society Newsletter*, no.31 (1979), 23; no.33 (1980), 19

E. B. Arnold and G. Weinrich: 'Acoustical Spectroscopy of Violins', *Journal of the Acoustical Society of America*, lxxii (1981), 1739

L. Cremer: *Physik der Geige* (Stuttgart, 1981; Eng. trans., 1984)

C. E. Gough: 'The Theory of String Resonances on Musical Instruments', *Acustica*, xlix (1981), 124

305

VIOLIN FAMILY

C. M. Hutchins: 'The Acoustics of Violin Plates', *Scientific American*, ccxlv (1981), Oct, 170

W. Y. Strong and E. Torick: 'Experimental Study of Vibration and Radiation Characteristics of a Violin', *Journal of the Acoustical Society of America*, lxxii (1982), suppl., p. 83 [abstract]

C. M. Hutchins: 'A History of Violin Research', *Journal of the Acoustical Society of America*, lxxiii (1983), 1421

K. Marshall: 'Modal Analysis of a Violin', *Journal of the Acoustical Society of America*, lxxvii (1985), 695

O. Rodgers: 'Initial Results on Finite Element Analysis of Violin Backs', *Catgut Acoustical Society Journal*, no.46 (1986), 18

C. M. Hutchins: 'Some Notes on Free Plate Tuning Frequencies for Violins, Violas and Cellos', *Catgut Acoustical Society Journal*, no.47 (1987), 39

B. E. Richardson, G. W. Roberts and G. P. Walker: 'Numerical Modelling of Two Violin Plates', *Catgut Acoustical Society Journal*, no.47 (1987), 12

C. Rubin and D. F. Farrar, jr: 'Finite Element Modelling of Violin Plate Vibrational Characteristics', *Catgut Acoustical Society Journal*, no.47 (1987), 8

Index

INDEX

INDEX

INDEX

Gerle, Hans, 155
Ghignone, G. P. See 'Guignon, Jean-Pierre'
Giardini, Felice, 110
Gibbons, Orlando, 186
Ginastera, Alberto, 128, 182, 197
Giornovichi, Giovanni Mane, 74
Giovannino del Violone, 195
Glazunov, Alexander Konstantinovich, 90, 124, 181
Glissando, 98–9
Gluck, Christoph Willibald, 145
Gnesin, Mikhail Fabianovich, 70
Goehr, Alexander, 128
Goffriller, Matteo, 28
Goldmark, Karl, 120
Goltermann, Georg, 170, 178
Goltermann, Julius, 170
Grancino family, 28, 155, 190
Graun, Johann Gottlieb, 112, 146
Graziani, Carlo, 163, 176
Grieg, Edvard, 123, 180
Gross, Robert, 79
Grümmer, Paul, 170
Grützmacher, Friedrich, 170, 177, 178
Guadagnini, Giovanni Battista [J. B.], 10, 28
Guadagnini, Lorenzo, 28
Guarneri, Andrea, 27, 155
Guarneri, Giuseppe, 'del Gesù', 27, 28, 35
Guarneri, Pietro, 28
Guarneri family, 27, 155
Guénin, Marie-Alexandre, 114
Guérin, Emmanuel, 163
Guhr, Karl, 92, 93
Guignon, Jean-Pierre, 113, 175
Guillemain, Louis-Gabriel, 113
Gullbrandsson, K., 195
Gunn, John, 162, 163, 166
Guy, Barry, 197

Habeneck, François-Antoine, 75
Hall, Marie, 102
Hammer, Franz Xaver, 163
Handel, George Frideric, 111, 140, 145, 176, 179
Hanslick, Eduard, 121
Hardanger fiddle, 66, 129
Harnoncourt, Nikolaus, 174
Harrell, Lynn, 174
Harris, Roy, 127
Harrison, Beatrice, 171

Hawkins, John, 207
Haydn, Joseph, 31, 52, 64, 73, 75, 108, 114–15, 146, 177, 178, 179, 195, 196, 209
Haydn, Michael, 148
Hegner, 195
Heifetz, Jascha, 76, 77, 82, 83, 84, 102
Heller, Kenneth, 182
Hellmesberger, Joseph, 77
Helmholtz, Hermann von, 218, 222, 223, 227
Henze, Hans Werner, 128, 151, 181, 198
Heron-Allen, Edward, 8
Hill family, 141
Himmelbauer, Wenzel, 163
Hindemith, Paul, 79, 105, 125, 151, 181
Hindle, J., 193–4
Hoffmeister Franz Anton, 146, 195
Hofstetter, Roman, 146
Holzbauer, Ignaz, 176
Honegger, Arthur, 125, 181
Hörlein, K. A., 143
Hrabě, Josef, 194, 196
Hubay, Jenö, 78
Hume, Tobias, 50
Hummel, Johann Nepomuk, 179, 196, 198
Hupfeld, L., 12
Hus-Desforges, Pierre Louis, 164
Hutchins, Carleen, 34, 144

Ibert, Jacques, 181
Indy, Vincent d', 123, 181
Ireland, John, 181
Ives, Charles, 125

Jacchini, Giuseppe, 161, 175, 176
Jambe de Fer, Philibert, 13, 19, 20, 36, 153, 154
Janigro, Antonio, 174
Janson, Jean-Baptiste-Aimé Joseph, 163, 164, 177
Janson, Louis-Auguste-Joseph, 163
Jarosy, Albert, 97
Joachim, Joseph, 15, 75, 76, 78, 82, 94, 95, 102, 106, 109, 116, 118, 119–20, 122, 124
John, Augustus, 171
Jolivet, André, 182

Kabalevsky, Dmitry Borisovich, 126, 127, 181

INDEX

Kagel, Mauricio, 182
Kämpfer, Josef, 195
Karayev, Kara, 126, 128
Karr, Gary, 197
Kelz, Mathias, 110
Kennedy, Thomas, 190
Kersting, Friedrich, 32
Khachaturian, Aram, 126, 181
Khandoshkin, Ivan, 65, 170
Khrennikov, Tikhon Nikolayevich, 126
Kindermann, Johann Erasmus, 70
Kirchner, Leon, 127–8
Kittel, Nicholas, 214
Klebe, Giselher, 128
Klengel, Julius, 170, 173, 178
Kochański, Pawel, 125
Kodály, Zoltán, 71, 181
Kogan, Leonid, 126
Kohne, Ridley, 76
Koussevitsky, Sergey, 197
Kraft, Anton, 163, 176, 177
Kraft, Nikolaus, 176
Krasner, Louis, 79
Kreisler, Fritz, 77–8, 83, 84, 97, 102, 122, 123
Krenek, Ernst, 125, 181
Kreutzer, Rodolphe, 31, 39, 73, 74, 77, 90, 92, 96, 105, 106, 108, 117, 139
Kriegck, Johann Jacob, 163, 170
Kubelík, Jan, 77
Kummer, Friedrich August, 167–9, 170

L'abbé le fils [Saint-Sévin, Joseph-Barnabé], 38, 39, 53, 58, 59, 85, 114
Labro, 194
Lafleur, Jacques, 211
Lafont, Charles, 124
La Laurencie, Lionel de, 114
Lalo, Edouard, 98, 118, 120, 180
Lamare, Jacques-Michel (Hurel de), 164, 177
Lanfranco, Giovanni, 17, 154
Lanzetti, Domenico, 176
Lanzetti, Salvatore, 163, 166, 175
Láska, Gustav, 197
Leaumont, Chevalier, de, 179
Leclair, Jean-Marie, l'aîné, 37, 57, 113–14
Leclair, Jean-Marie, le cadet, 57, 59
Lee, Sebastian, 170
Lees, Benjamin, 127
Legrenzi, Giovanni, 106

Leipp, Emile, 8
Lemaire, J., 70
Leo, Leonardo, 176
Leonard, Hubert, 75, 94
Levasseur, Jean Henri, 165, 170
Levasseur, Pierre François, 163, 164
Ligeti, György, 182
Linarol, Ventura, 21, 186, 188
Lindley, Robert, 170
Liszt, Franz, 32, 196
Locatelli, Pietro Antonio, 28, 38, 105, 107
Löhlein, Georg Simon, 89
Lolli, Antonio, 66, 70, 74
Lombardini, Maddalena, 60
Lonati, Carl'Ambrogio, 66, 70
Lott, John Frederick, 190
Louis XIII, King of France, 38, 140
Louis XIV, King of France, 111, 113
Lully, Jean-Baptiste, 24, 42, 43, 111, 113
Lupot, François, 214
Lupot, Nicolas, 31, 35
Lutosławski, Witold, 182

Mace, Thomas, 25
Maggini, Giovanni Paolo, 21, 25, 35, 141, 155, 186, 188
Mahler, Gustav, 71, 149, 197
Mainardi, Enrico, 170
Malipiero, Gian Francesco, 127
Mara, J. B., 163
Marais, Marin, 100
Marcello, Benedetto, 175
Marini, Biagio, 22, 37, 66, 70, 106, 110
Martin, François, 163, 176
Martin, Frank, 127
Martinn, Jacob-Joseph-Balthasar, 149
Martinů, Bohuslav, 127, 181
Marx, Klaus, 164
Mascitti, Michele, 113
Messart, (Joseph) Lambert, 75, 77
Matteis, Nicola, 109
Meauchand, 211
Medici, Catherine de', 36
Meinel, H. F., 226
Mell, Davis, 109
Mendelssohn, Felix, 75, 76, 102, 105, 116, 118–19, 122, 179, 180
Mennin, Peter, 127
Menotti, Gian Carlo, 127
Menuhin, Yehudi, 78, 102, 125
Menzel, Adolf, 15

311

INDEX

Merck, Daniel, 100
Merk, Joseph, 170
Mersenne, Marin, 22, 24, 42, 71, 91, 100, 140, 153, 203, 208
Metsu, Gabriel, 158
Milhaud, Darius, 125, 151, 181
Milstein, Nathan, 76
Möchel, 195
Mondonville, Jean-Joseph Cassanéa de, 105, 113
Monn, Georg Mathias, 176
Montagnana, Domenico, 28
Monteverdi, Claudio, 20, 22, 37, 52, 104, 145, 155
Montichiaro, Zanetto, 17
Moore, Douglas, 127
Moscheles, Ignaz, 124
Mozart, Leopold, 28, 38, 39, 40, 41, 42, 45, 47, 52, 53, 57, 61, 63–4, 73, 83, 101, 107, 108, 114, 115, 166, 186, *206*, 207
Mozart, Wolfgang Amadeus, 31, 52, 66, 68, 73, 85, 105, 108, 113, 114–16, 145, 146–8, 177, 179, 195, 197, 209
Muffat, Georg, 42, 43
Mukel, May, 171
Muntzberger, Joseph, 164
Musorgsky, Modest Petrovich, 197
Myaskovsky, Nikolay Yakovlevich, 126

Nanny, Edouard, 194, 196
Nardini, Pietro, 69, 70, 73, 74, 104, 105, 107–8
Navarra, André, 174
Nelsova, Zara, 174
Nielsen, Carl, 124
Nono, Luigi, 128
Norblin, Louis Pierre Martin, 170
Norris & Barnes, 211
North, Roger, 101, 109

Oistrakh, David, 78, 125
Ondříček, František, 120
Onslow, Georges, 179, 198
Osborne, George, 124

Pachelbel, Johann, 70
Paganini, Nicolò, 27, 32, 68, 73, 74, 75, 82, 87, 89, 92, 93, 96, 105, 106, 107, 114, 118, 121, 122, 124, 150
Palm, Siegfried, 174, 182
Patouart, 176

Paxton, William, 163
Peccatte, Dominique, 35, 161, 214
Penderecki, Krzysztof, 128, 181, 182
Perle, George, 127
Perroni, Carlo, 176
Perroni, Giovanni, 176
Persinger, Louis, 78
Petits Violons, 113
Petracchi, Francesco, 194
Pfitzner, Hans, 125, 180, 181
Piani, Giovanni Antonio [Desplanes, Jean-Antoine], 113
Piatigorsky, Gregor, 170
Piatti, Alfredo, 170, 178
Pischelberger, Friedrich, 195
Pisendel, Johann Georg, 111, 112
Piston, Walter, 127, 151
Pizzetti, Ildebrando, 127, 181
Pizzicato, 51–2, 89–90
Planyavsky, Alfred, 186, 197
Platel, Nicolas Joseph, 170
Platner, Michael, 28
Platti, Giovanni, 175, 176
Playford, John, 52, 70, 105
Pleyel, Ignace, 146
Popper, David, 170, 178
Porpora, Nicola, 104, 175, 176
Porter, Quincy, 127
Pošta, František, 197
Poulenc, Francis, 181
Praetorius, Michael, 5, 19, 22, 153, *154*, 155, 186
Prell, A. C., 170
Prell, J. N., 170
Pressenda, Giovanni Francesco, 35
Primrose, William, 141, 149, 151
Prinner, Johann Jacob, 186
Prokofiev, Sergey, 90, 105, 126, 151, 181, 197, 198
Prospero, 186
Puccini, Giacomo, 178
Pugnani, Gaetano, 27, 73, 108
Purcell, Henry, 24, 109, 145

Quantz, Johann Joachim, 45–6, 47, 68, 112, 144

Rakhmaninov, Sergey, 180
Rathaus, Karol, 125
Ravel, Maurice, 79, 90, 126, 149, 151, 181, 197

312

INDEX

Rebel, Jean-Féry, 113
Reger, Max, 105, 124–5, 180, 181
Reicha, Josef, 146, 163
Reinagle, Joseph, 163
Respighi, Ottorino, 127
Rey, Louis, Charles Joseph, 164
Richardson, Arthur, 143
Riegger, Wallingford, 127
Ries, Ferdinand, 116, 179
Rieti, Vittorio, 127
Rimsky-Korsakov, Nikolay Andreyevich, 121
Ritter, Hermann, 34, 143, 150
Ritter, Peter, 163, 177
Robineau, Alexandre-Auguste, Abbé, 114
Rode, Pierre, 31, 39, 73, 74, 77, 90, 101, 105, 106, 108, 117, 118
Rodrigo, Joaquín, 181
Rogeri, Giovanni Baptista, 155
Rogeri family, 155
Rognoni, Francesco, 42
Rognoni, Riccardo, 42
Rolla, Alessandro, 146
Romberg, Bernhard, 161, 163, 167, 170, 178
Rose, Leonard, 174
Rossi, Salomone, 104
Rossini, Gioachino, 178, 196, 197
Rostal, Max, 78
Rostropovich, Mstislav, 172, 173, 174
Roth [Roth-Sihon] mute, 24
Rousseau, Jean, 100
Roussel, Albert, 125, 181
Rowe, Walter, 110
Rubbra, Edmund, 181
Rubinstein, Anton, 124
Rugeri, Francesco, 155
Rugeri family, 155
Rühm, 195
Rust, Friedrich Wilhelm, 112

Saint-Georges, Joseph Boulogne, 114
Saint-Saëns, Camille, 106, 118, 120, 123, 124, 180, 197
Saint-Sévin, Joseph-Barnabé. See 'L'abbé le fils'
Salmanov, V. N., 128
Salomons, David, 196
Sanders, L. C., 225
Sarasate, Pablo, 74, 120, 124
Saunders, Frederick, 144

Saunders, Wilfred, 138
Savart, Félix, 33, 217
Schelling, J. C., 223, 226
Schetky, Johann Georg Christoph, 163
Schindlöker, Philipp, 163
Schlick, Johann Conrad, 163
Schmelzer, Johann Heinrich, 70, 110
Schneider, Georg Abraham, 146
Schobert, Johann, 105, 113, 116
Schoenberg, Arnold, 50, 73, 79, 88, 125, 149, 151, 197
Schubert, Franz, 114, 117, 124, 151, 178, 179, 197
Schubert, Joseph, 146
Schuberth, Carl, 170
Schuman, William, 127, 182
Schumann, Clara, 15
Schumann, Robert, 70, 105, 118, 119, 122, 124, 179, 180
Schwarz, Anton, 163
Scipriani, Francesco, 164
Scordatura, 65–71
Scott, Cyril, 125
Senaillé, Jean Baptiste, 113
Senn, Walter, 8
Seraphin, Sanctus, 28
Serly, Tibor, 151
Servais, Adrien, François, 169, 170, 178
Sessions, Roger, 127
Ševčík, Otakar, 77, 95, 139
Shnitke, Alfred, 128
Shostakovich, Dmitry, 126–7, 128, 151, 181
Sibelius, Jean, 105, 124
Simandl, Franz, 193, 194, 196
Simpson, Christopher, 100
Simpson, Thomas, 109, 110
Sinding, Christian, 123
Slonimsky, Sergey, 128
Smetana, Bedřich, 106, 124
Somis, Giovanni Battista, 107, 113
Sotheby's, London, 35
Sperger, Johannes, 195
Spivakovsky, Tossy, 82
Spohr, Louis, 33, 34, 74, 75, 80, 82, 93, 94, 95, 101, 105, 108, 109, 112, 116, 118, 169, 178, 196, 197, 211
Stainer, Jacob, 10, 25, 26, 27, 28, 38, 71, 190, 225
Stamitz, Anton, 112
Stamitz, Antonín Tadeáš, 163

313

INDEX

Stamitz, Carl, 66, 73, 112, 146, 148, 177, 195
Stamitz, Johann, 112
Stamitz family, 146
Starker, Janos, 174
Šťastný, Bernard, 163
Šťastný, Jan, 163
Staufer, J. G., 156
Stelzner, Alfred, 156
Stern, Isaac, 13, *15*, 78, 83
Stern, Leo, 170
Stoll, Klaus, 197
Stolyarsky, Pyotr Solomonovich, 78
Stradivari, Antonio, *2*, 5, 10, 11, 27, 28, *30*, 31, 33, 35, 38, 71, 73, 141, 143, 150, 155–6
  Betts' violin, 28, *29*
  'Messiah' violin, 6
  'Tuscan' viola, *10*
  'Lady Blount' violin, 35
Straeten, Edmund van der, 156, 170
Strauss, Richard, 120, 123, 149, 178, 180, 197
Stravinsky, Igor, 70, 71, 79, 94, 105, 126, 150, 197
Streicher, Ludwig, 197
Strinasacchi, Regina, 116
Strungk, Nicolaus Adam, 70
Stuck, Jean Baptiste ['Batistin'], 163
Suggia, Guilhermina, 171
Svendsen, Johan, 180
Swert, Jules de, 170
Szigeti, Joseph, 70, 78, 83, 97–8, 173, 174
Szymanowski, Karol, 124
Talbot, James, 25
Talietti, Luigi, 175
Tarisio, Luigi, 35
Tarr, William, 190, *191*
Tartini, Giuseppe, 31, 44, 45, 60, 70, 73, 74, 80, 104, 105, 106, 107, 108, 118, 128, 163, 176, 209
Tchaikovsky, Pyotr Il'yich, 73, 77, 89, 106, 118, 121, 124, 149, 180
Tecchler, David, 28, 155
Telemann, Georg Philipp, 111–12, 145
Tertis, Lionel, *138*, 143–5, 151
Testore family, 28, 155, 190
Theile, Johann, 70
Thompson, Virgil, 127, 181
Tillière, Joseph Bonaventure, 164
Toch, Ernst, 125

Tomasini, Luigi, 116
Tononi, Giovanni [Joannes], 28
Tononi family, 155
Torelli, Giuseppe, 28, 107
Tortelier, Paul, 173, 174
Tourte, François, 31, 32, 38, 73, 90, 143, 156, 161, *205*, 209, 211–14
Tourte *père*, 31, 209, *210*, 211
Tremais, de, 70
Tricklir, Jean Balthasar, 163, 164
Tubbs, James, 214
Turetzky, Bertram, 197
24 Violons du Roi, 25, 38, 113, 140, 161

Uccellini, Marco, 70, 106
Uhlrich, 116
Ustvol'skaya, Galina Ivanovna, 128

Valentin de Boullongne, *23*
Vandini, Antonio, 163, 176
Vanhal, Johann Baptist, 146, 148, 195
Vaughan Williams, Ralph, 127
Veracini, Francesco Maria, 28, 107
Verdi, Giuseppe, 149, 178, 196
Vestergaard, Knud, *51*
Vibrato, 99–103
Vieuxtemps, Henry, 75, 77, 105, 106, 116, 118, 121, 122, 124
Villa-Lobos, Heitor, 181
Viotti, Giovanni Battista, 25, 27, 31, 38, 73, 80, 82, 89, 90, 92, 104, 105, 108–9, 114, 117, 209, 212, 214
Vitali, Giovanni Battista, 37, 106
Vivaldi, Antonio, 38, 70, 105, 107, 111, 145, 175, 176
Vogel, Hanns, 186, *187*
Voirin, François Nicolas, 35, 161, 214
Volkmann, Robert, 180
Viullaume, Jean-Baptiste, *26*, 35, 184, 214

Wagenseil, Georg Christoph, 176
Wagner, Richard, 88, 143, 149, 178
Walls, Peter, 59
Walther, Johann Jakob, 27, 37, 47, 52, 71, 100, 111 .
Walton, William, 127, 151, 181
Webber, Julian Lloyd, 174
Weber, Ben, 127
Webern, Anton, 79, 125, 151, 181
Weigl, Joseph Franz, 163
Weill, Kurt, 125

314

INDEX

INDEX